Speaking in the Spirit

Speaking in the Spirit

A Study of New Testament Prophecy

STEPHEN WEXLER

WIPF & STOCK · Eugene, Oregon

SPEAKING IN THE SPIRIT
A Study of New Testament Prophecy

Copyright © 2019 Stephen Wexler. All rights reserved. Except for brief quotations in critical publications or reviews, no part of this book may be reproduced in any manner without prior written permission from the publisher. Write: Permissions, Wipf and Stock Publishers, 199 W. 8th Ave., Suite 3, Eugene, OR 97401.

Wipf & Stock
An Imprint of Wipf and Stock Publishers
199 W. 8th Ave., Suite 3
Eugene, OR 97401

www.wipfandstock.com

PAPERBACK ISBN: 978-1-5326-5620-0
HARDCOVER ISBN: 978-1-5326-5621-7
EBOOK ISBN: 978-1-5326-5622-4

Manufactured in the U.S.A.   JULY 3, 2019

Unless otherwise indicated, all Scripture quotations are from The ESV® Bible (The Holy Bible, English Standard Version®), copyright © 2001 by Crossway, a publishing ministry of Good News Publishers. Used by permission. All rights reserved.

To Raya and Rose

Nothing is so difficult as not deceiving oneself.
Ludwig Wittgenstein

It ain't what you don't know that gets you into trouble.

It's what you know for sure that just ain't so.
Mark Twain

Contents

Acknowledgments | xiii

Abbreviations | xiv

Introduction | 1

Part One: Groundwork | 7

Chapter 1: An Introduction to Old Testament Prophecy | 9

>Prophets are men and women through whom God speaks to his people. Prophecy has many forms and modes of production, but it always originates in the Spirit, and always involves a divine encounter. Two of its chief purposes are to declare God's covenant and to recall God's people to that covenant, that is, to relationship with him.

Chapter 2: An Inadequate Introduction to New Testament Prophecy | 34

>The vocabulary of prophecy is surprisingly rare in the New Testament. How are we to account for this? We highlight the dangers of assuming all prophecy is so labelled, of seeing only what we expect to see, and of generalizing from particular events.

Chapter 3: Toward an Interpretative Framework for Prophecy—Part 1 | 46

>We consider the nature of the superiority of every Christian over the Old Testament prophets (Matt 11:9-11), and argue that Acts 2:14-21 describes a new age of the Spirit in which all God's people are able to speak in the power of his Spirit.

CONTENTS

Chapter 4: Toward an Interpretative Framework for Prophecy—Part 2 | 52

> We consider cessationist and continuationist readings of Eph 2:20, 3:4–6, and conclude that they are not as opposed as they appear: both agree that a version of prophecy has ceased, and a version of prophecy (even if only figurative) continues.

Chapter 5: Old Testament Prophets, New Testament Apostles | 60

> Grudem contends that the New Testament counterparts of the Old Testament prophets are not the New Testament prophets but the *apostles*, and that New Testament prophets therefore do not speak with absolute authority. We argue that the apostles are *model* prophets, but that other prophets do indeed speak authoritatively from God, albeit in submission to apostolic doctrine.

Part Two: The Prophets at Corinth | 67

Chapter 6: Prophecy as Gospel (1 Cor 1–2) | 69

> We consider Gillespie's claim that prophecy is the unlabeled subject matter of Cor 2:6–16, and the implication that Paul's gospel preaching is his prophesying.

Chapter 7: Babes and Apostles (1 Cor 3–4) | 81

> What constitutes "spiritual" behavior? Christ-likeness. What constitutes "spiritual" speech? Preaching that is aligned to Christ. We are to imitate Paul both in his life and speech—and this includes his *prophesying*.

Chapter 8: The Pneumatics (1 Cor 12) | 85

> Gillespie argues that 1 Cor 12:3 offers the standard by which prophetic speech is to be assessed: it exalts Christ. We consider the claim of Ellis that the *pneumatika* are not simply "spiritual gifts" but "*the gifts of Spirit-inspired speech.*"

Chapter 9: Vagueness, Uncertainty, and Error (1 Cor 13:9–12) | 92

> From the phrase "now we see in a mirror dimly" Grudem argues that "the prophet may not always understand . . . just what has been revealed to him, and at times may not even be sure that he has received a revelation."

Contents

> We dispute that claim, which opens the way to prophecy as the report of a vague impression.

Chapter 10: Prophecy as Loving Speech (1 Cor 14) | 96

> 1 Corinthians 14 is to be read as a comprehensive contrast between tongues and prophecy, with prophecy being an expression of love (following 1 Cor 13), since it involves the prophet actively considering how to build up others in Christ.

Chapter 11: The Missing Contrast of 1 Corinthians 14:1 | 99

> "Earnestly desire the *pneumatika, especially* that you may prophesy." Translations tend to miss Paul's correction here: "*or rather.*" A revised translation of *pneumatika* may help to restore the missing contrast and indicate the nature of prophecy.

Chapter 12: A Definition of Prophecy? (1 Cor 14:3) | 103

> We examine the three effects of prophecy in this verse and suggest that they all imply that prophesying must involve Christ-centered preaching, which alone can have these effects.

Chapter 13: Revealing Secrets (1 Cor 14:24–25) | 111

> The effect on an unbeliever of exposure to prophecy is that "the secrets of his heart are disclosed." Grudem argues that this means the prophets have miraculous insight into a person's secret sins. We argue that Paul is describing an individual who is exposed to gospel-based speech of some kind and comes under conviction of sin.

Chapter 14: Judging and Fallibility (1 Cor 14:29) | 117

> Grudem considers that the fact that we are to "weigh" (*diakrinō*) prophecies implies that there will be true and false elements within them. We argue that the word means "pass judgement" and probably implies a verbal assessment of what has been said against Scripture.

Chapter 15: Spontaneity and Interruption (1 Cor 14:30) | 126

> Grudem argues that this text indicates that all prophecy is spontaneous, and the fact that one prophet could interrupt another means that they

Contents

cannot have been thought to be speaking the very words of God. We argue that interruption is not required by the text, which may simply describe the to and fro of discussion.

Chapter 16: Impression and Revelation (1 Cor 14:30) | 133

Prophecy is based on revelation. Grudem argues that this could be "words, thoughts or mental pictures that suddenly impressed themselves forcefully on the mind of the prophet." We argue that revelation includes *realizations*, that is, the fresh understanding of Biblical truth that we might come to every day. In other words, it can involve both new-to-the-person as well as new-to-the-world truth. Either way, revelation normally involves thinking things through.

Chapter 17: Women Prophets (1 Cor 14:34–35) | 140

We argue that the command for women to be silent may in fact be a command for wives not to take part in the discussion of prophecies given by their own husbands.

Part Three: Agabus | 145

Chapter 18: Agabus and the Disciples at Tyre | 147

Grudem claims that a certain "vagueness" attaches to the phrase "Agabus . . . foretold *by the Spirit*" (Acts 11:28). We dispute this. The disciples at Tyre then tell Paul "through the Spirit" not to go to Jerusalem. Is this the Spirit speaking vaguely or a misinterpretation of the Spirit's voice?

Chapter 19: Agabus Predicts the Arrest of Paul | 151

Grudem claims that there are "two small errors" in Agabus' prediction of the arrest of Paul by the Jews. This suggests to him that prophecy might sometimes be only partly accurate. But is Grudem correct?

Chapter 20: Does Agabus Model Prophecy for Today? | 160

Do the predictions of Agabus serve as examples of normative prophesying today? We suggest some characteristics of his prophecies that make him an unsuitable model for prophesying today.

Contents

Part Four: Synthesis | 165

Chapter 21: Foundational and Congregational Prophecy | 167

> We consider the role played by prophets in the explanation and communication of the apostolic letter from the Jerusalem Council to Gentile believers (Acts 15:22–32). Their prophetic gift seems to have confirmed to them, and enabled them to confirm and explain to others, the doctrine of Gentile inclusion.

Chapter 22: Prophecy as *Paraklēsis* and Hermeneutics | 172

> We look at the tight correlation between prophesying, the interpretation of Scripture, and *paraklēsis*, and conclude that New Testament prophecy exhorts the church by the Spirit-enabled interpretation of Old Testament Scripture in light of the Christ event.

Chapter 23: The Doctrinal Content of Prophecy (Rom 12:6) | 178

> When Paul says that prophecy is to be "in agreement with the faith" is he hinting that prophecy must have doctrinal content?

Chapter 24: Addressing Perceived Need | 180

> Prophecy frequently begins with people rather than with a text: it addresses perceived *local* need with the gospel. But it also addresses the *universal* need for the gospel. The key principle is that prophets are effective gospel communicators.

Chapter 25: Speaking God's Word Today | 184

> We argue that whenever we faithfully communicate Scripture today, *God speaks* through his word. To that extent, we can indeed speak the very words of God (1 Pet 4:11).

Chapter 26: Prophecy as Eschatology | 189

> Prophesying is inherently predictive inasmuch as it proclaims the gospel message of salvation and judgment. It frequently also declares material evidences that we are living in the last days, and exhorts the church, in the light of this, to stay faithful to her Christ.

CONTENTS

Chapter 27: Is All Spirit-Enabled Speech Prophecy? | 192

>The word "preaching" is only used in the New Testament to describe evangelistic discourse. There is no obvious word for describing an equivalent address to a believing audience: "teaching" seems inadequate. We consider whether "prophesying" might be that word.

Chapter 28: Conclusion | 198

>We summarize our argument that all speech that exalts Christ constitutes prophecy, and suggest that, rather than describing prophecy as either continuing or ceasing, it might be more accurate to think it as *transforming* in the New Testament. We consider whether or not we should continue to use the term today.

Appendix I: *The Interpretation of Tongues* | 207

>Thiselton argues that Paul expects people to interpret *their own tongues*, and that *diermeneuō* ("interpret") refers to putting into words thoughts or feelings that are difficult to articulate.

Appendix II: *The Danger of Narrow Appeals to History* | 212

>Charles Spurgeon has been quoted in support of completely opposing views of prophecy. This demonstrates that we need to be as careful in our study of history as in our study of theology.

Bibliography | 215

Acknowledgments

I owe huge thanks to Dr. Rob Knowles for his support. Without his positive reaction to the first few scribbles, I would not have written more, without his careful commenting on my early drafts, my work would have been much weaker, and without his belief that I could write this book, I would not have believed it myself.

I am thankful also to Anthony C. Thiselton for his positive reaction, and to Richard Coekin for his generous encouragement.

Finally, I am extremely grateful also to my wife, Raya, for her patience over the years it has taken me to complete this study.

Abbreviations

AG	William F. Arndt and F. Wilbur Gingrich. *A Greek-English Lexicon of the New Testament*. Cambridge: Cambridge University Press, 1957.
EDNT	Horst Balz and Gerhard Schnieder. *Exegetical Dictionary of the New Testament*. 3 vols. Grand Rapids: Eerdmans, 1994.
ESV	The Holy Bible. *The English Standard Version*. Wheaton, IL: Crossway, 2002.
FEC	Anthony C. Thiselton. *First Epistle to the Corinthians*. Grand Rapids: Eerdmans, 2000.
GP	Wayne Grudem. *The Gift of Prophecy*. Wheaton, IL: Crossway, 2000.
KJV	The Holy Bible. *The King James Version*. Peabody, MA: Hendrickson, 2004.
LS	Henry George Liddell and Robert Scott. *A Greek-English Lexicon*. Oxford, UK: Oxford University Press, 1861.
mg	marginal reading
NASB	The Holy Bible. *The New American Standard Bible*. Foundation, 1995.
NBD	*The New Bible Dictionary*. Downers Grove, IL: IVP, 1962.
NIV	The Holy Bible. *The New International Version*. Grand Rapids: Zondervan, 1984.
NLT	Holy Bible. *The New Living Translation*. Carol Stream, IL: Tyndale, 2015.
OED	*The Shorter Oxford English Dictionary*. Oxford: Oxford University Press, 2007.
RSV	The Holy Bible. *The Revised Standard Version*. Downers Grove, IL: InterVarsity, 1969.
TDNT	*Theological Dictionary of the New Testament*. Edited by G. Kittel and G. Friedrich. Grand Rapids: Eerdmans, 1978.

Introduction

ALL THEOLOGY IS, OF course, dialogue: dialogue with Scripture, and dialogue with other scholars by means of their texts. I have chosen to dialogue extensively, but not exclusively, with two writers and two works: *The Gift of Prophecy* by Wayne Grudem, and *The First Theologians* by Thomas W. Gillespie.

Grudem's book is a highly regarded elaboration of a very popular view of prophecy, and this is why I focus on it so intently. Don Carson says, "That Grudem has rightly delineated some distinguishing marks of New Testament prophecy is in my judgment beyond cavil."[1] J. I. Packer describes the book as "careful, thorough, wise, and to my mind convincing."

When a work is so respected it might seem a presumptuous task to take issue with it! But of course I do not undertake the task alone; I draw heavily from other writing, perhaps mainly Thomas Gillespie's *The First Theologians*. As with Grudem's book, Gillespie's work started life as a PhD thesis, recast some twenty years later for wider publication; but whereas Grudem chose to write for a popular audience, Gillespie kept an academic audience in view.

I also draw on the work of a range of other scholars, principally Anthony C. Thiselton, whose larger commentary on 1 Corinthians (he has written two!) must surely qualify as one of the finest commentaries ever written.

Our Pre-understanding

When anyone asks the question, "Do you think prophecy continues today?" there is really only one possible answer, namely, "It depends what you

---

1. Carson, *Showing the Spirit*, 99.

Introduction

mean by the word 'prophecy!'" If you then ask for a definition of prophecy, you are likely to get a range of answers:

- "It's predicting the future."
- "It's God speaking through people."
- "It's the word of God."
- "It's mainly in the Old Testament."
- "It's a sense of something the Spirit is saying."
- "It's the Holy Spirit speaking through people."
- "It's infallible speech."
- "It's not infallible speech."

These responses show the level of confusion surrounding the topic today. Since we will all bring our own pre-understanding to any discussion of prophecy, it will be helpful to clarify that pre-understanding at the outset of our discussion; you may find your own described in one or more of the following definitions of prophecy offered by various scholars in the field:

> Prophecy . . . consisted of spontaneous, Spirit-inspired, intelligible messages, orally delivered in the gathered assembly, intended for the edification or encouragement of the people.[2]

> The early Christian prophet was an immediately-inspired spokesman for the risen Jesus who received intelligible oracles that he felt impelled to deliver to the Christian community.[3]

> A Christian prophet is a Christian who functions within the Church, occasionally or regularly, as a divinely called and divinely inspired speaker who receives intelligible and authoritative revelations or messages which he is impelled to deliver publicly, in oral or written form, to Christian individuals and/or the Christian community.[4]

> For Paul prophecy apparently is a formal term embracing certain kinds of inspired teaching.[5]

---

2. Fee, *First Epistle to the Corinthians*, 595.
3. Boring, *Sayings of the Risen Jesus*, 16.
4. Hill, *New Testament Prophecy*, 8.
5. Ellis, *Prophecy & Hermeneutic*, 141.

Introduction

> The prophet is the spirit-endowed counsellor of the community who tells it what to do in specific situations, who blames and praises, whose preaching contains admonition and comfort, the call for repentance and promise.[6]
>
> For Paul prophecy is the reception and subsequent communication of spontaneous, divinely given *apokalypsis* . . . the declaring of a revelatory experience.[7]
>
> Prophecy is the reception and subsequent public declaration of (usually) verbal revelation. Such revelation is normally spontaneous . . . and the subsequent declaration is normally immediate.[8]
>
> Prophecy . . . should be defined as . . . "telling something that God has spontaneously brought to mind."[9]
>
> Prophesying in Paul's theology . . . is the performing of intelligible, articulate, communicative speech-acts, the operative currency of which depends on the active agency of the Holy Spirit mediated through human minds and lives to build up, to encourage, to judge, to exhort, and to comfort others in the context of interpersonal relations.[10]
>
> By this term [prophets] he [Paul] means . . . those who were endowed with a peculiar gift, not merely for interpreting Scripture, but also for applying it wisely for present use . . . Let us, then, by Prophets in this passage understand, first of all, eminent interpreters of Scripture, and farther, persons who are endowed with no common wisdom and dexterity in taking a right view of the present necessity of the church, that they may speak suitably to it, and in this way be, in a manner, ambassadors to communicate the divine will.[11]

By the end of his study, Hill includes "pastoral preaching,"[12] and concludes:

> Perhaps—and we can put it no stronger than that—it is those who have grasped the meaning of Scripture, perceived its powerful

---

6. Friedrich, *TDNT*, VI (*sub prophētēs*), 855, in Panagopoulos, *Prophetic Vocation*, 119.
7. Turner, *Holy Spirit and Spiritual Gifts*, 10–11.
8. Forbes, *Prophecy and Inspired Speech*, 229.
9. *GP*, 284.
10. *FEC*, 1094.
11. Calvin, *Commentary on the Epistles*, 415.
12. Hill, *New Testament Prophecy*, 126.

INTRODUCTION

> relevance to the life of the individual, the Church and society, and declare that message fearlessly who are the true successors of . . . the prophets in the New Testament.[13]

There is a considerable degree of consensus among these definitions; but there are also hints of some key differences, which we will explore in our study. For example, one difference is the extent to which prophecy is believed to be always or normally "spontaneous" or "immediately-inspired" (Fee, Boring, Forbes, Turner, and Grudem above), and another is the extent to which "revelation" forms the basis of the gift of prophecy, or perhaps rather, as we shall see, what the term "revelation" is understood to mean.

Continuationism and Cessationism

In the course of our study, from time to time we use the terms "cessationist" and "continuationist." As far as possible, I try to avoid using these terms (and in particular to avoid applying them to individuals rather than to the viewpoints they hold). This is partly because these labels do not do a very good job of delineating key differences when it comes to prophecy: they oppose the views of people who fundamentally hold similar reformed views (such as Gaffin and Thiselton), and they unite the views of others who substantially disagree on prophecy (such as Grudem and Thiselton). So as labels they are not really fit for purpose. It may be better to refer to the "reformed continuationist" and the "charismatic continuationist" positions, although even these can sometimes be crude caricatures of nuanced positions.

There is a further reason for trying to avoid using these labels, and that is that they are simply misunderstood. Many assume, for example, that cessationism denies that miracles happen today. While some scholars with such views do indeed believe that miracles have ceased, many believe that they continue: Thomas Schreiner, for example, describes himself as a cessationist and yet believes that miracles and healings continue; only the *gifts* of miracles and healing have ceased.[14]

Since some scholars believe that only some miraculous gifts have ceased, it might be more accurate to say that someone is, for example, "cessationist *on prophecy*" or "cessationist *on tongues.*" In these terms, *all* the

---

13. Hill, *New Testament Prophecy*, 213.
14. Schreiner, "Why I am a Cessationist."

Introduction

main scholars we consider are cessationist *on apostleship* in the strictest sense of the word "apostleship," and, as we will see, they are all continuationist on prophecy in at least *some sense* of the word "prophecy."

A Summary of Views of Prophecy

In the course of our study we will find ourselves focusing on three popular positions, two of which maintain that prophecy continues today, and one which claims that it has ceased:

"Prophecy continues today"	"Prophecy has ceased"
Prophecy is proclaiming the message of Christ to the church. *Key text: Acts 2:17*	Prophecy is the infallible word of God. *Key text: Eph 2:20*
Prophecy is spontaneously-received revelation from God which is given in merely human words. *Key text: 1 Cor 14:29–30*	

Three Popular Positions on Prophecy

Of course, none of these views depends entirely on a single verse for their case; nevertheless, the arguments for each position do seem to gravitate toward the particular texts shown. The challenge before us is to reconcile these three texts—among many more!

My Approach

My approach will be as follows:

1. *The Old Testament.* We need to gain some broad sense of the nature of Old Testament prophecy and its mode of inspiration, transmission, content, purpose, and forms. We will then need to distinguish the key features of the Old Testament phenomenon so we can compare it with the New Testament gift.

2. *Exegesis of New Testament Texts.* This is where we need to spend most of our time. In the case of 1 Corinthians, we will also need an understanding of the key themes of the book as a whole, and not simply of the passages in which our topic appears to be explicitly addressed.

3. *Dialogue with Scholars.* As we do all of this we will spend much of our time in the company of leading scholars.

4. *Synthesis.* We will then need to draw the strands together. Our task here will be a bit like completing a jigsaw puzzle; areas of the puzzle may be complete (a tree, a lake . . .), but the overall picture may still be unclear. The synthesis is the attempt to determine how these areas fit together to form a comprehensive whole, and then to draw any lessons for today. Where things still remain unclear, we should not be afraid of *failing to conclude*.

What I Don't Cover

This is a study of biblical texts, not of the contemporary practice of prophecy. I aim to give a clear enough picture of the nature of the gift to enable a reader to assess contemporary expressions, but I do not discuss examples of contemporary practice because I want to build biblical convictions, rather than make a case through weight of anecdote. Nor do I explore the history of the understanding of the gift of prophecy by the church; for that, I refer readers to Thiselton's excellent study, *The Holy Spirit*.

A Dialogue with You

I began by saying that all theology is dialogue. That implies that this book is also a dialogue *with you*. I am very fallible: some of what I say here may be quite wrong, but I look forward to discussing it with you, so that together we can get closer to the truth. This book is the continuation of a discussion, not the end of one.

Part One
GROUNDWORK

Chapter 1

An Introduction to Old Testament Prophecy

It is impossible to investigate the New Testament gift of prophecy properly without considering its Old Testament counterpart. We therefore need to undertake a brief survey of the phenomenon of prophecy in the Old Testament and consider how it might bear on the nature of the New Testament gift.

What "Prophecy" Means

The Greek word for prophet (*prophētēs*) is composed of the prefix *pro-* and the verb *phēmi* ("speak"). Some key meanings that the prefix *pro-* brings to composites are:

1. *Standing in another's place* (as in "pronoun" in English)
2. *Forth and publicly* (as in "proclaim")
3. *Beforehand* (*pro-* becomes *pre-* in Latin, as in "predict")[1]

Although etymology is valuable, we should never feel constrained by it: D. A. Carson, following James Barr, rightly warns against an overreliance on etymology in understanding words, which he calls "the root fallacy,"[2] and

---

1. *LS*, 1208.
2. Carson, *Exegetical Fallacies*, 28.

talks about "semantic obsolescence"[3]: it is clear that words only mean what they mean when they are used, not what they may once have meant, or may mean elsewhere. Nevertheless, etymology is useful as an indicator of *possible meaning*. Prophecy is commonly described as both "foretelling" and "forth-telling" (that is, as prediction and proclamation), but these cover only two of the three etymological possibilities above, and omit, as we shall now see, arguably the most significant.

An Initial Definition

In the Old Testament, prophecy seems to be *God speaking through people*, that is, people speaking in God's name, on his behalf and with his authority to declare his plans and purposes. Prophecy announces unequivocally the very words of God. No Old Testament prophet ever says, "God *may* be saying this." This is why prophecy often appears in the first person: it is often unequivocal direct speech, rather than a potentially unreliable report.

Because the prophecy recorded in Old Testament Scripture comes as the very words of God, it has an absolute authority, and cannot be challenged. Grudem rightly says, "We do not find in the Old Testament any instance where the prophecy of . . . a true prophet is 'evaluated' or 'sifted' so that the good might be sorted from the bad, the true from the false."[4] People never ask, "Which *parts* are true, and which *parts* are false?" This is certainly correct: Jeremiah's prophecy, recorded in Scripture, is *wholly* true, despite the fact that many failed to acknowledge it as such in his own day. As the widow of Zarephath proclaims to Elijah, "Now I know that you are a man of God, and that the word of the Lord from your mouth is the *truth*" (1 Kgs 17:24).

The First Prophets

Michael Heiser says, "If we define prophets simply as spokespeople for God, prophets go all the way back to the beginning."[5] Adam clearly encountered

---

3. Carson, *Exegetical Fallacies*, 35.
4. *GP*, 24.
5. Heiser, *Unseen Realm*, 233.

An Introduction to Old Testament Prophecy

God and heard his voice (e.g., Gen 3:17–19); he must also have reported this to others, and so could by that token be considered the first prophet.[6]

Jesus refers to Abel as a prophet (Luke 11:50–51). Enoch is described as prophesying by the New Testament (Jude 14–16), and his prophecy consists of proclaiming God's judgment on the ungodly. It is also possible to describe Noah as a prophet: Peter calls him a "herald of righteousness" (2 Pet 2:5), and his warnings about the impending flood might well be called prophetic; the building of the ark could also be viewed as a prophetic act.

However, it is Abraham who is the first person to be explicitly identified as a prophet by the Old Testament itself: we are told that because he is a prophet, his prayer will be heard (Gen 20:7). Indeed, God may be referring to *all* the patriarchs as prophets when he says, "Touch not my anointed ones, do my prophets no harm" (Ps 105:15)!

Although these figures may all be designated as prophets, it is with Moses that we get the clearest articulation of the term, and its prime example. First, God says to Moses, "your brother Aaron shall be *your prophet* [Heb. *nabi'*]" (Exod 7:1), where the meaning is clearly "spokesman," "mouthpiece," or "representative": Aaron will speak on behalf of Moses. This verse reveals the core notion of one person faithfully conveying the words of another; and so a prophet of God is someone who acts as a faithful spokesman for God, someone through whom God speaks.

Although Aaron was Moses' spokesman, Moses was God's spokesman, that is, God would speak through him (Exod 4:15). Nevertheless, the term "prophet" seems to be used of Moses only retrospectively, to highlight his superiority over other prophets: "no prophet has risen since in Israel like Moses, whom the Lord knew face to face" (Deut 34:10, cf. Deut 18:18). Moses was not just *a* prophet, he was *the* Old Testament prophet.

The prophetic role of Moses involved speech ("I will be with your mouth and teach you what you shall speak"—Exod 4:12), and it also included authenticating *action*: "I will be with your mouth . . . and will teach you . . . what to *do*" (Exod 4:15). Thus Moses was given miraculous signs to authenticate his words, and armed with these gifts of both speech and action, he played his part in the rescue of Israel. Subsequent prophets were men and women of authoritative speech, sometimes also authenticated by

---

6. Heiser refers to Job 15:7–8, which he says implies that Adam had listened in at the council of God (Heiser, *Unseen Realm*, 233). As we shall see later (from Jeremiah 23:22), being present in God's council is a key qualification of the true prophet.

miraculous action. Elisha, for example, says that Naaman is healed "that he may know that there is a prophet in Israel" (2 Kgs 5:8).

The Attributes of Prophecy

It may be helpful to distinguish and discuss three key attributes of Old Testament prophecy:

1. The nature of prophecy: what it *was*.
2. The purposes of prophecy: what it was *for*.
3. The forms and characteristics of prophecy: what it typically *looked like*.

THE NATURE OF PROPHECY

The Spirit and Prophecy

Throughout Scripture it is clear that prophecy is always speech that is empowered, directed, inspired, given or enabled by the Holy Spirit: all prophets speak in the power of the Holy Spirit (2 Pet 1:19–21).[7] Prophesying and speaking in the power of the Spirit are frequently equated (1 Sam 10:6; Num 11:25; Neh 9:30), and the Spirit is described as coming upon prophets before they speak. We see this made explicit with, for example, Micaiah (1 Kgs 22:24), Azariah (2 Chr 15:1), Jehaziel (2 Chr 20:14), Zechariah (2 Chr 24:20), and both with Saul (1 Sam 19:23) and his messengers (1 Sam 19:20).

Of course, this should not surprise us—for how can one speak from God except under the influence of his Spirit (1 Cor 2:11)? However, while it is beyond question that all prophecy is Spirit-inspired, what we will need to consider is whether the converse is also true: that is, *is all Spirit-inspired speech prophecy?*

Prophecy was certainly a sign of Spirit-filling. Thus, in Numbers 11, God says he will take some of the Spirit that is on Moses and put it on the seventy elders, so that they might be able to share the burden of leading

---

7. IMPORTANT NOTE: In this study I normally use the term "Spirit-inspired" to refer to the infallible writings of Scripture. I use terms such as or "Spirit-empowered" or "Spirit-enabled" to refer to speech that is given under the influence of the Holy Spirit, but is not infallible (such as in a powerful sermon today). Nevertheless, I do also occasionally describe both forms of speech broadly as "Spirit-inspired."

God's people. We read, "as soon as the Spirit rested on them, they prophesied. But they did not continue doing it" (Num 11:25). Here it seems that prophesying is a temporary, visible sign to indicate the long-term, invisible enabling of the elders by the Spirit to lead God's people. The focus here is firmly on the fact that the Spirit enables the elders to serve, rather than on the actual content of the prophecy, which is not reported; their prophesying was simply some verbal evidence of the presence of the Spirit. Further examples of the tight association between Spirit-enabled speech and prophecy are found, for example, in 1 Samuel 10:6, 10:10, and 19:20.

Scripture as Prophecy

If prophecy is God speaking through people, Moses was prophesying not just when he was addressing Pharaoh, but, equally (assuming he was the author), when he wrote the first five books of the Bible, which include not only the records of God speaking to and through Moses, but also all the connecting narrative material, for chronicling the works of God in history was a common function of Old Testament prophets (1 Chr 29:29). Indeed, the whole Bible is the fully authoritative and reliable word of God, and those God used to write it are his spokesmen, his prophets. Thus, the common rabbinic phrase "the law and the prophets" can be used to refer to Old Testament Scripture as a whole (Acts 13:15; 24:14; 28:23; Rom 3:21). Grudem acknowledges this:

> There is some indication that all of the Old Testament was thought to have been written by those who were functioning as "prophets," for we read in Luke's Gospel: "And beginning with Moses and *all the prophets*, he interpreted to them in *all the scriptures* the things concerning himself" (Luke 24:27, RSV).[8]

A Focus on the Covenant People of God

The primary audience of prophecy is the covenant people of God. Nevertheless, prophecy can also be directed beyond Israel to her enemies—such as in Moses' prophecy to Pharaoh, and Jeremiah's prophecies about Egypt, Assyria, and Babylon, which are all speeches *against* the enemies of Israel.

---

8. *GP*, 26.

God promised Abraham that he would bless all the nations of the earth through him (Gen 22:18); in other words, God's covenant people were always intended to stretch beyond Israel. Thus, Isaiah's words of comfort (e.g., Isa 40:1–2), although addressed to Israel, surely anticipate the proclamation of the gospel to the nations, and this suggests that we should be wary of drawing too strong a distinction today between gospel preaching and prophecy.

A Prophetic People

Whilst particular individuals are designated as prophets in the Old Testament, there is also an important sense in which *all Israel* is to be a prophetic people. Thus,

> "Declare his glory among the nations, his marvelous works among all the peoples!" (Ps 96:3)

> "And as for me, this is my covenant with them," says the Lord: "My Spirit that is upon you, and my words that I have put in your mouth, shall not depart out of your mouth, or out of the mouth of your offspring, or out of the mouth of your children's offspring," says the Lord, "from this time forth and forevermore." (Isa 59:21)

Divine Encounter and the Prophetic Call

Every prophet in the Old Testament operates following an encounter with and a call from God. Many have noted a standard, recurring structure in the commissioning narratives. The following diagram (based on a similar model by Dennis Bratcher[9]) suggests a pattern, applied to three particular cases:

---

9. Bratcher, "Prophetic 'Call' Narrative."

	Moses	Gideon	Isaiah
A crisis in which God determines to act (sometimes in response to fervent prayer)	Exod 3:7-9	Judg 6:1-7	
Encounter with the holy God brings awareness of sinfulness	Exod 3:5-6	Judg 6:22	Isa 6:1-5
A commissioning of the prophet as God's agent	Exod 3:10	Judg 6:12-14	Isa 6:9
The prophet's reluctance and sense of inadequacy	Exod 3:11	Judg 6:15	
The adequacy of God: the promise of the ongoing presence and support of God, sometimes accompanied by signs	Exod 3:12	Judg 6:16-17	
God guarantees the results of the mission	Exod 3:17-22	Judg 6:16	Isa 6:11-13
God details the mission	Exod 3:14-17	Judg 6:25-27	Isa 6:9-10
God's patient dealing with the prophet's inadequacy, including signs to demonstrate God's adequacy	Exod 4	Judg 6:36-40	

The Structure of Commissioning Narratives

The prophet's encounter with God always entails a clash between the human and the divine. Exposure to the holiness of God produces a traumatic awareness in the prophet of his own sinfulness, and this is a foretaste of what is to come when the prophet reports the divine viewpoint to those to whom he is sent. The prophet thus commonly proclaims a clash of viewpoints: "*You think and do x, but God says y and will do z.*"

Divine encounter is not only fundamental to the call of the prophet; it is essential also to every prophetic act. Quite simply, without divine encounter, there is no prophecy.

Prophets as Men and Women of God and of His Word

The term "man of God" was closely associated with the word "prophet," particularly in the ministries of Elijah and Elisha, although the term is not used of any of the literary prophets (Isaiah, Jeremiah, etc.). It indicates that prophets were far more than transmitters of divinely received messages: they were normally (but not always) men and women of unusual devotion to God. They spoke whatever God may have required them to say without apology, equivocation, or compromise, even to their own extreme detriment (Jer 20:7–8). As Dunn says, "The prophetic spirit is always uncomfortable, both for the prophet himself and for those to whom he speaks."[10] Isaiah, for example, walked around Jerusalem naked for three years, Ezekiel lay on one side for a year, and Hosea married a prostitute. *A prophet put his life where his mouth was.*

As people of God, Old Testament prophets were also men and women of God's word, who would have memorized the Pentateuch in its entirety as an integral part of their loving devotion to God (Deut 6:4–9; Prov 7:3). As they meditated on Scripture day and night (Josh 1:8; Ps 1:2), they found that it *talked* to them, guiding their path and giving them wisdom (Prov 6:22). They continually sought to align their thoughts with the thoughts of God (Isa 55:8–9).

Although God clearly does speak *originally* through the prophet, God's voice to the prophet can never be entirely separated from God's voice to him or her *in Scripture*. This is why the words of prophets are steeped in the words of the prophets who preceded them, and this is most clearly evident in the heavy dependence of all the prophets on the words of Moses.

The Divine Council

Every true prophet encounters God, and this encounter is described as taking place in the "divine council." Thus, Jeremiah complains that false prophets have not "stood in the council of the Lord, to see and hear his word . . . But if they had stood in my council, then they would have proclaimed my words to my people, and they would have turned them from their evil way, and from the evil of their deeds" (Jer 23:18, 22).

Michael Heiser has written compellingly about this council,[11] which he describes as a council of God and other divine spirit beings ("*eloihim*"), who are called "gods" in Psalm 82: "God has taken his place in the divine council; in the midst of the *gods* he holds judgment" (Ps 82:1).

---

10. Dunn, *Christ and the Spirit*, 25.
11. Heiser, *Unseen Realm*, 23–37.

We see the inner workings of this council in 1 Kings 22:13–23. The Lord has determined that Ahab is to die, but not yet the means by which this is to happen. This then is what "the host of heaven" is meeting to discuss. One spirit proposes to act as a lying spirit in the mouth of the prophets (v. 22), and God accepts this proposal. Micaiah is a spectator during all these discussions.

Heiser points out that this plural nature of the council is also evident when Isaiah meets God. God says, "Whom shall I send and who will go for *us*" (Isa 6:8)?

In summary, the prophet engages with the Lord in his heavenly council of divine spirit beings and waits for him to speak.

THE PURPOSES OF PROPHECY

In the following paragraphs we identify a number of key purposes of Old Testament prophecy.

To Establish Covenant—Covenantal Prophecy

As well as his involvement in rescuing God's people from Egypt with his prophetic powers, Moses is also the major covenantal prophet of the Old Testament; that is, on Mount Sinai, and later in the Tent of Meeting, he was given and reported the terms of God's covenant with his people, and the Law of God (in Exodus, Leviticus, Numbers, and Deuteronomy).

To Recall to Covenant—Reformational Prophecy

God's revelation in Scripture is *gradual and developing*, that is, the writing of every Old Testament prophet brings fresh insights into the heart of God and the Christ to come. Nevertheless, it is also true that the role of all Old Testament prophets after Moses was also to recall God's people to their covenant relationship with God. We could call this "reformational prophecy." For example,

> Yet the Lord warned Israel by every prophet and every seer, saying, "Turn from your evil ways and keep my commandments and my statutes, in accordance with all the Law that I commanded

Part One—Groundwork

> your fathers, and that I sent to you by my servants the prophets." (2 Kgs 17:13)

> But this command I gave them: "Obey my voice, and I will be your God and you shall be my people. And walk in all the ways that I command you, that it may be well with you." But they did not obey ... I have persistently sent all my servants the prophets, day after day. Yet they did not listen to me ... (Jer 7:23–26)

Moses says to those who love God and walk in his ways, "you shall live," and to those who follow other gods, "you shall surely perish" (Deut 30:16–18), and he proclaims a number of blessings and curses in Deuteronomy 28. Subsequent prophets draw deeply from that chapter, which warns, for example, of exile (Deut 28:36) and foreign oppression (Deut 28:33, 49). This means that the predictions by later prophets of exile to Assyria and Babylon are Spirit-given applications of these Mosaic warnings.

J. Daniel Hays summarizes the standard message of the preexilic prophets as consisting of three points:

1. You have broken the covenant (through idolatry, social injustice, religious ritualism), so repent!
2. No repentance? Then Judgment! Judgment will also come to the nations.
3. Yet there is hope beyond the Judgment for a glorious future restoration both for Judah/Israel and for the nations.[12]

The role of the prophet is thus to contend for the faith by declaring sin and error to individuals, communities, cultures, and nations:

> But as for me, I am filled with power, with the Spirit of the Lord, and with justice and might, to declare to Jacob his transgression and to Israel his sin. (Mic 3:8)

Micah's work involved a diagnosis and declaration of cultural sin. The message of the prophets was always divinely appropriate to the audience to whom it was addressed. However, although it was Spirit-given, this discernment of sin was rarely miraculous.

In short, Old Testament prophets offered critiques of culture; they had the role of what we would call preachers; yes, they occasionally displayed

---

12. Hays, *Message of the Prophets*, 99.

An Introduction to Old Testament Prophecy

miraculous powers beyond any preacher today, but they were preachers nonetheless, and preachers today, as their successors, have much to learn from them.

To Reveal the End Times—Eschatological Prophecy

The Old Testament also includes eschatological prophecy, delivered largely through visions, and often expressed using extensive symbolism. Daniel, for example, looks not only back to the covenant, but also forward to the end times. Ezekiel, Joel, Isaiah, Jeremiah, and Zechariah are sometimes described as "proto-apocalyptic" because their prophecies include elements of an apocalyptic vision of the future. Of course, such prophecy is closely related to messianic prophecy and the proclamation of the ultimate triumph of God's kingdom.

To Pre-proclaim Christ—Messianic Prophecy

Although prophets recalled people to the Mosaic covenant, Ezekiel, Isaiah, Jeremiah, Joel, and many others also pointed forward to a new covenant relationship with God. So throughout the Old Testament there are messianic predictions pointing to the coming Christ, such as the predictions of the suffering servant in Isaiah 53.

Some have counted over 350 predictions relating to Christ in the Old Testament. But the Old Testament should not be seen as containing prophecies of the Christ in the sense that a bun contains currants; rather, Christ and the gospel are in the DNA of Scripture, and therefore present (albeit often hidden) in every part, and one task of preachers today is to expose and expound the gospel theme in all Scripture. This is what Jesus was doing when we read of him that, "beginning with Moses and all the prophets, he interpreted to them in all the Scriptures the things concerning himself" (Luke 24:27). Jesus is not simply saying here that the Old Testament often predicts him; he is saying that he is the *all-pervasive* theme of the Old Testament both revealed and concealed within it; thus, according to Peter, "*all the prophets* who have spoken, from Samuel and those who came after him, also proclaimed these days" (Acts 3:24).

Gillespie concludes that Old Testament prophets both "proclaim God's promise (realized in the gospel) and bear witness to God's righteousness (revealed in the gospel)."[13] The Old Testament is as christocentric as the New Testament. As we will see later, the teaching ministry of the New Testament apostles consists largely of christological readings of Old Testament texts.

To Guide the People of God—Domestic Prophecy

Finally, in our rough classification of types of prophecy, there is what we might call *domestic prophecy*, which deals with the need for day-to-day guidance. So, for example, a prophet might advise a king when to attack an enemy. We can easily assume that the ministries of Elijah and Elisha were filled with many rather casual miracles of this type. But this is to overstate matters: Jesus tells us that there were many lepers in Elisha's day, but he healed *only one*—Naaman the Syrian (Luke 4:27). Of course, there is nothing casual about the healing of Naaman: it is an event that is key to demonstrating God's love for people of all nations.

Likewise, Samuel's miraculous knowledge of the whereabouts of lost donkeys (1 Sam 9) may seem a trivial use of his gift. But the lost donkeys are providential in getting Saul to visit Samuel and therefore key to his anointing as king, and the fact that Samuel knows their location reinforces his authority to anoint Saul. So although miraculous prophecy in the Old Testament may sometimes appear casual, it is usually anything but: a miracle often advances God's overall purposes for his people at key points in salvation history.

THE FORMS AND CHARACTERISTICS OF PROPHECY

The Word of the Lord

God frequently reveals himself by putting words into the mouths of prophets: God, the *Word*, reveals himself chiefly *in words*.

The phrase "Thus says the Lord" followed by direct, first-person speech appears 415 times in the Old Testament (150 times in Jeremiah alone), and the phrase "The word of the Lord came to" appears 128 times (e.g., Gen 15:1; 1 Sam 15:10; Hos 1:1; Joel 1:1). The word "came" here in Hebrew is the verb "to be," and according to Motyer the sense is something

---

13. Gillespie, *First Theologians*, 136.

An Introduction to Old Testament Prophecy

like "the word of the Lord *became actively present to.*"[14] This key phrase is a signal of the production of Scripture and shows how closely associated prophecy is with Scripture.

In their prophesying, true prophets spoke *only* the words that God gave them to speak: they are "my words in your mouth" (Jer 1:9, 5:14; Isa 51:16, 59:21). Prophets speak under a strong sense of compulsion and direction; thus Balaam says, "Have I now any power of my own to speak anything? The word that God puts in my mouth, that must I speak" (Num 22:38). Peter, thinking of Old Testament prophecy, says, "no prophecy of Scripture comes from someone's own interpretation [Gk: *epilysis*, explanation, interpretation]. For no prophecy was ever produced by the will of man, but men spoke from God as they were carried along by the Holy Spirit" (2 Pet 1:21–22).

The phrase "the word of the Lord came to" means, of course, that the revelation came as words: there was no prior perception of a truth that subsequently had to be verbalized. This implies that there was no possibility of a degradation of the message during transmission, and therefore the word of the prophets was *the fully authoritative word of God.*

It is also clear that "the word of the Lord" is frequently associated with a vision of the Lord:

- *The word of the Lord* came to Abram in a *vision.* (Gen 15:1)
- *The word of the Lord* came to him saying . . . and he [i.e., the word of the Lord] brought him outside. (Gen 15:4–5)
- And God *spoke* to Israel in *visions* of the night. (Gen 46:2)
- The *word of the Lord* was rare those days; there was no frequent *vision.* (1 Sam 3:1)
- And the Lord *appeared* again at Shiloh, for the Lord revealed himself to Samuel at Shiloh by *the word of the Lord.* (1 Sam 3:21)
- The *word* that Isaiah the son of Amoz *saw.* (Isa 2:1)
- The *words* of Amos . . . which he *saw* concerning Israel. (Amos 1:1)
- The *oracle* that Habakkuk the prophet *saw.* (Hab 1:1)
- Write the *vision*; make it plain on tablets, so that he may run who *reads* it. (Hab 2:2)

---

14. Motyer, "Prophecy," 1039.

As Michael Heiser says, in these texts "the word of the Lord came" seems to imply "*a visible manifestation of Yahweh.*"[15] In other words, "the word of the Lord" is a *divine name*, and "came" seems to mean that the Lord appeared in visible form. But, as well as being God, "the word of the Lord" also has his own distinct identity: as John says, the Word *was* God, but was also *with* God (see John 1:1).

Although the phrase "the word of the Lord came" is not always explicitly mentioned in every Old Testament prophecy, it is possible that it is always implied whenever a prophet says, "Thus says the Lord . . ." So it is even possible, therefore, that *all Old Testament prophecy may have involved both an auditory and a visual experience of God.* God the Word appeared to prophets in embodied form before he was made flesh in Jesus Christ (John 1:14).

Dreams and Visions

"Vision" seems to be the generic term to describe the means by which God communicates to prophets. For example,

- If there is a prophet among you, I the Lord make myself known to him in a *vision*; I speak with him in a dream. (Num 12:6)
- Where there is no prophetic *vision* the people cast off restraint. (Prov 29:18)[16]

Some prophets use the word "vision" to introduce the verbal revelations they received (Isa 1:1; 2 Chr 32:32; Nah 1:1; Obad 1:1), just as other prophets use the phrase "the word of the Lord" (Hos 1:1; Zech 1:1).

God may speak to a prophet through either a dream or a vision (Num 12:6), and the terms "dreams" and "visions of the night" sometimes appear to be synonyms (Job 20:8, 33:15; Isa 29:7). However, gentile unbelievers seem exclusively to have dreams rather than visions (Abimelech, Laban, Pharaoh, Nebuchadnezzar, etc.), and the prophetic involvement is to provide interpretation.

On the other hand, when prophets have revelatory dreams, these are normally referred to as "visions at night". Thus, Solomon meets God in his

---

15. Heiser, *Unseen Realm*, 129; italics mine.

16. See also Genesis 15:1; Numbers 24:4; 1 Samuel 3:15; 2 Samuel 7:17; 2 Chronicles 9:29; Lamentations 2:9, 14; Ezekiel 1:1, 7:26.

dream (1 Kgs 3:4–6), and when Jacob awakes from his dream of a ladder, he knows he has been in the very presence of God: "How awesome is this place! This is none other than the house of God and this is the gate of heaven" (Gen 28:17). Daniel's experience of the Four Beasts is described as "a dream and visions of his head" (Dan 7:1) and "night visions" (Dan 7:13), perhaps as a way of emphasizing that this is an experience beyond conventional dream.

The experience of the boy Samuel (1 Sam 3:1–18) is intriguing. When he hears God calling, he is "lying down" but apparently not asleep. The experience appears to consist of a disembodied voice from God. However, it is later described as a "vision" (1 Sam 3:15) and, taken with the phrase "the Lord came and stood" (1 Sam 3:10), the text makes it clear that the experience involved an embodied manifestation of God.

So God communicates to prophets through dreams and visions; but the dreams are normally more than dreams—they are visions (often of God) at night. This may explain why, as a method of divine communication, the Bible sometimes seems to view dreams with some skepticism:

- For when dreams increase and words grow many, there is vanity; but God is the one you must fear. (Eccl 5:7)
- Let the prophet who has a dream tell the dream, but let him who has my word speak my word faithfully. What has straw in common with wheat? declares the Lord. (Jer 23:28)

Dreams are as dead as straw, but the word of God is a living seed.

Prediction

Prediction clearly occupies a special place within prophecy. Indeed, prediction and prophecy are so closely aligned that Moses' key test for false prophecy is whether or not the word it announces comes to pass (Deut 18:22). According to Motyer, "Almost every prophet appears as a foreteller."[17] Moses' basic message to Pharaoh from God is a simple command: "Let my people go," and each time a plague is threatened. Motyer says,

> We ... find in Moses the combination of proclamation and prediction which is found in all the prophets ... In the interests of

17. Motyer, "Prophecy," 1038.

speaking to the present situation the prophet often undertakes to enlarge upon events yet to come. It is this interlocking of proclamation and prediction which distinguishes the true prophet . . . Calls to repentance (e.g., Isa 30:6–9) and calls to practical holiness (e.g., Isa 2:5) are equally based on a word concerning the future; the vision of the wrath to come is made the basis for a present seeking of the mercy of God; the vision of the bliss to come calls to a walking in the light now.[18]

Revelation: Miraculous and Ordinary Insight

All prophecy is the report of a divine revelation: quite simply, without revelation there is no prophecy. Thus Amos talks of God "*revealing* himself to his servants the prophets" (Amos 3:7). We hear that, as a child, Samuel "did not yet know the Lord, and the word of the Lord had not yet been *revealed* to him" (1 Sam 3:7; cf. 1 Sam 3:21). Isaiah describes the process of the word of the Lord coming to him as God "*revealing* himself in my ears" (Isa 22:14).

The revelation that comes to the prophet is clearly often miraculous. We frequently read of some miraculous knowledge or perception given to prophets, such as Nathan's knowledge of David's adultery (2 Sam 12), Elisha's vision of the greed of Gehazi (2 Kgs 5:26), and knowledge about whether someone would recover from an illness (2 Kgs 1:4). Not only prophets, but priests also were assumed on occasion to be able to access such insights (Judg 18:4–5).

Prophetic revelation also includes the *less-obviously miraculous*—for example, the extraordinary wisdom of Solomon. We read, in Proverbs: "God gave Solomon wisdom and understanding beyond measure, and breadth of mind like the sand on the seashore" (1 Kgs 4:29). The book of Proverbs is clearly the product of divine wisdom, yet it is, nevertheless, a wisdom of ordinary things, an ordinary *type* of wisdom. Likewise, we also see, in the prophecies of Isaiah, Jeremiah, and many others, not only miraculous insight and predictions, but also Spirit-enabled "ordinary" wisdom: piercing sermonic diatribes against personal and cultural sin, idolatry, the neglect of God's law, greed, selfishness, and immorality of all kinds. Such speech is not the product of miraculous insight, but it is Spirit-inspired, and therefore prophetic.

18. Motyer, "Prophecy," 1037–38.

Songs and Prayers of Praise and Thanksgiving

It seems clear that prophecy often took the form of songwriting, singing, or spoken praise. Thus, Miriam, a prophetess, took up a tambourine and sang a praise song (Exod 15:20–21). Deborah's praise song in Judges 5 also has a strong element of historical narrative.

We know that bands of prophets prophesied in song as they walked along (1 Sam 10:5). We are told that Asaph "prophesied under the direction of the king" (1 Chr 25:2); since we know that he was a musician, and the author of a dozen psalms (Psalm 50 and Psalms 73–83), this suggests that these psalms may be the output of the prophetic activity referred to in 1 Chronicles. We are also told that Asaph, Heman, Jeduthun and their sons had a ministry of prophesying with music (1 Chr 25:1–8): they "prophesied with lyres, with harps, and with cymbals" (1 Chr 25:1), and "prophesied with the lyre *in thanksgiving and praise* to the Lord" (1 Chr 25:3).

These examples are interesting on several accounts: they suggest that prophecy need not always be addressed solely to people, as Paul says in 1 Corinthians 14:3, but might also include thanksgiving and praise *addressed to God*—although praise songs are often also addressed to people (the common exhortation of the Psalms, "Praise the Lord!," is both praise addressed to God and exhortation to others to praise him). Also, the need to sing in unison (2 Chr 5:13), and to co-ordinate songs with music, does not suggest a spontaneous or impromptu activity.

When Saul meets a band of (presumably) singing prophets (1 Sam 10:5), we are told "the Spirit of God rushed upon him, and he prophesied among them" (1 Sam 10:10). This suggests that Saul was caught up compellingly in the praise songs of the prophets. Turner describes this as "some kind of invasively inspired worship."[19] He distinguishes this from "non-invasive" prophecy, which he sees as the norm. A similar form of irresistible prophesying is described in 1 Samuel 19:20–24 and Jeremiah 20:9.

These examples all demonstrate that the term "prophecy" can be used to include some forms of prayer. As such, although prophecy is always Spirit-enabled, it need not always involve obviously miraculous revelations, nor first-person speech, nor include a preface claiming it to be from the Lord. The term is certainly broader than we may have imagined.

---

19. Turner, *Holy Spirit and Spiritual Gifts*, 189.

PART ONE—GROUNDWORK

Modes of Prophetic Inspiration

D. A. Carson suggests that there are several modes of prophetic inspiration,[20] including:

- *Direct dictation.* God dictates words, for example, through Jeremiah to Baruch, who writes them down (Jer 36:4). When the scroll is destroyed, the original content is easily reproduced (Jer 36:32) because, as Carson says, "God's mental disks never get wiped clean!"[21]
- *By vision and word* that the human agent himself may not always understand (as in Daniel 8).
- *Out of the fullness of the prophet's heart and experience,* borne along by the Spirit of God. Psalm 23 is clearly David speaking from the heart.
- *After long meditation on Scripture.* Carson argues that David's understanding of Melchizedek in Psalm 110 originates from his meditation on Genesis 14:18–20.

In other words, as well as being *multiform,* prophecy is also *multimodal,* that is, it is produced in many ways. It is possible that the idea of direct dictation may be overplayed here: just because Jeremiah dictates to Baruch does not mean that God dictated to Jeremiah. We simply have no idea how Jeremiah reproduced the first scroll, and are told only that he includes "all the words" of the first scroll and adds "many similar words" (Jer 36:32).

As Carson suggests, Scripture seems often to have been produced by God providentially employing the prophet's *actively engaged mind and personality* (the historical narrative of the books of Samuel serve as an example of this). J. I. Packer says,

> *Psychologically,* from the standpoint of form, it is clear that the human writers contributed much to the making of Scripture—historical research, theological meditation, linguistic style, etc. . . . But *theologically,* from the standpoint of content, the Bible regards the human writers as having contributed nothing, and Scripture as being entirely the creation of God.[22]

---

20. Carson's talk, "Getting Excited about Melchizedek."
21. Carson, "Getting Excited about Melchizedek."
22. Packer, "Inspiration," 565; italics mine.

Some argue that automatic writing of some sort was involved; they point to Peter's words: "For no prophecy was ever produced by the will of man, but men spoke from God as they were carried along *[pheromenoi]* by the Holy Spirit" (2 Pet 1:21). This verse is often compared to another verse that uses the same verb: "And when the ship was caught and could not face the wind, we gave way to it and were driven along *[epherometha]*" (Acts 27:15). Just as this ship was controlled by and at the mercy of the wind—it is argued—so the Scripture authors wrote under the control of the Spirit.

However, the Scripture writers were not inanimate objects, like boats; they had active minds, and to suggest that these minds were often actively involved in the process is not to deny the divine nature of Scripture; it is simply to maintain that in divine purposes there are often both an ultimate cause (God) and proximate or immediate causes (people) (see Gen 50:20).

First-person Speech

The prefaces "The word of the Lord came to" and "Thus says the Lord" are commonly followed by first-person speech in Old Testament prophecy. Such prefaces are, as we have already said, key markers of prophetic speech and of Scripture.

But, as we saw when we looked at prophetic songs of praise, it would be wrong to assume that all prophetic speech must be given in the first person. Many speeches in Scripture are clearly Spirit-enabled, and even include predictions, but are not given in the first person (for example, Jacob's blessing on his sons in Genesis 49, Moses' song in Deuteronomy 32, and his blessing on Israel in Deuteronomy 33). First-person speech is a frequent, but certainly not an essential, marker of prophecy: God speaks through people both directly and indirectly.

Primary and Secondary Prophets

We have said much about prophets who contributed to Scripture (with Grudem, we could call them "primary" prophets). But what about those who never made such a contribution—such as the bands or schools of "secondary" prophets who were associated with primary prophets like Elijah, Elisha, and Obadiah (who hid a hundred prophets in a cave)? How did their gift differ from that of those who contributed to Scripture?

Grudem says of these secondary prophets:

> None of their prophetic utterances are preserved in the canonical Scriptures, which *may suggest* that their prophesying was not ordinarily counted as equal in value or *equal in authority* to the messages of the primary, established prophets such as Samuel or Elijah. The wider distribution of the gift of prophecy to these bands of prophets foreshadows the outpouring of prophecy . . . (Acts 2:17–18) . . . in the New Covenant.[23]

If Grudem is suggesting here that the prophesying of the schools of prophets *lacked authority* or may have been *partly inaccurate*, caution is needed. There is clearly a hierarchy in prophets: Elisha led a band of some 100 disciples, referred to as "sons of the prophets" (2 Kgs 4:38, 44). But the bands of prophets at Bethel and Jericho both accurately foretold Elijah's last day on earth (2 Kgs 2:3, 5). The important point is that, inspired by God, all faithful prophets spoke his words *accurately*.

Poetic Prophecy

Much prophecy consists of rather brief utterances (for example, in the historical books, such as Samuel, Kings, and Chronicles). But the writings of the literary prophets (the authors of the books listed among the Major and Minor Prophets) are much more expansive. These extended prophecies start with Amos (or perhaps Joel) around 850 BC and introduce a largely new genre of prophetic discourse.

These literary prophets wrote primarily in poetry and with much use of figurative speech and imagery to strengthen their argument. They also make constant use of parallelism, in which one line is restated slightly differently in the next, to extend the meaning, as in, for example: "Fear not, for you will not be ashamed; be not confounded, for you will not be disgraced" (Isa 54:4).

Hays lists a range of further poetic devices used by the literary prophets:[24]

- *Metaphor*: "I will make you . . . a light to the nations."

- *Hypocatastasis*: "The storm of Yahweh will burst out in wrath."

---

23. GP, 275; italics mine.

24. Hays, *Message of the Prophets*, 52–56.

An Introduction to Old Testament Prophecy

- *Hyperbole*: "Let my eyes overflow with tears night and day."
- *Personification*: "Hear, O heavens! Listen, O earth!"
- *Metonymy*: "Every garment rolled in blood will be fuel for the fire."
- *Synecdoche*: e.g., using "Jerusalem" to refer to the southern kingdom of Judah.

This kind of poetic prophecy seems to be closely related to the prophetic songwriting we saw in the psalms. It consists largely of sermons recalling Israel to her God and to his Law, and its emotional force derives from its poetic quality. Clearly, what we have here is a radically different form of prophecy from, say, the historical narrative of the books of Samuel.

False Prophecy

False prophets are those who speak when the Lord has not spoken (Deut 18:20; Jer 14:14). Their speech is called the sin of *presumption*, and in the Old Testament was punishable by death: "But the prophet who presumes to speak a word in my name that I have not commanded him to speak, or [or 'and'] who speaks in the name of other gods, *that same prophet shall die*" (Deut 18:20).

This verse should give pause to anyone who claims to be speaking for God today. The Hebrew word for "or" here could mean either "or" or "and," which has prompted Grudem to assert that "there was no death penalty simply for speaking a false prophecy"[25] on the grounds that the penalty applied only if one *also* spoke in the name of other gods.

But perhaps we should not be so sanguine about the fate of the presumptuous prophet: it seems unlikely that the same person would speak *both* on behalf of both God *and* of other gods, and therefore Deuteronomy 18:20 is probably describing two individuals, one speaking presumptuously in the name of God, and the other speaking in the name of other gods. A further reason for considering Grudem mistaken on this point is the fact that we know that calling people to follow other gods was alone sufficient to warrant the death penalty (e.g., Deut 13:6–9). But whatever the case, to speak in the name of God when he had not spoken was then, and remains today, a great wickedness.

---

25. *GP*, 274.

Part One — Groundwork

We know that a prophet has spoken presumptuously if his prediction does not come to pass (Deut 18:22). However, although the fulfillment of any prediction is a necessary condition of prophecy, it is not a sufficient one: we read that God might allow a false prophet (meaning particularly, but not exclusively, one who calls people to idolatry) to predict events accurately—even accompanied by miracle—as a way of testing his people (Deut 13:1–3). God's people must therefore test not just the prophecy itself, but also the orthodoxy and orthopraxy of the prophet, and indeed their own hearts, being careful not to be unduly swayed by miracles, either real or apparent. Prophecy tests both the prophet and his hearers.

False prophets, unlike the true, have not *encountered God*; they have not "stood in the council of the Lord" (Jer 23:18), for if they had done so they would have spoken the truth (Jer 23:22). They are also described in the Old Testament as speaking from their *own hearts or imagination* (Ezek 13:2; Jer 23:26), following their *own spirits*, and speaking the delusions of their *own minds* (Ezek 13:3; Jer 14:14).

False prophets say, "'Declares the Lord,' when the Lord has not sent them, *and yet they expect him to fulfil their word*" (Ezek 13:6, italics mine). There is certainly no question of their sincerity (the deceiver is the first casualty of his own deceit!), but the real tragedy of false prophecy lies in the impact on those it deceives: false prophets are effectively "putting to death souls who should not die and keeping alive souls who should not live" (Ezek 13:19). They whitewash walls that God is promising to knock down (Ezek 13:14), they dishearten the righteous, and encourage the wicked (Ezek 13:22).

Those who cannot bear the truth say to the prophets, "Do not prophesy to us what is right; speak to us *smooth things*, prophesy illusions" (Isa 30:10), and the prophets readily oblige: their message often involves "saying peace when there is no peace" (Ezek 13:10; Jer 6:14; cf. 23:17), simply because that is the message most likely to be well received.

Unlike the true prophets, false prophets do not mend what is broken: "Your prophets have seen for you false and deceptive visions; they have not exposed your iniquity to restore your fortunes" (Lam 2:14). So, as Hosea says, "it shall be like people, like priest" (Hos 4:9): people will get the prophets they deserve (Hos 9:7).

Finally, God himself may deceive a prophet: if someone separates himself from God, goes after idols, and yet still comes to enquire of a prophet of God, there will be *no message* for him, and if any prophet does venture to speak to such an enquirer, God promises to deceive and destroy the prophet: "I, the Lord, have deceived that prophet, and I will stretch out my hand against him and will destroy him" (Ezek 14:9). Both prophet and enquirer share the same fate: false prophecy can be a sign of God's judgment on prophet and hearers alike.

Conclusion

We have seen that prophecy involved people speaking as God's spokesmen and spokeswomen, never at the prophet's own initiative, but always directed by God, down to the very words the prophet uses. Through prophecy God reveals himself to his people.

In our consideration of the purposes and characteristics of prophecy, we have noticed that in its manifestations it is richly diverse: it can appear as direct commands from God, songs of praise and thanksgiving, poetry, wisdom, historical narrative, sermons, and so on; it can be characterized both by miraculous insight and by ordinary (although Spirit-enabled) wisdom; its content covers everything from the nature of the Messiah and predictions about the end times to the whereabouts of lost donkeys! God's voice will not be limited by our narrow expectations of the speech forms he might use.

The fact that it appears in such a wide breadth of forms means that we should be wary of seeking to define prophecy in terms of its outward characteristics. Can spontaneity, for example, really be a *defining characteristic* of prophecy? Surely not, since so much prophetic writing (for example, the historical narratives) bears evidence of the active engagement of the prophet's mind. God himself is, of course, the cause and source of prophecy, but he is not necessarily the sole or immediate cause.

While the characteristics of prophecy are broad, its purposes are relatively narrow: the main purposes seem to be to reveal God's covenant with his people, to recall God's people to that covenant, and to pre-proclaim Christ. This leads us to suggest that prophecy is not to be defined by its outward characteristics, but rather, perhaps, by its *purposes*.

Above all, however, the primary defining characteristic of prophetic speech must surely simply be its *origin in the Spirit*.

Part One — Groundwork

Prophecy in the Old and New Testaments

What might our study of prophecy in the Old Testament lead us to expect to find in New Testament prophecy?

- We would expect prophecy in the New Testament to be *God speaking through people,* that is, people speaking with God's authority to declare his plans and purposes. It will be a faithful report of a miraculous revelation.

- We would expect the gift of prophecy to be closely related to speaking *in the Spirit,* and perhaps even synonymous with it.

- The gift of prophecy will deliver New Testament Scripture just as it delivered Old Testament Scripture.

- Just as Old Testament prophecy recalled God's people to the Mosaic covenant, so we would expect New Testament prophecy to recall God's people to the gospel of Christ.

- We would expect New Testament prophets to be men and women of God, operating following a divine encounter and call.

- We would expect New Testament prophets to confront sin, whether in the behavior of individuals, in the practices of church communities, or in wider cultural trends.

- We would expect prophecy in the New Testament to proclaim *the infallible word of God.* We would expect it always to be *true* because it proceeds from the Spirit of truth (John 14:17).

- Just as the Old Testament prophets announced Christ in their prediction, so we would expect New Testament prophets to announce him in their proclamation.

- Old Testament prophets *sometimes* performed miracles to authenticate their ministry. In the New Testament we would expect, at least sometimes, to see prophets continuing to manifest similar divine authentications of their words.

- We would expect to see predictions in the form of warnings and promises about the future as a significant part of New Testament prophecy.

- We would expect to see evidence of the working of the human mind in the production of prophecy.

- We would expect false prophecy to persist in the New Testament, and to be just as wicked.
- We would expect to see a gift richly diverse in its manifestations, but narrower in it purposes and functions.
- We have seen hints that Israel was a prophetic people, proclaiming God to the nations, and we would expect to see this theme taken up in the New Testament.

Chapter 2

An Inadequate Introduction to New Testament Prophecy

This chapter offers only an initial—and, as we shall see, *inadequate*—introduction to the subject of prophecy in the New Testament, as a prelude to our more detailed discussion in later chapters.

When we compare the New Testament with the Old, we see a distinct change in the vocabulary of prophecy. In the Old Testament, both the concept and the terminology of prophecy are ubiquitous. Men described as "prophets" wrote every book of the Old Testament, and we have seen that the phrase "the law and the prophets" refers to the Old Testament in its entirety.

In the New Testament, however, although the concept of people speaking in the Spirit with the authority of God is very much alive, the vocabulary of prophecy is much diminished. So, for example, although Jesus has all the gifts (and more) of any Old Testament prophet, and although people often refer to him as a prophet, he does not commonly refer to himself by the term; nor do the apostles refer to themselves as prophets, although they clearly have the ability to speak authoritatively from God. This change between the testaments will need to be accounted for in due course; in this chapter we simply highlight the issue.

An Inadequate Introduction

Communication and Incarnation

The most obvious reason why Jesus hesitates to refer to himself as a prophet is clear from Hebrews, in which Jesus is contrasted with the prophets: "Long ago, at many times and in many ways, God spoke to our fathers by the prophets, but in these last days he has spoken to us by his Son" (Heb 1:1–2). Jesus is not merely a spokesman for God, but God's very Son, who bears "the exact imprint of his nature" (Heb 1:3). The God whom the prophets could only speak of indirectly and in part, we have now come to encounter directly and fully in Christ, who has made "purification for sins" (Heb 1:3). This implies that some aspects of Old Testament prophecy have now been *superseded*.

Prophets and the Indwelling Spirit

In Old Testament times, the Holy Spirit was not universally available to the people of God, and in their relationship with God they were therefore reliant on intermediaries: they needed priests to teach them God's Law and mediate on their behalf to God, and they needed Spirit-directed prophets to access the wisdom of God.

By contrast, as Christians today, we have access to the wisdom of God through the indwelling Holy Spirit who glorifies Christ (John 16:13–14) by guiding us in gospel truth, and in the completed Scriptures, through whose prophetic voice God continues to speak. It is therefore dangerous to assume that New Testament prophets must have an identical role to that of their Old Testament counterparts: there are important covenantal differences that we need to account for.

On this basis, we might well expect the concept of prophecy to disappear altogether in the New Testament. It does not: indeed, we see prophecy described as a gift of the Spirit, referred to in several lists of the gifts, principally Ephesians 4:11, 1 Corinthians 12:10, and Romans 12:6. However, although it does not disappear, the gift does seem to undergo a number of key changes or transformations from its Old Testament counterpart, as we shall see.

Announcement of the Messiah

At the beginning of Luke's Gospel, we see examples of Spirit-inspired speech from Mary (Luke 1:46–55), Zechariah (Luke 1:68–79), and Simeon (Luke

2:29–32, 34–35). Anna, who is described as a "prophetess," gives thanks to God and speaks of him "to all who were waiting for the redemption of Israel" (Luke 2:38). Although only Zechariah's speech is explicitly described as prophecy, since they are all Spirit-inspired announcements of the arrival of the Messiah, Luke would surely have been happy to describe all these speech-acts as prophetic.

Still Spirit-inspired Speech

At Pentecost, we hear that when the Holy Spirit was given, "they were all filled with the Holy Spirit and began to speak in tongues" (Acts 2:4). The tongues speech proclaims "the mighty works of God" (Acts 2:11), that is, surely, God's mighty works *in Christ*. Peter then explains this event as the fulfillment of a prophecy by Joel: "And in the last days it shall be, God declares, that I will pour out my Spirit on all flesh, and your sons and your daughters shall prophesy'" (Acts 2:17).

Peter is saying, in effect, "What you are hearing is speech inspired by the Spirit—don't you remember that Joel said that people would prophesy?" Of course, he is not implying that the tongues speech at Pentecost is infallible Scripture; he is simply saying that the tongues speech of Pentecost is outward evidence of an inner filling with the Spirit, which he equates with prophecy.[1] Here again, as we saw in Numbers 11, prophecy and Spirit-inspired speech seem to be synonymous notions, and this provides evidence that not only is all prophetic speech Spirit-enabled, but also that all Spirit-enabled speech may be described as prophecy. We will return to Acts 2 in our next chapter.

We see something similar in the story of the conversion of the Ephesian disciples in Acts, where we read that, "when Paul had laid his hands on them, the Holy Spirit came on them, and they began speaking in tongues and prophesying" (Acts 19:6). These "disciples" were, in effect, Old Testament believers, having received the baptism of John, but knowing little or nothing of Jesus. Immediately after their conversion at the hands of Paul, they start speaking in tongues and prophesying. Their speech gives outward evidence of an inward change and demonstrates continuity with the events of Pentecost (despite the fact that here tongues and prophesying are

---

1. Although Paul *contrasts* tongues and prophecy in 1 Corinthians 14, Peter *equates* them in Acts 2. Many take this to indicate that the passages described different kinds of tongue gifts.

distinguished). The prophecy here (as at Pentecost) probably consisted of proclaiming the mighty works of God in Christ; in other words, its content matched the tongues speech. It does indeed seem that, as Christopher Forbes notices, "For Luke, however, virtually *any speech inspired by the spirit* may be described as prophetic."[2]

Prediction

Because prediction and prophecy are so strongly correlated in the Old Testament, it would be natural to assume that they are also tightly correlated in the New. It would be easy to collect a number of apparent predictions in the New Testament and to declare them to be prime or typical examples of New Testament prophecy; but this could be a circular argument.

So, for example, we could single out these texts:

- Agabus's prediction of a famine (Acts 11:28)
- Agabus's prediction of the arrest of Paul at Jerusalem (Acts 21:11)
- The warning to Paul by the disciples at Tyre (Acts 21:4)
- An unspecified prophecy about Timothy (1 Tim 1:18; 4:14)
- Peter's prediction of the death of Sapphira (Acts 5:9)
- Paul's rebuke of Elymas and the prediction of his blindness (Acts 13:10–11).

Of course, these are indeed examples of prophetic speech, but are they *normative* examples of New Testament congregational prophecy? Are they the kind of speech that Paul is seeking to encourage in 1 Corinthians 14? This is a question we will explore in due course.

Eschatological Prediction

The apostles seem to have been given a clear vision of the last days, and make a number of eschatological predictions:

> "But you must remember, beloved, the predictions of the apostles of our Lord Jesus Christ. They said to you, 'In the last time there will be scoffers, following their own ungodly passions.'" (Jude 17–18; see also 2 Pet 3:3–4; 2 Tim 3:1–5)

2. Forbes, *Prophecy and Inspired Speech*, 219; italics mine.

Part One — Groundwork

Of course, by far the most extensive example of eschatological prediction in the New Testament is the book of Revelation, which we are told constitutes a prophecy in its entirety (Rev 1:3; 22:19). The book is clearly a New Testament example of the kind of apocalyptic prophecy we noted in the Old Testament; but whereas the end times there were indeterminably distant, in Revelation they have become *imminent*: it concerns "the things that must *soon* take place" (Rev 1:1). The book is not given to satisfy idle curiosity about the future, but in order to encourage the church to live in the light of the imminence of the judgment to come: that is, to *repent* (Rev 2:5, 16, 22; 3:3, 19), and to *persevere* (Rev 2:10; 3:11). Its prophetic nature must consist at least partly in the fact that it is *exhortation, encouragement, and consolation* of the church (cf. 1 Cor 14:3) *in the light of these future events*.

Dreams and Visions

In the Old Testament we saw that visions of God frequently seem to accompany prophecy, and that what might appear to be revelatory dreams were normally visions (often of God) at night. After Pentecost, we hear of several day-time visions (Acts 9:10; 10:3; 2 Cor 12:1–3; the extensive visions of Revelation), and a couple of incidents are referred to as "visions in the night" (Acts 16:9; 18:9). These experiences are often received in a state described as a "trance" ("*ekstasis*") (Acts 10:10; 11:5; 22:17), are so intense that action undertaken as part of them is confused with reality (Acts 12:9; 2 Cor 12:3).

There are very few revelatory dreams in the New Testament. Joseph has a couple (Matt 1:20; 2:13), and there is the dream of Pilate's wife (Matt 27:19). But there are no other revelatory dreams recorded in the Gospels. In Acts 2:17, Peter quotes Joel's prediction of a new age in which "your old men shall dream dreams, and your young men shall see visions." This might lead us to expect an upsurge in the occurrence of prophetic dreams after Pentecost. However, curiously, this is the last mention of dreams in Acts; indeed, they are only mentioned once after this in the rest of the New Testament, and then in a negative sense, to describe those who wrongly rely on them (Jude 1:8).

So there is no evidence for widespread prophetic dreams in the New Testament age, and very few visions at night. This may well suggest that the words of Joel, quoted in Acts 2:17, are to be taken somewhat figuratively. Joel would then be using familiar theophanic language to describe an unfamiliar future age in which God would reveal himself to all his people through the new birth. So, one could say, all Christians have had a vision of God.[3]

Miraculous Insights

After Pentecost, the prophecies of Agabus are perhaps the most striking examples of miraculous, Spirit-given insight, and we explore these separately in later chapters. Apart from these, there are surprisingly few examples of miraculous insight. For example, we know that the Spirit prevents Paul from preaching in Asia (Acts 16:6), but the means is unclear. In the case of Ananias and Sapphira in Acts 5, Peter's knowledge of their lie to the Holy Spirit may well have come through a miraculous revelation. There is a similar example in Paul's rebuke of Elymas (Acts 13:10–11), which is accompanied by a prediction.

We may conclude that, even among the apostles, miraculous insight is rather rare after Pentecost.

"The word of the Lord"

In the Old Testament, we saw that the phrase "the word of the Lord came" was a signature of prophetic speech. Might there be a parallel in Acts, in which the apostles are described as "speaking the word of God" (Acts 4:31; 6:2)? Clearly there are fundamental differences in the meanings of these phrases: in the Old Testament, "the word of the Lord" referred to God in a visible form, whereas, in the New Testament "the word of the Lord" or "the word of God" means "the gospel" or the gospel message. But there are also parallels between the two usages. In both cases, "the word of the Lord" seems to have an agency that is beyond and independent of those who are speaking it: in the Old Testament the word of God "came" to particular individuals, and in the New Testament we read that the word of God "increased and multiplied" (Acts 12:24), and "continued to increase and prevail mightily" (Acts 19:20). Furthermore, in the New Testament, as in the Old, the expression is explicitly tied to the filling of the Holy Spirit:

---

3. This is not to deny the possibility of more literal visions of God or Christ today, or prophetic dreams. However, since both are extremely rare in the New Testament we would expect them to be extremely rare today too..

"they were all filled with the Holy Spirit and continued to speak the word of God with boldness" (Acts 4:31).

However, there is also a key difference between the two usages: "the word of the Lord" that came to the prophets is the infallible word of God; but when we read of the apostles and others preaching "the word of the Lord," *there is no implication that they always spoke infallibly*, and yet they spoke powerfully and effectively, because their message was rooted in biblical truth. So the phrase "the word of the Lord" was a signal of *original Scripture* in the Old Testament, but after Pentecost "the word of God" indicates *Scripture-based gospel preaching*.

False Prophecy

We saw that in the in the Old Testament false prophets do not tell people the hard truth they need to hear, but the "smooth things" (Isa 30:10) they want to hear. It is no different in the New Testament:

- "People will not endure sound teaching, but having itching ears they will accumulate for themselves teachers to suit their own passions." (2 Tim 4:3)
- "Many false prophets have gone out into the world . . . They are from the world; therefore they speak from the world, and the world listens to them." (1 John 4:1, 5)

Jesus warns specifically against those who employ miracles as evidence of spirituality: "On that day many will say to me, 'Lord, Lord, did we not prophesy in your name, and cast out demons in your name, and do many mighty works in your name'" (Matt 7:22)? These false prophets are astonished to find themselves rejected by Jesus, just like their Old Testament counterparts who spoke lies and yet expected God to fulfill their words (Ezek 13:6). Their sincerity is not in question; nor, indeed, is their miraculous ability.

A miracle is certainly not, as many assume, a sure sign of blessing. Rather, the prophet is to be assessed by whether his message conforms to the message of Christ (1 John 4:2). So when Jesus says that we will recognize false prophets "by their fruits" (Matt 7:20), he implies that they are to be assessed not just by the fruit of their lives (their orthopraxy), but also by the fruit *of their lips* (cf. Prov 12:14; 13:2), that is, by the orthodoxy of their speech.

An Inadequate Introduction

Scripture as Prophecy

Since it is the word of God, the New Testament, like the Old, can be described as "prophecy" in its entirety. This means that the letters of Paul constitute prophecy just as much as the book of Revelation; clearly, they are different *types* of prophecy, but this difference merely shows what a broad spectrum of speech and literary forms is covered by the term. Paul is certainly no less aware than John that he is a spokesman of God: as he says, "Christ is speaking in me" (2 Cor 13:3). This means that all who contributed to the New Testament canon, that is, the apostles, Mark, Luke, and the writer of Hebrews, may be described as "prophets."

So Scripture both *contains* prophecy (inasmuch as it reports direct speech from God) and *is* prophecy (inasmuch as it is all the word of God). Prophecy is the gift through which Scripture was given. This is not the sole purpose of the gift, but it is both its primary purpose and its supreme manifestation.

Prophecy, Scripture, and the Spirit

We should therefore also note the very tight association of prophecy with both Scripture and the Holy Spirit in both testaments. Since Scripture and the Holy Spirit are also tightly correlated (see Eph 6:17; 2 Tim 3:16; 2 Pet 1:21), we can describe a three-way relationship, with the terms closely orbiting each other: prophecy is Spirit-enabled, prophecy produces Scripture, and Scripture is both produced by the Spirit (2 Tim 3:16) and used by Spirit (Eph 6:17).

Prophecy

Holy Spirit   *Scripture*

Figure 1

PART ONE—GROUNDWORK

The Vanishing Act

Our search has unearthed very few examples of speech explicitly described as prophecy in the New Testament church. This means that our understanding of the nature of New Testament prophecy is based on rather a small dataset. As Forbes says, our understanding is "based on implications drawn from narrative (in the case of Luke) and occasional comments which may be situationally or polemically conditioned (in the case of Paul)."[4] It is not at all clear why the examples should be so few, especially since at Pentecost, Peter had suggested that prophecy in the new age would actually be abundant and widespread (Acts 2:17).

Why is the word "prophecy" not as common in the New Testament as the words "preaching" and "teaching?" Consider the number of times the word "prophecy" and its associated terms are mentioned in the two testaments, compared to "preaching" and "teaching":

Occurrences in NIV	OT	NT
Prophesy, Prophecy, Prophet	429	44*
Preach, Preacher	7	97
Teach, Teacher	119	242

*excluding references to OT prophecy

This scarcity creates a substantial hermeneutical issue: with so little data, how are we to determine what is typical and what is exceptional? The prophecies of Agabus may demonstrate typical examples of New Testament prophecy; but, on the other hand, they might be reported because they are exceptional. How are we to account for this vanishing act? We can begin to account for it, I think, once we acknowledge that, even at this early stage in our analysis, we are already in danger of falling into three serious errors.

Error 1: Assuming All Prophecy is so Described

We have only been concerned with occurrences of the word group "prophet," "prophecy," and "prophesy." That is, we have assumed a one-to-one correspondence between the Bible's use of the term "prophecy" and the manifestation of the gift—that prophecy will invariably be so described; but that would be like assuming that every time someone prays in the Bible, the

---

4. Forbes, *Prophecy and Inspired Speech*, 221.

word "pray" must appear, and to ignore words like "praise" and "thanksgiving." In other words, we have not given adequate consideration to New Testament texts that clearly involve prophecy but *do not use the term*—we haven't been looking in all the right places. For example, what of the great speeches of Peter and Stephen in the early part of Acts, and indeed, the epistles of Paul—do these teach us anything about the New Testament gift of prophecy? And what of the ministry of Barnabas? He is identified as a prophet—but where is his prophesying? As M. E. Boring says: "Some studies of early Christian prophecy have been too dominated by the occurrence or non-occurrence of the word *prophētēs*."[5] Hill would agree:

> Why not then simply concentrate attention on the occurrences of the word and word-group? This approach assumes that the phenomenon to be defined will *always* be so labeled . . . This procedure . . . is of little assistance in understanding a particular phenomenon which may occur in connection with a given word *as well as apart from it*.[6]

It is hard to overestimate the significance of these comments; if we accept them in principle, our study will take a radically different turn. But if we ignore them, and restrict ourselves to occurrences of the word group, it may be impossible to build a coherent picture of our subject.

Error 2: Seeing What We Expect to See

This is related to the previous error. *We have allowed our own preunderstanding to determine what constitutes prophecy rather than the text.* So we have looked for predictions and have assumed that the few examples of prediction are the only examples of prophecy. So we have assumed, for example, that the warning from the disciples at Tyre (Acts 21:4) constitutes "prophecy," although the text does not mention the term, but simply reports that it is speech made "in the Spirit."

Of course, if we decide that all speech made "in the Spirit" may be described as prophecy, we may describe such speech as prophecy on that basis; but we must be wary of limiting our understanding of prophecy to prediction, and we should certainly not assume that Paul has prediction in mind when he encourages prophecy in 1 Corinthians 14. It is far from clear

---

5. Boring, *Sayings of the Risen Jesus*, 15.
6. Hill, *New Testament Prophecy*, 2–3; italics his.

that prophecy is as tightly associated with prediction in the New Testament as it was in the Old.

Error 3: Operating With an Inadequate Interpretative Framework

In coming to an understanding of a biblical phenomenon, not all texts are equal. In particular, we should be wary of generalizing from particular, often remarkable, events; rather, we need to seek out and give weight to passages which seem to offer an *interpretative framework* or lens through which to view and understand the phenomenon more widely.

Conclusion

With the arrival of Christ, there are indications that some aspects of the gift of prophecy might cease (Matt 11:13; Heb 1:1); but far from disappearing, we are told in Acts 2 that prophecy has (in some sense) become a widespread phenomenon among the people of God.

Surprisingly, however, there are not nearly as many examples of prophecy in the New Testament as we might expect: the gift seems to have performed something of a vanishing act. This is all the more surprising since we recall from our study of the Old Testament gift that "prophecy" was a broad, polymorphic term, which could describe many types of speech-act.

We have seen how the phrase "the word of God" is used differently in the two testaments, and wondered if we might be beginning to see a transformation in the gift of prophecy itself. Might the gift that produced infallible Scripture in the Old Testament proclaim the gospel using that Scripture in the New Testament? Could this account for the vanishing act?

Prophecy, as we have seen, comes in many and various forms. So when Paul encourages the Corinthians to seek the gift of prophecy "earnestly" (1 Cor 14:39), which of these forms does he have in mind? Is he encouraging the Corinthians (and us) to engage in praise songs? Or to receive miraculous original insights? Or make predictions? Or to preach a sermon? Or to share the gospel with a friend? Or to contribute to the canon of Scripture? Or to share some insight into the last days? Or all the above? Clearly, without more analysis, it would be dangerous to become fixated on any one of these possible forms and declare it to be a model or paradigm of what Paul has in mind.

An Inadequate Introduction

What our study so far has lacked is an adequate interpretative framework for understanding the gift of prophecy. We need to ask whether there might be some key texts that would help us to build such a framework. In the next couple of chapters we will propose and examine a few such texts.

CHAPTER 3

Towards an Interpretative Framework for Prophecy—Part 1

SEVERAL PASSAGES IN THE New Testament are particularly significant for our understanding of the gift of prophecy. We will start by examining three such texts, and we will come across more later in our study.

John the Baptist: More than a Prophet (Matt 11:9–13)

With the arrival of John the Baptist, prophecy takes an important turn. John predicts the imminent arrival of the Messiah: "Repent, for the kingdom of heaven is at hand" (Matt 3:2). We then immediately see Jesus "proclaiming the gospel of the kingdom and healing every disease" (Matt 4:23). Proclamation of the kingdom has replaced prediction of it; and since both activities depend on revelation, both can equally be termed as "prophetic." Prophecy seems now to have as much to do with *proclaiming* Christ as it formerly had to do with *predicting* him.

Jesus points to the superiority of John the Baptist over the prophets who came before, and yet also stresses the superiority of every Christian over John:

> What then did you go out to see? A prophet? Yes, I tell you, and more than a prophet . . . Truly I tell you, among those born of women there has not risen anyone greater than John the Baptist. Yet the one who is least in the kingdom of heaven is greater than

Towards an Interpretative Framework — Part 1

he . . . For all the Prophets and the Law prophesied until John. (Matt 11:9–11, 13)

Jesus is saying that in some sense all Christians are greater than John the Baptist. What then is the nature of this superiority?

- First, John's superiority over earlier prophets must surely consist in the fact that he had the privilege of proclaiming the arrival of the Messiah whom his predecessors could only distantly predict.
- On the other hand, our superiority over John must consist in the fact that, as those indwelt by the Spirit of God, we inhabit a kingdom he could only indicate, we are the heirs of a kingdom of which he was merely the herald.

We have a fuller understanding of the purposes of God than any Old Testament prophet and a far greater knowledge of Christ (why then only a fraction of their zeal?). We have the indwelling Spirit transforming us into the likeness of Christ. We can speak, not infallible Scripture as Isaiah did, but nevertheless a complete gospel message under the authority of Christ (Matt 28:18–20). We are indeed "greater" than the prophets; they, as our servants, supplied pieces of the jigsaw but never saw the whole picture (1 Pet 1:12).

Jesus seems to imply that prophecy might end altogether with John: "For all the Prophets and the Law prophesied until John" (Matt 11:13). Indeed, the Old Testament phrase, "The word of the Lord came to" is used for the last time in Scripture in relation to John (in Luke 3:2, although in the form, "The word of *God* came to"). Clearly *something* is ending, but what exactly? Certainly, prophecy as messianic prediction passes away. But what is replacing it?

Are We All Now Prophets? (Acts 2:14–21)

We already touched on this passage in our last chapter. At Pentecost, *everyone* in the house was filled with the Spirit and spoke in tongues (Acts 2:4). Peter explains this event as the beginning of the last days predicted by Joel, and as the dawning of the new age of the Spirit, characterized by the pouring out of the Holy Spirit *universally* upon the people of God (Acts 2:14–18).

Joel had said that the Spirit would be poured out on "all flesh" and that as a consequence,

> your sons and your daughters shall prophesy, your old men shall
> dream dreams, and your young men shall see visions. (Joel 2:28)

So Peter is equating the tongues speech at Pentecost with Joel's promise of an outpouring of prophecy. The new age of the Spirit has begun.

When Peter quotes the next verse, "Even on the male and female servants in those days I will pour out my Spirit" (Joel 2:29), he adds a phrase of his own: "*and they shall prophesy*" (Acts 2:18), and so creates what is in effect a new promise that strongly suggests that *all Christians will actually prophesy*. Peter thus seems to indicate what Roger Stronstad, David Garland, Richard Gaffin and others have called the "prophethood" of all believers, to mirror the doctrine of the priesthood of all believers (1 Pet 2:9–10), and that of the kingship of all believers (Eph 2:6; Rom 5:17). Timothy Keller suggests that the prophethood, priesthood, and kingship of all believers are all implied in 1 Peter 2:9, in which believers are described as "a royal priesthood [kings and priests], that you may proclaim [prophets] the excellences of him who called you out of darkness into his marvelous light."[1]

On this reading, Joel's text has echoes of Jeremiah's description of the age of the Spirit, in which he declared that the knowledge of God would one day be universally available to the people of God:

> I will put my law within them, and I will write it on their hearts.
> And I will be their God, and they shall be my people. And no longer shall each one teach his neighbor and each his brother, saying,
> "Know the Lord," for they shall all know me, from the least of them
> to the greatest, declares the Lord. (Jer 31:33–34)

Of course, this universal knowledge of God does not mean an end to the need for the gift of teaching in the church: it is simply Jeremiah explaining a mysterious future reality in terms of a then-familiar practice. In much the same way, it seems that Joel was explaining the mysterious future age of the Spirit in terms of a well-known term: prophesying—*believers will speak authoritatively for the God they know personally.*

Carson agrees; he compares Joel 2 with Jeremiah 31 and concludes,

> Joel's concern is not simply with a picky point—more people will
> prophesy some day—but with a massive eschatological worldview.
> What was anticipated was an entirely new age, a new relationship

---

1. Keller, *Center Church*, 344–46.

Towards an Interpretative Framework—Part 1

> between God and his people, a new covenant . . . *All* who live under this new covenant enjoy the gift of this prophetic Spirit.[2]

The phrase, "I will pour out my Spirit, and they shall prophesy" seems simply to be describing the consequences of the Spirit being poured out—namely, that people will speak under the Spirit's direction. There is thus further evidence here that "prophesying" is synonymous with "speaking in the Spirit" in the New Testament, just as it appeared to be in the Old.

There are alternative ways of reading Acts 2:17–18. Peter could be referring to:

- A widespread, but not universal outpouring of prophecy at Pentecost that was short-lived, and lasted only for the time of the apostles
- A widespread, but not universal outpouring of prophecy that continues to today
- A universal *potential* for prophecy that continues to today

These three readings are all possible, but none really does full justice to Peter's announcement of a new age in which the Spirit is poured out universally upon the people of God, which is evidenced by their speech.

Some maintain that Peter must be referring to a widespread rather than a universal distribution of the prophetic gift because when Paul asks the question, "Are all prophets?" (1 Cor 12:29) he surely expects the answer "No." But it is perfectly possible that prophesying, like teaching, is an activity of which all believers are capable to an extent, but in which only some are particularly gifted. (All may prophesy without being prophets just as all may teach without being teachers.)

It is also possible, however, that Peter's reference to prophecy is to be taken *metaphorically* in some sense; Peter could be saying that all God's people will speak in the Spirit *like prophets*. That would allow for an additional New Testament gift of prophecy. The case for this metaphorical reading is strengthened by the fact that, as we have already seen, it is possible to read the prediction of an abundance of dreams and visions at least somewhat figuratively.

Gaffin, for example, seems to hold a figurative view of the Joel text. On the one hand, he acknowledges that, according to the passage, "*all* believers are prophets; the whole church is a congregation of prophets,"[3] but

2. Carson, *Showing the Spirit*, 153.
3. Gaffin, *Perspectives on Pentecost*, 59.

he claims that, *"Apparently without exception, however, the New Testament vocabulary for prophecy is not used in this sense."*[4] We will need to assess this claim as we examine the relevant passages.

The Prophetic Call of Every Christian (Matt 28:18–20)

As we saw when we examined Old Testament prophecy, every prophet in the Old Testament operated under the call of God following a divine encounter. This call always includes a command to *speak*, and often also a command to *go*, sometimes with an explicit promise of God's *presence*. Consider these examples of God's commissioning words to prophets:

- To Moses: "I will *send* you . . . I will be *with* you . . . *Say* this" (Exod 3:10, 12, 15).
- To Jeremiah: "To all whom I *send* you, you shall *go*, and whatever I command you, you shall *speak*. Do not be afraid of them, *for I am with you to deliver you*" (Jer 1:7–8).
- To Isaiah: "*Go*, and *say* to this people . . ." (Isa 6:9).
- To Ezekiel: "*Go* to the house of Israel and speak *with my words* to them" (Ezek 3:4).

We see hints of this pattern in the calling of Paul: "But when he who had set me apart before I was born, and who called me by his grace, was pleased to reveal his Son to me, in order that I might *preach* him *among the Gentiles* . . ." (Gal 1:15–16).

The other apostles received a similar prophetic call in the words of the Great Commission when Christ announced,

> All authority in heaven and on earth has been given to me. *Go* therefore and make disciples of all nations, baptizing them in the name of the Father and of the Son and of the Holy Spirit, *teaching* them to observe all that I have commanded you. And behold I am *with you* always to the close of the age. (Matt 28:18–20; italics mine)

This command includes the standard elements of Old Testament prophetic calling ("*go* . . . *speak* . . . *with* . . ."). But one significant difference is that here the apostles are to speak not "whatever I command you" but "all that I

---

4. Gaffin, *Perspectives on Pentecost*, 59.

Towards an Interpretative Framework—Part 1

have commanded you." In other words, the speech enjoined on the apostles is rooted in the *already-revealed* message of Christ (although certain aspects of Christian doctrine were revealed only later).

Since nothing that is promised to the apostles here does not also apply to all believers today, Christians have long viewed this passage as an ongoing call to every believer to be involved in the ministry of making disciples. By that token, it could also be described as the ongoing *prophetic* call of every believer. If it is correct to view this as a prophetic call then, by definition, what is proclaimed as a result of it must be prophecy. In other words, prophecy is concerned both with teaching and securing wholehearted, active obedience to everything Christ commands.

Conclusion

We are those to whom God's gospel plan of redemption through the cross has been fully revealed. We are therefore also able to proclaim a clearer, fuller, more authoritative message than any Old Testament prophet, and so in that sense are greater prophets than they were. We understand that judgment and salvation depend on a person's response to the message of Christ. The ministry of Moses, although glorious, brought condemnation and death, but we have the far more glorious, life-giving ministry of the Spirit and righteousness (2 Cor 3:7–9).

Taken with the Joel passage quoted in Acts 2, in this chapter we have seen two passages in Matthew which allow us to consider *all God's people as prophets* since, as those who have had a personal encounter with God, all Christians are called to proclaim the message of Christ with his authority.

From Jesus' statement that "all the Prophets and the Law prophesied until John" (Matt 11:13), it is clear that some properties of prophecy end with John (most obviously, prophecy as messianic prediction). Prophecy does not disappear, but it does appear to undergo a substantial transformation. It is the nature of this transformation that must be the focus of the rest of our study.

Chapter 4

Toward an Interpretative Framework for Prophecy—Part 2

Foundational Prophecy

WE COME NOW TO some of the most intriguing and contentious texts on prophecy in the New Testament. In Ephesians, we read of

> the household of God, built on the foundation of the apostles and prophets, Christ Jesus himself being the cornerstone. (Eph 2:19–20)

A little further on we read of

> the mystery of Christ, which was not made known to the sons of men in other generations as it has now been revealed to his holy apostles and prophets by the Spirit. This mystery is that the Gentiles are fellow heirs, members of the same body, and partakers of the promise in Christ Jesus through the gospel. (Eph 3:4–6)

These passages are often used (e.g., by Gaffin, MacArthur, and others) to claim that prophecy (like apostleship) was concerned with establishing the foundational doctrines of the early church and therefore, like apostleship, has ceased.

Others, however, argue that the "foundational" version of the gift indicated in Ephesians 2:20 is distinct from the "congregational" version we read about in 1 Corinthians 14. Congregational prophecy, the argument goes, must consist of lower-order, locally relevant, and possibly less-reliable utterances. The need for two classes of prophecy springs from the difficulty of marrying the role of prophecy in the delivery of foundational gospel truth with the fact that Paul expects a number of prophecies to be given at each church meeting. Clearly, it would be unrealistic to expect such a volume of "Scripture-quality" prophecy to have been delivered week by week in local churches.

Apostle-prophets?

Grudem sees the most likely meaning of Ephesians 2:20 as "the apostle-prophets," that is "the apostles who are also prophets."[1] In other words, he sees this verse as referring simply to the apostles. This is a possible meaning, he claims, because of the lack of the definite article before the word "prophets." He says that he cannot find a similar construction in Paul's writing referring to two sets of people. On the other hand, Grudem argues that even if it does refer to two groups, then it refers not to all New Testament prophets, but to "a group of prophets who are closely associated with the apostles and who have the authority to write Scripture."[2]

On the notion of a single group of "apostle-prophets," Grudem's appeal is to a rule in Greek grammar known as "Granville Sharp's Rule," which describes the construction "article-noun-*kai* ('and')-noun." Much ink has been spilt trying to argue this grammatical point one way or another.

But the confusion seems to clear if we consider the similar phrase in Ephesians 3:5: "his holy apostles and prophets." In this case, the word order of the Greek seems to be decisive:

> ... *tois hagiois apostolois*   *autou*   *kai prophetais*
> ... to the holy apostles   his   and prophets

Here, as O'Brien says, "The *autou* ('his') divides the two nouns 'apostles' and 'prophets,' rather than coming after both, and because of this *hagiois* ('holy') appears to qualify only *apostolois* ('apostles')"[3] This indicates strongly that Paul has two groups of people in mind rather than one.

1. *GP*, 331.
2. *GP*, 307.
3. O'Brien, *Letter to the Ephesians*, 233.

Furthermore, in his list of gifts shortly after, Paul distinguishes two groups: "the apostles, the prophets" (Eph 4:11). It seems highly unlikely that Paul would repeat the same word in such close proximity but with radically different meanings. On these grounds, I think we can safely reject Grudem's view of "apostle-prophets."

A. T. Robertson's comment may also be appropriate here: "Sometimes groups more or less distinct are treated as one for the purpose in hand, and hence use one article."[4] So the use of one article to describe two groups surely indicates the close collaboration of apostles and prophets, and seems to suggest that the role of prophets *supports the ministry of the apostles*. It is surely this integration between the ministries of the apostles and prophets that is the key reason for the use of only one definite article in Ephesians 2:20.

To explore this text further, we need to answer a number of questions.

Old Testament Prophets or New?

O'Brien, Hoehner, and other commentators agree that the phrase "the apostles and prophets" in Ephesians 2:20 must refer to New Testament rather than Old Testament prophets. Hoehner lists five reasons for this, including the word order, and the fact that in Ephesians 3:5 Paul talks about the gospel mystery "which . . . has *now* been revealed to his holy apostles and prophets by the Spirit." Paul is clearly talking about revelation in the New Testament era.

Cornerstone or Capstone?

According to O'Brien, "Current New Testament scholarship is divided as to whether the unusual word used here refers to the foundation stone (i.e., cornerstone) of the building or the crowning stone at the top of the edifice."[5] O'Brien suggests that "cornerstone" "makes better meaning in the immediate context, especially the relation of Christ to the apostles, and the picture of the growing and unfinished building."[6] The parallel with another passage in which the Septuagint uses the same word, *akrogōniaios*, adds further (for me, decisive) weight to this conclusion: "Behold, I am the one who has laid

---

4. Robertson, *Grammar of the Greek New Testament*, 787.
5. O'Brien, *Letter to the Ephesians*, 216.
6. O'Brien, *Letter to the Ephesians*, 217.

Towards an Interpretative Framework—Part 2

as a foundation in Zion, a stone, a tested stone, a precious cornerstone, of a sure foundation" (Isa 28:16).

What Kind of Genitive?

The most controversial part of the whole passage is the phrase "the foundation of the apostles and prophets." The cessationist argument is that this means that the apostles and prophets form the foundation of the church, which was laid one for all, and that both groups have therefore now ceased.

The question is, what kind of genitive is being used here? Hoehner discusses three possibilities:

1. *Genitive of possession*. This would imply that "the foundation *belonged to* the apostles and prophets, but Christ is the cornerstone. Therefore, Christ *belongs to* the apostles and prophets."[7] For this reason, and others, Hoehner discounts this reading.

2. *Subjective genitive, or genitive of agency or originating cause*: "the foundation *by* the apostles and prophets." Examples are "loved *by* God" (Rom 1:7), and "known *by* the high priest" (John 18:16). Hoehner presents a number of issues with this reading, to which we could add the fact that according to Daniel Wallace,[8] this use is normally applied to adjectives rather than nouns.

3. *Genitive of apposition*: "the foundation *which is* the apostles and prophets." There are similar genitives in the phrase "the deposit *of* the Spirit" (2 Cor 5:5), and "the temple *of* his body" (John 2:21). This is Hoehner's preferred reading.

Most commentators agree with Hoehner that this is indeed a genitive of apposition, which would make it mean, as O'Brien puts it, the foundation "*consisting of* the apostles and prophets."[9] On this reading, every element of the household of God consists of people: Christ *is* the cornerstone, the apostles and prophets *are* the foundation, and Christians *are* the superstructure.

So Paul seems to be making a point about the *overall role and function* of the apostles and prophets, which was to *be* the foundation of the church. Does it really make sense to suggest that the apostles somehow did *more*

---

7. Hoehner, *Ephesians*, 398.
8. Wallace, *Greek Grammar Beyond the Basics*, 126.
9. O'Brien, *Letter to the Ephesians*, 213; italics mine.

than form the foundation of the church? No, Paul here seems to be viewing the *totality of their ministry* as foundational.

The Cessationist View

The cessationist position holds that, since the foundation has now been laid, there is no further need for any ongoing ministry devoted to laying it. When the apostles died, they were not replaced because the body of doctrine on which the church is built had been *fully delivered*. Their role simply became defunct. Gaffin relates this text to the bounded apostolic "tradition" that is to be held fast (2 Thess 2:15; 3:6), the "deposit" to be kept . . . (1 Tim 6:20; 2 Tim 1:14), and on the "faith *once and for all* delivered to the saints (Jude 3)."[10] This is now finished and complete, and the apostles are no more.

Gaffin maintains that prophecy had a *custodial* function during the early days of the church:

> It is . . . important to appreciate that the church in its foundational period of apostles and prophets did *not* possess a "sufficient" Scripture . . . At the time, say, Paul wrote 1 Corinthians, his readers did not have access to, for example, all four Gospels . . . nor to . . . Acts . . . nor to Romans, or Hebrews . . . or Revelation. We must ask ourselves whether we grasp our profound advantage in the access granted to us to God's completed statement in his Word.[11]

He maintains that prophecy

> is a foundational word-gift in two distinct respects: (a) in producing what is eventually recognized to be canonical . . . (b) in meeting contemporary needs in the church that are bound up with and peculiar to the foundational, that is, incomplete canon situation.[12]

So prophecy that was not incorporated into Scripture had a purely *local relevance,* useful in establishing the church in its infancy:

> The same distinctive applies to the ministry of the apostles. While several [apostles], notably Paul, are prominent in producing (inscripturated) revelation that permanently serves the church . . . the

---

10. Gaffin, *Perspectives on Pentecost*, 93.
11. Gaffin, *Perspectives on Pentecost*, 100.
12. Gaffin, *Perspectives on Pentecost*, 99.

majority, along with the prophets, bring revelation that is intended only for the church in their own (foundational) time.[13]

It seems difficult to object to the possibility that God may have given particular *nonenduring* gifts to support the church in its infancy, since such a principle is evidenced in the gifting of the apostles.

Two Responses

The cessationist argument from this verse is a strong one. There seem to be two possible responses to it. First, there is the view expressed by Storms: "To use an analogy, once a man establishes a company . . . he does not necessarily cease to exist or to serve the company in other capacities."[14]

The problem with this view (as with, for example, that of Ruthven[15]) is that it doesn't do full justice to *the genitive of apposition*, treating it rather as a genitive of possession, and therefore it doesn't view the *totality of the ministry* of the apostles as providing the foundation of the church.

Another argument runs as follows: Christ is alive! The fact that Christ is the cornerstone of the church clearly cannot imply that he is dead; but neither need it imply that *his role as cornerstone* has ceased. Thus, Robert Knowles says,

> We should be wary of pushing the building metaphor too far. The church of God is not a static temple, but a living entity; Christ is its ongoing, living cornerstone, the apostles and prophets constitute its ongoing, living foundation, and we are its living stones.[16]

In other words, Knowles suggests, since this verse cannot mean that Christ has ceased, neither need it necessarily mean that prophets have ceased either; prophets do continue today, and their role continues to be in some sense *"foundational"* because they continue to propound foundational doctrine today. In other words, prophets today re-present Scripture so that it continues to exercise its church-forming prophetic power.

---

13. Gaffin, *Perspectives on Pentecost*, 99.

14. Storms, "Third Wave Response," 78–79.

15. See Ruthven, *On the Cessation*. Ruthven argues that the foundation represents the apostolic confession.

16. Dr. Robert Knowles, in an email correspondence with the author. Knowles is the author of several works of theology, and the leading scholar on the work of Anthony C. Thiselton.

Conclusion

We have tried to present both sides of the argument on Ephesians 2:20. The text does provide some evidence that prophecy may have ceased. Nevertheless, this verse has to be explained in light of other texts, (not least of which is Acts 2:17). As Carson says, "It is . . . illegitimate for Gaffin to use this verse as the controlling factor in his understanding of the gift of New Testament prophecy."[17]

Ultimately, I think those who argue heatedly about Ephesians 2:20 agree far more than they think because, however we read the verse, both sides would agree that

- *some form of prophecy* (if not all) *has ceased*. Fully authoritative, apostolic prophecy has ceased, specifically that which led to the writing of Scripture.

On the other hand, both sides also agree that

- *some form of prophecy* (if only figurative, as Gaffin might suggest) *continues*. Prophecy may continue in either a literal or a figurative sense. As we have seen, even Gaffin, who argues the cessationist position on Ephesians 2:20, nevertheless also believes that Acts 2:17 indicates that "*all* believers are prophets; the whole church is a congregation of prophets."[18]

So our task then becomes simply to determine in which sense prophecy continues and in which sense it has ceased. We must also not ignore the obvious implication in Ephesians 3:5, which is that the role of prophets was to support the ministry of the apostles.

So this verse allows us to make a clear proposition about the nature of New Testament prophecy:

- The role of New Testament prophets (as of apostles) included the receipt and faithful explanation of apostolic Christian doctrine.

Since we know the receipt of original doctrine must have ceased, it seems likely that

- The prophecy that continues today includes the faithful explanation of doctrine, or more broadly of Scripture.

---

17. Carson, *Showing the Spirit*, 97.
18. Gaffin, *Perspectives on Pentecost*, 59.

We will need to do more to confirm these propositions in the course of our study. But they are in line with what we saw in the Old Testament, where we identified two key roles prophecy had, namely to *establish* covenant (particularly Moses), and to *recall* to covenant (prophets after Moses). So we could add a further clarifying proposition:

- The prophecy that continues today includes the recalling of God's people to their covenant relationship with God.

We know, then, from Ephesians 3:5, that the truth of gentile inclusion in the church was revealed to prophets as well as to apostles. What we have not yet explored is *how this revelation happened*. We will do that in chapter 21 below, when we will return to these key Ephesian texts and explore how Acts 15 sheds further important light on their meaning.

Chapter 5

Old Testament Prophets, New Testament Apostles

IS A PROPHET NECESSARILY someone who speaks *the very words of God*? Or might a prophet's speech contain error?

Having established that the Old Testament prophets "spoke the very words of God," Grudem looks to the New Testament and discovers a group of men there who speak with the same authority—the apostles.[1] The apostles, like the Old Testament prophets before them, were messengers of God. They were those appointed by Christ as "witnesses to his resurrection" (Acts 1:22; see also Acts 26:16), and they are connected with the Old Testament prophets in phrases such as "I will send them prophets and apostles" (Luke 11:49). But, Grudem claims, "The most significant parallel between Old Testament prophets and New Testament apostles, however, is *the ability to write words of Scripture*."[2] He says, "The apostles, then, have authority to write words that are God's own words."[3]

Grudem wonders why the New Testament uses the word "apostle" instead of "prophet," and concludes that "The New Covenant age was expected to be an age when all God's people would be able to prophesy,"[4] so

---

1. See *GP*, 27. This strong equation between Old Testament prophets and New Testament apostles can be found in an earlier work: Myers and Freed, "Is Paul also among the Prophets?," 40–53.
2. *GP*, 29; italics mine.
3. *GP*, 33.
4. *GP*, 34.

the word "prophet" would have been too broad a term to apply to such a special group of men as the apostles. Following Erich Fascher[5] he argues that the word "prophet" in the ancient world had become "a 'frame-word' without a narrowly defined meaning of its own" and "would not automatically suggest 'one who speaks with absolute divine authority.'"[6]

So Grudem argues that in the New Testament the word "prophet" does not imply someone speaking the very words of God. He argues that Jesus chose the word "apostle" because it was largely free of the potentially misleading contemporary connotations of the word "prophet" (although he rightly maintains that there are hints that the apostles may have seen themselves as having prophetic gifts, e.g., 1 Cor 13:9; 14:6).

Grudem considers the book of Revelation, which John refers to as "prophecy" (Rev 1:3; 10:11; 22:7, 10, 18, 19), but considers that its authority is derived not from the fact that it is prophecy, but from the fact that it was written by an apostle. He asks:

> But should we look at the Book of Revelation as evidence of what the gift of prophecy was like in ordinary New Testament churches? No, it would not be appropriate to do so. This is not a prophecy given by some ordinary Christian but rather by a very prominent apostle of Jesus Christ.[7]

Grudem sees this prophecy as differing from that which functioned among ordinary Christians in first-century churches,[8] and so he asks whether there might then be two kinds of prophecy—the authoritative, apostolic, "foundational" version, and the ordinary, "congregational" version. He decides against this and draws a parallel with the case of teaching or preaching, which clearly has greater authority when it is apostolic. There is no difference in "kind," but only in the "authority that attaches to the words spoken."[9]

---

5. Fascher, *Prophētēs*, 51–54.
6. *GP*, 35.
7. *GP*, 44.
8. *GP*, 45.
9. *GP*, 48.

Comment

We have seen that Grudem says that, "the apostles are the New Testament counterpart of the divinely authoritative Old Testament prophets" and "have authority to write words that are God's own words."[10] He talks of their "ability to write words of Scripture."[11] But, of course, the New Testament was not written entirely by apostles: Luke, for example, contributed to Scripture but is not an apostle, and most of the apostles made no contribution to Scripture. The correspondence between being an apostle and having the authority to write Scripture is a little simplistic: rather, the New Testament was not written by apostles but, just like the Old Testament, by *prophets*.

The New Testament was written through the gift of prophecy, just as was the Old Testament (2 Pet 1:20–21). The implication is that we should consider the New Testament as a whole to be prophecy by virtue of the fact that it is Scripture, and the apostles who wrote it as *apostolic prophets*.

The book of Revelation does indeed specifically refer to itself as prophecy, but it is not the only work of prophecy in the New Testament, any more than apocalyptic books such as Daniel and Ezekiel are the only works of prophecy in the Old Testament.

Are the Apostles Prophets?

If, according to Grudem's argument, the apostles are the New Testament counterparts of the Old Testament prophets, with the same authority as those prophets, it must surely be accurate to describe the apostles as "prophets."

Grudem claims that the apostles were not called "prophets" because in the first century "prophet" had lost its distinctive meaning as someone speaking the very words of God. But if the reason for not using the word "prophet" were largely a matter of contemporary secular understanding of the term, the apostles would nonetheless still be prophets *in biblical terms*. In other words, if "apostle" was chosen because it more accurately captured what the word "prophet" had previously meant, then the apostles were not just, as Grudem calls them, "the *counterpart* of the prophets," *they were prophets*.

10. *GP*, 33.
11. *GP*, 29.

The other reason Grudem gives to explain why the term "apostle" was chosen is that in the New Testament the gift of prophecy was to be widespread among the people of God and so the word "prophet" would have been too broad a term to apply to a special group. This seems absolutely correct: the office of apostleship clearly *surpasses* the widespread congregational gift of prophecy. But it surpasses it by *subsuming* it: according to David Hill, "the attributes of the apostle were sufficiently extensive to include most if not all of those belonging to the prophet."[12] This is surely correct: indeed, the term "apostle" seems to embrace many other gifts (prophet, teacher, evangelist, etc.) to an exceptional degree.

Grudem ought to have no issue with the idea that the apostles are prophets, since he sees Ephesians 2:20 as referring to the fact that the foundation of the church was laid by the "apostle-prophets," that is, "the apostles *who are also prophets.*"[13] But he doesn't really explore the full implications of that notion.

The reason the apostles are not referred to as prophets seems to be because, like John the Baptist, an apostle is to be understood as "*more than a prophet*" (Matt 11:9; Luke 7:26; italics mine)—just as a university professor might not commonly refer to himself as a "student." To call Paul a prophet would be an accurate description, but not an adequate one. We find the same reticence to use the term "prophet" in biblical descriptions of both Moses and Christ: both were clearly prophets, both were clearly far more.

Paul's Awareness of His Prophetic Calling

Prophecy, in both the Old and New Testaments, is always associated with the proclaiming of revelation, and Paul is clear that he is preaching a gospel that came "by revelation of Jesus Christ" (Gal 1:12). His description of his apostolic function as planting and building (1 Cor 3:6, 10) clearly parallels the terminology used to describe the prophetic call of Jeremiah, who is appointed "to build and to plant" (Jer 1:10), and provides an important hint that Paul conceived his ministry in prophetic terms. This self-awareness is perhaps at its clearest in Paul's description of his call: "But when he who had set me apart before I was born, and who *called* me by his grace, was pleased to *reveal* his Son to me, in order that I might *preach* him *among the Gentiles* . . ." (Gal 1:15–16, italics mine).

12. Hill, *New Testament Prophecy*, 116.
13. *GP*, 340; italics mine.

The calling of Paul to go and speak closely matches that of Old Testament prophets (Exod 3:10, 12, 15; Jer 1:7; Isa 6:9; Ezek 3:4), and so may be called both an apostolic *and* a prophetic calling. It was a prophetic calling to preach the gospel, and this strongly suggests that *Paul's preaching constituted his prophesying*.

Hill finds close parallels between Paul's call and that of both Isaiah (Isa 49:1–6) and Jeremiah (Jer 1:5).[14] Boring would agree: "Paul's account of his call in Gal 1:15–16 is replete with prophetic allusions and shows that he understands himself in the succession of prophets."[15]

Karl Olav Sandnes would also agree: he suggests one reason why Paul does not designate himself as a prophet is because he sees himself as "standing on the shoulders of the prophets."[16] His prophetic awareness is also apparent, as Sandnes points out, in the fact that Paul operates under *prophetic compulsion*: "necessity is laid upon me" (1 Cor 9:16).[17] The same compulsion is evident among several Old Testament prophets (see, e.g., Jer 4:19, 20:9; Amos 3:8) and seems to be a mark of true prophetic calling.

Paul writes under the sense that "Christ is speaking through me" (2 Cor 13:3), and this qualifies him as a prophet of God. But it is also often suggested that Paul's writing includes specific instances of what seem to be more direct prophetic oracles (notably, Rom 11:25–26; 1 Cor 15:51–52; 1 Thess 4:15–17).[18]

Hill concludes that Paul was indeed a prophet: "there is no doubt that Paul was divinely called and commissioned, that he received revelations, and that he felt himself to be under divine constraint to proclaim, in word and letter, what he had been given."[19]

---

14. Hill, *New Testament Prophecy*, 111–12.
15. Boring, *Sayings of the Risen Jesus*, 31.
16. Sandnes, *Paul*, 243–44.
17. Sandnes, *Paul*, 117–30.

18. Boring reports on Ulrich Müller's great methodological care in picking out prophetic elements in Paul's letters, including: introductory and authorization formulae, function and content, traditional speech forms of prophets, the congruency of the text with our picture of New Testament prophecy as we otherwise know it, the congruency of the text with oral speech patterns, and the sudden departure from the literary style of the context. Boring says, "Müller's use of these criteria shows how pervasive prophetic speech was in Paul's letters, including both prophetic oracles and the incidental fragments of prophetic forms that are not part of a prophetic oracle per se" (Boring, *Continuing Voice of Jesus*, 63).

19. Hill, *New Testament Prophecy*, 111.

Apostles and the Covenant

In our study of Old Testament prophecy, we made a rough distinction between "covenantal prophecy" (which set out the terms of the covenant) and "reformational prophecy" (which recalled people to that covenant). It is clear that the apostles played a uniquely covenantal (or "foundational") role in the New Testament: that is, they were the messengers of the covenantal revelation of the gospel of grace, just as Moses was the messenger of the covenantal revelation of the Law.

If we are happy to describe all New Testament apostolic writing as "apostolic prophecy," the question then raised is, how does apostolic prophecy relate to the congregational version we see in 1 Corinthians 14? Is Grudem correct to say that the congregational prophets did not speak with "absolute divine authority?"[20]

New Testament prophets (particularly congregational prophets) are clearly submitted to the apostles in authority (1 Cor 14:37), but this need not suggest that they did not speak authoritatively from God. It seems possible that they had a *reformational* role, recalling God's people to their covenant, thereby mirroring a similar function of Old Testament prophets. It also seems possible that the apostles serve as our model prophets, just as they serve as our model teachers and evangelists, and we will begin to explore how in a couple of chapters.

Before we can explore this issue, we will first need to explore the nature of Paul's prophesying in more detail; in order to do that, we now need to turn to 1 Corinthians.

20. *GP*, 48.

Part Two

THE PROPHETS AT CORINTH

CHAPTER 6

Prophecy as Gospel (1 Cor 1–2)

Introduction

IN THIS SECTION WE look at the early chapters of 1 Corinthians, mainly through the eyes of Thomas Gillespie and his book *The First Theologians*, and discover that they lay the groundwork for a proper understanding of Paul's later discussion of prophecy in chapters 12–14.

Paul says,

> Now we have received not the spirit of the world, but the Spirit who is from God, that we might understand the things freely given us by God. And we impart this in words not taught by human wisdom but taught by the Spirit, interpreting spiritual truths to those who are spiritual. (1 Cor 2:12–13)

In other words, Paul speaks *Spirit-revealed truth in Spirit-taught words to spiritual people.* In this chapter we explore what Paul means by the phrase "words . . . taught by the Spirit," and what is the content of such speech.

In his breakthrough discovery, Gillespie contends that this is a clear description of *prophetic speech*; he argues that 1 Corinthians 2:6–16 "is a text in which early Christian prophecy *is the unlabeled subject matter* and that the function of such prophecy was the interpretation of the apostolic kerygma."[1]

---

1. Gillespie, *First Theologians*, 165; italics mine.

PART TWO—THE PROPHETS AT CORINTH

To see if there is merit in this claim, we first need to build a careful understanding of Paul's preceding argument, and so below I include a summary of Gillespie's view of 1 Corinthians 2, with some observations of my own.[2]

Paul's Evangelistic Message

It is widely agreed that one of Paul's main concerns in 1 Corinthians is to challenge, reframe, and refocus Corinthian understanding of spirituality generally, and of Spirit-enabled speech in particular, around *the message of the cross*. We see this in his description of his evangelistic message to the Corinthians as tightly focused on "the cross of Christ" (1:17), "the word of the cross" (1:18) or "*cross-speech*," and "Christ crucified" (1:23). It was "*nothing except* Jesus Christ and him crucified" (2:2).

The Jews demand miraculous signs of power in their preachers, including apparently miraculous speech forms, whilst the Greeks prefer impressive rhetorical displays of wisdom ("*sophia*," 1:22). Such speech is variously described as excellency of speech (2:1), and persuasive wisdom speech (2:4), but is dismissed by Paul as "the wisdom of men" (2:5) and "the wisdom of this age" (2:6). In preaching the gospel, Paul resists the temptation to use such displays of wisdom "lest the cross of Christ be emptied of its power" (1:17). The locus of God's power is the message of the cross: "For the word of the cross is folly to those who are perishing, but to us who are being saved it is the power of God." (1:18).

In verse 18, Paul repeats his equation of the word of the cross with the power of God from verse 17. At this point we might have expected him to assert that the word of the cross is the wisdom of God, but he does not do so, at least initially, because he agrees that his message is indeed (apparently) foolish: "it pleased God through the folly of what we preach to save those who believe" (1:21). As Gordon Fee comments, "he says in effect, '. . . Look at [the gospel's] message: it is based on the story of a crucified Messiah. Who in the name of wisdom would have dreamed that up? Only God is so wise as to be so foolish' (1:18–25)."[3]

Gillespie points out that Paul sets up two antitheses: wisdom/foolishness on the one hand, and power/weakness on the other:

2. Gillespie, *First Theologians*, 165-198.
3. Fee, *First Epistle to the Corinthians*, 67.

> Curiously, the antithetical terms of each set are never juxtaposed in the text. In no statement is wisdom played off against foolishness or power against weakness. Rather, foolishness is opposed to power in 1:18, and wisdom to power (twice) in 2:4–5 ... Through this coordination, the two logical sets of antitheses are reduced to one.[4]

The message of Christ crucified satisfies neither the impulse for wisdom nor that for powerful signs, but rather offends them both by appearing to be both weak and foolish.

Having acknowledged the "foolishness" of the message, Paul then turns to describe it as "the wisdom of God" to those who are being called (1:24), and Christ Jesus as "wisdom from God" (1:30). So the message is not *inherently* unwise or foolish, but folly only "to those who are perishing," only foolish "in the world" and weak "in the world," that is, in the world's eyes (1:27).

So, Gillespie argues, the conflict is between the Corinthian conception of power/wisdom and the Pauline view of power/wisdom.[5] For Paul, there is simply no message more powerful than the message of Christ and the cross, and no message wiser.

The Spirit

In 2:1–2, Paul contrasts "lofty speech or wisdom" with the message of Christ crucified. The two are utterly opposed. He then appears to be about to repeat himself: "my speech and my message were not in plausible words of wisdom, but . . ." (2:4). One might have expected him to repeat himself and say, ". . . I spoke only of Christ crucified." Instead Paul introduces the theme of the Holy Spirit into the letter "in demonstration of the Spirit and of power." By this parallel, Paul immediately binds the work of the Spirit to the communication of the message of the cross.

Paul also associates the Spirit with the "power of God." He has already established "the power of God" as inhabiting his message of the cross of Christ (1:17, 18, 24). By now associating the Spirit also with the power of God, Paul again binds *Spirit-speech* to *cross-speech*. He seems to be carefully

---

4. Gillespie, *First Theologians*, 170–71.
5. Gillespie, *First Theologians*, 175.

reframing a Corinthian understanding of spirituality that had become dislocated from the cross.

It is as if the Corinthians had asked Paul something along these lines, "Yes, of course, in your evangelism the focus is rightly on Christ and the cross. But with mature Christians—*like us!*—surely you move beyond the message of the cross to something a bit more *powerful*, a bit more *spiritual*?" In 2:6–16, we get Paul's answer. In summary, he says, "Among mature Christians, as with unbelievers, our teaching is grounded in Christ and the gospel, because the gospel is the deep mystery of God, revealed by the Spirit through Christ."

The Content of Paul's Message to Mature Christians

We learn that when dealing with "mature" Christians, Paul does indeed engage in wisdom-speech: "we do impart wisdom, although it is not a wisdom of this age" (2:6), but "of God" (2:7). As Gerd Thiessen points out, this wisdom is cognitive: it enables people to understand (2:12), to interpret (2:13), and to judge (2:14, 15).[6]

What, then, is the content of Paul's wisdom-speech? It is a secret wisdom, foreordained by God before the ages (2:7), but which at some point he *revealed* (aorist, i.e., a past tense), and whose focus is "the depths of God" (2:10). In other words, the content of Paul's speech to Christians focuses on God's mystery now revealed in Christ, who is "the wisdom of God" (1:24). This "secret and hidden wisdom of God" is essentially the gospel, which Paul describes elsewhere as "the mystery *which is Christ*" (Col 2:2), "the mystery *of Christ*" (Eph 3:4; Col 4:3), "the mystery *of Christ in you*" (Col 1:27), and "the mystery *of the gospel*" (Eph 6:19).

The conclusion must be that the wisdom Paul delivers to the "mature" (2:6) has the same core content as the evangelistic message he first delivered to Corinth (1:17; 2:1): "It is precisely this *meaning* of the cross that Paul claims to articulate in the wisdom spoken among the mature."[7] This focus is confirmed a few verses later when we hear that the Spirit helps us to "understand the things freely given us by God" (2:12). Fee says this "gives us a clear glimpse into the *content* of the wisdom that God has revealed to his people by his Spirit. The verb (*charizomai*) [lit. 'give graciously'] seems to

---

6. Thiessen, *Psychological Aspects*, 386, in Gillespie, *First Theologians*, 179.
7. Gillespie, *First Theologians*, 181.

be a deliberate allusion to the 'grace' (*charis*) of God, or the 'gift' (*charisma*) of salvation (as in Rom 6:23)."[8]

The Spirit enables us to understand the grace of God in Christ. David Garland agrees:

> Paul does not intend to imply that he imparted esoteric ideas only to a small circle of clever students and kept it from the immature ... This mystery is the word of a crucified Christ (2:1–2), which heretofore had been hidden to human enquiry ... It is the same teaching ... he first spoke to them.[9]

The Source of Paul's Message

The wisdom we have been discussing clearly comes only by revelation from God, through the activity of the Spirit: "What no eye has seen, nor ear heard ... these things God has revealed to us through the Spirit" (2:9–10).

Just as only the spirit of a person knows a person's thoughts, so only the Spirit of God knows the thoughts of God: "For the Spirit searches everything, even the depths of God" (2:11). Here Paul binds the focus of the Spirit to the thoughts of God, and "the depths of God" (literally "the deep things of God") (2:10), that is, God's purposes *in Christ*.

Speaking Wisdom by the Spirit

When Paul communicates these Spirit-revealed truths, the words he uses are Spirit-taught: "And we impart this in words not taught by human wisdom but taught by the Spirit, interpreting spiritual truths to those who are spiritual" (2:13). So as well as revealing gospel truth, the Spirit also directs Paul's word to communicate it accurately. Actually, the text reads literally, "things of the Spirit" rather than "truths." We thus have *Spirit-revealed things communicated in Spirit-taught words to spiritual people*.

This is the big picture of what Paul is saying. However, the detail is a little harder to pin down. The phrase at the end of verse 13 ("*pneumatikois pneumatika sunkrinontes*") is unclear:

---

8. Fee, *First Epistle to the Corinthians*, 113.
9. Garland, *1 Corinthians*, 95.

Part Two—The Prophets at Corinth

- *sunkrinō* can mean "bring together," "combine," "compare," "explain," or "interpret."

- *pneumatikois* could be either neuter or masculine, and if masculine, could either mean "spiritual people" or refer back to *logois* ("spiritual words"). If it is masculine (as it clearly is in 3:1), then it may parallel *en tois teleios*, "among the mature" (2:6).

Most commentators prefer one of the following possible meanings:

- "*expressing spiritual truths in spiritual words*" (NIV)
- "*interpreting spiritual truths to those who are spiritual*" (ESV and NIV mg.)
- "*comparing spiritual things with spiritual*" (KJV, RSV mg.).

Fee prefers the first option here ("explaining the things of the Spirit by means of the words taught by the Spirit"[10]), Gillespie the second,[11] and Thiselton a variation of the second.[12] "Interpreting" seems appropriate to Édouard Cothenet because of the use of the same word in LXX to describe the interpretation of dreams (Gen 40:22; 41:12; Judg 7:15), and the writing on the wall in Daniel (Dan 5:8, 13).[13]

Being fully aware of the ambiguities and resonances of his Greek, Paul may be playing here with multiple meanings. If the phrase is read as "interpreting spiritual truths to those who are spiritual," there is a hint here that Paul is concerned with meeting the specific spiritual needs of the people he addresses. However, it is perhaps easiest to read *pneumatikois* in 2:13 as referring to the words (*logois*) Paul has just been talking about. (Then *pneumatika* seems to refer back to *ta charisthenta* of verse 12.) This would bring us to the NIV reading, "expressing spiritual truths in spiritual words," although "*explaining* (or *interpreting*) spiritual things in spiritual words" seems preferable.

---

10. Fee, *First Epistle to the Corinthians*, 115.
11. Gillespie, *First Theologians*, 184–85.
12. *FEC*, 264.
13. See Cothenet, "Les prophètes chrétiens comme exégètes," 95.

Prophecy as Gospel (1 Cor 1–2)

The Interpretation of Scripture

Any of the main translations of 1 Corinthians 2:13 can be read as referring to the interpretation of Scripture. Cothenet, taking a reading along the lines of "comparing spiritual things with spiritual" (RSV mg.) suggests that Paul is referring to *the interpretation of Scripture by Scripture*. He discerns hints of this in 1 Corinthians 2:10: "The Spirit searches (*epauna*) everything, even the depths of God." He points out that *epaunan* has "its technical sense of *interpreting* Scripture (cf. John 5:39; 7:52; 1 Pet 1:11)."[14]

So the phrase could be referring to the interpretation of new covenant revelation in light of Old Testament Scripture, a constant concern of Paul, and one he has just demonstrated (particularly in 2:9). Incidentally, this reading is in line with the AG translation of the verse as "*comparing the spiritual gifts and revelations* (which we already possess) *with the spiritual gifts and revelations* (which we are to receive) and judging them thereby."[15]

How did the apostles receive their revelation of the mystery of God? The risen Christ "opened their minds to understand the Scriptures" (Luke 24:45), and in particular, gave them insight into the Christ-centered nature of the Old Testament (Luke 24:27). This suggests that their understanding of the gospel mystery was revealed to the apostles *through Scripture*. This is why Paul talks of "the revelation of the mystery that was kept secret for long ages but has now been disclosed and *through the prophetic writings* has been made known to all nations" (Rom 16:25b, 26a NIV). Paul is talking broadly about *Biblical wisdom*.

A Trinitarian Project

In Paul's evolving catalogue of different speech types (*logoi*), he has already established and united *cross-speech* (1:18) and *godly wisdom-speech* (2:6). To this he now adds *Spirit-taught speech* (2:13), which is grounded in the cross.

Paul has established a thoroughly trinitarian project: it involves a mystery now revealed by *God* through the *Spirit*, which is grounded in *Christ* who is "the wisdom of God" (1:24), communicated effectively in words taught by the *Spirit*. Paul also describes how the *Spirit* searches the

---

14. Cothenet, "Les prophètes chrétiens comme exégètes," 94.
15. *AG*, 782.

thoughts of *God* (2:10–11), and then finally attributes to *Christ* what he has previously attributed to the *Spirit* and to *God*: "'For who has understood the mind of the *Lord* so as to instruct him?' But we have the mind of *Christ*" (2:16).

The binding of the work of the Spirit to Christ seems to be complete. Paul is talking about *God's Spirit-revealed mystery of Christ, communicated in Spirit-taught words*. Given its deep dependence on the Spirit at every point, and its origin in God, it seems beyond dispute that such speech must qualify as "prophecy" under any reasonable understanding of the term: indeed, this text could serve as a definition of Pauline apostolic prophecy and should therefore form the basis for our understanding of its congregational counterpart.

Cross-shaped Living

Gillespie points out that *pneumatikos* ("spiritual person," 2:15) is used in contrast to *psychikos* ("natural person," 2:14), and so, "clearly identifies the believer and the unbeliever respectively."[16] But, Gillespie says, Paul also uses *pneumatikoi* in contrast to both *sarkinoi* ("people of the flesh," 3:1) and *nepioi* ("infants in Christ," 3:1) that is, in the sense of mature believers as opposed to immature believers.

Paul is saying that the Corinthians are not the mature spiritual believers they claim to be (3:1): their divisive, partisan behavior shows them to be operating under an altogether different spirit (3:2–3), one entirely inconsistent with the cross of Christ.

Comparing 1 Corinthians 2 with 1 Corinthians 12–14

The crucial question, Gillespie acknowledges, is whether the wisdom spoken in "words . . . taught by the Spirit" (2:13) can be identified as prophetic speech despite the fact that it is not so described. To forge this link, he highlights a number of key terms that appear both in 1 Corinthians 2 and in the discussion of prophecy in 1 Corinthians 12–14:[17]

1. *apokalyptein* (reveal) 2:10; 14:20

---

16. Gillespie, *First Theologians*, 185.
17. See Gillespie, *First Theologians*, 187.

Prophecy as Gospel (1 Cor 1–2)

2. *pneumatikoi* (spiritual ones) 2:13; 12:1
3. *pneumatikos* (spiritual one) 2:15; 14:37
4. *pneuma* (Spirit) 2:10, 13; 12:4, 7, 8
5. *pneuma theou* (Spirit of God) 2:11, 12, 14; 12:3
6. *sophia* (wisdom) 2:6, 7; 12:8
7. *teleioi* (mature) 2:6; 14:20
8. *anakrinein* (judge) 2:15; 14:24
9. *mystērion* (mystery) 2:1, 7; 13:2; 14:2

If we include chapter 3, we could also add:

10. *oikodomē* (building) 3:9–15; 14:3

Both passages are about "what counts as genuine inspired utterance"[18] and share common elements:

1. the revelation
2. of God's mystery
3. through human agents
4. who speak in the Spirit
5. and whose utterances must be judged on the basis of their content.

To these we could add,

6. and who speak to build the church.

The implication, according to Gillespie, is that we have solid evidence that the content of the prophecy Paul commends in 1 Corinthians 14, although not clear in that passage, is described clearly in 1 Corinthians 2, and involves explaining the implications of the message of Christ to believers. In 1 Corinthians 1:18–25,

> Paul critiques the Corinthians' wisdom discourse—venerated among them as inspired utterance—for *having lost its substantive relationship to the kerygma*. In 2:6–16 he counters their claim by advocating a wisdom grounded in the kerygma of Christ crucified (2:8), revealed through the Spirit of God (2:10), and articulated in words taught by the Spirit (2:13). The question, in other words,

---

18. Gillespie, *First Theologians*, 188.

concerns what counts as genuine inspired utterance—the same problem that dominates the discussion in chapters 12–14.[19]

In chapter 3, Paul goes on to describe his ministry of proclaiming Christ to the Corinthians as laying the foundation "which is Jesus Christ" (3:10–11), and he expects others to continue his work and to build on the same foundation (3:10b–11). In other words, their teaching (and by extension their *prophesying*) is to be as faithfully Christ-centered as Paul's own.

Apostolic and Congregational Prophesying

In the face of Gillespie's argument, it seems hard to deny that 1 Corinthians 2:13 describes Paul's *apostolic prophesying*. The question that arises is, how does this prophecy relate to the wider *congregational* prophesying described in chapter 14?

To answer this question, we need to consider the identity of the "we" mentioned several times in 2:6–16. Fee (referring to 2:6) proposes: "The shift in this first instance (and in verses 7 and 13) represents his common editorial 'we,' and refers at least to Paul, and perhaps to other preachers/teachers."[20]

Garland says:

> Paul may use an editorial "we speak" here to refer to his own preaching . . . or may refer collectively to his fellow apostles and the unanimity of the apostolic witness . . . It is more likely, however, that he attests to the unanimity of the Christian witness. Although Paul primarily has his own preaching in mind, *all who proclaim the Christian gospel* speak this wisdom.[21]

An alternative view is that the word "we" refers to the *apostles and prophets*, since Paul makes it clear elsewhere (Eph 2:20, 3:5) that it is to the apostles and prophets that the foundational truths of the gospel were revealed.

However we read it, some of what Paul says here must surely be taken as common Christian practice: all Christians receive the revelation of the gospel (v. 10), all have at least some ability to understand what the Spirit gives (v. 12), all have in some sense the mind of Christ (v. 16), and all have

---

19. Gillespie, *First Theologians*, 187–88; italics mine.
20. Fee, *First Epistle to the Corinthians*, 101n13.
21. Garland, *1 Corinthians*, 91; italics mine.

in some sense the ability to impart gospel revelation in "Spirit-taught words" (v. 13).

It may well be, therefore, that in this passage Paul has both apostolic *and* congregational prophesying in mind; that is, that he is describing his apostolic prophesying as a pattern for the derived congregational prophesying of those who follow him.

Conclusion

Gillespie has shown (to my mind, conclusively) that 1 Corinthians 2 delineates not simply the parameters of Paul's teaching ministry to Christians, but also his practice of prophesying: the communication of the mystery of the gospel revealed by the Spirit, understood by the Spirit, and imparted in words taught by the Spirit. Throughout Scripture we have seen that Spirit-inspired speech is a signal of prophecy, and here we see the Spirit at work in the theological enterprise of communicating the mystery of Christ.

Prophecy has thus begun to manifest itself as the proclamation of the message of Christ, and as the interpretation of the message of Christ, which is undertaken by comparing Scripture with Scripture. This does not mean that Paul talked narrowly about the cross all the time; his message is one of *Christ-centred Biblical wisdom* in a broad sense.

Even without this understanding of the passage, since 1 Corinthians is prophecy inasmuch as it is inspired Scripture, we should be aware that Paul is prophesying when, for example, he rebukes the Christians at Corinth, just as Jeremiah was when he rebuked the inhabitants of Jerusalem. We should not let differences of style fool us; but we should let the radically new writing project of Paul (for example his careful theological reasoning) inform our understanding of how prophecy has transformed since the days of Jeremiah.

This is an activity involving both the mind and the Spirit. The apostles have introduced a new form of prophetic speech, namely, *reasoned theological discourse*, dependent on the power of the Holy Spirit in all its phases. Gillespie would say that Paul *defines* prophecy in chapter 2, *orders its practice* in chapter 14, and *models* it throughout (particularly, he argues, in chapter 15). Gillespie's conclusion is that the New Testament prophets were "*the first theologians of the church.*"[22]

22. Gillespie, *First Theologians*, 263; italics mine.

PART TWO—THE PROPHETS AT CORINTH

We can agree with Gillespie that the prophesying Paul practices in 1 Corinthians 2 must be the prophesying he promotes in 1 Corinthians 14. We could define prophecy as *"the Christ-centered, Spirit-revealed wisdom of God interpreted in Spirit-taught words."* This all seems to be implied in 1 Corinthians 2:13. This chapter has therefore offered strong support for the propositions we have already suggested (but can now slightly improve):

- The role of New Testament prophets (as of apostles) included the receipt and faithful explanation of Christ-centered biblical wisdom.
- The prophecy that continues today includes the faithful explanation of Christ-centered biblical wisdom.

CHAPTER 7

Babes and Apostles (1 Cor 3–4)

WE HAVE ALREADY SEEN that the work of the Spirit is to glorify Christ, and this theme continues through 1 Corinthians 3–4. What constitutes "spiritual" behavior? Not amazing experiences, Paul seems to say, but a Christlike attitude. What constitutes "spiritual" speech? Not amazing speech gifts, but teaching that is carefully aligned with Christ.

Baby Is as Baby Does

Although the Corinthians think of themselves as spiritual (*pneumatikoi*, 3:1), Paul says they are of the flesh (*sarkinoi*, 3:1) and behaving in a fleshly way (*sarkikoi*, 3:3). They might think of themselves as mature, but they are in fact "babies" or "mere infants" (*nepioi*, 3:1). The immature Corinthians are simply not ready for the solid food reserved for mature Christians. Paul has already explained (in 2:6-13) what this solid food is; as Fee says,

> for Paul the gospel of the crucified one is both 'milk' and 'solid food.' As milk it is the good news of salvation; as solid food it is understanding that the entire Christian life is predicated on the same reality—and those who have the Spirit should so understand the 'mystery.'[1]

---

1. Fee, *First Epistle to the Corinthians*, 125.

Indeed, "The fact is that 'his meat does not differ from his milk.'"[2] If the meat and the milk are the same, what is the point Paul is making? The Corinthians seem to have considered that they had progressed beyond the simple message of the cross.

Paul calls the Corinthians "babies" because of their partisan attitude (vv. 3–4); to consider oneself spiritual whilst behaving in a partisan manner is as nonsensical as a round square. Paul has already said that the spiritual person has "the mind of Christ," and this must imply not just the understanding of Christ, but also the attitude of Christ, as in Philippians 2:5–7, particularly his humility, which is so lacking in the Corinthians, who are "behaving only in a human way" (3:3). Garland talks of "their failure to appreciate and incarnate the message of the cross."[3]

Paul spends much of the rest of the epistle addressing moral shortcomings in Corinth that result from their spiritual immaturity, and all of these may be ultimately traceable to their failure, unlike Paul, "to understand, accept and live out this basic message of the cross."[4] True spirituality has to do with following the way of the cross of Christ.

Building on a Foundation

> I laid a foundation as a wise builder, and someone else is building on it. But each one should build with care. For no one can lay any foundation other than the one already laid, which is Jesus Christ. (1 Cor 3:10–11)

Paul has carefully laid the foundation of Jesus Christ in the church at Corinth like a skilled (*sophos,* "wise") master-builder. His claim to wisdom picks up the references to Christ as the wisdom of God (1:24), and the consequent wisdom Paul uses among the mature (2:6): the wise builder builds on Christ, the wisdom of God. The foundation, being Jesus Christ, is clearly "him crucified," that is, the gospel.

The work of the builder is to be assessed by whether the building is rightly aligned with and centered on Christ as its foundation. The work will also be judged by the quality of the materials used in the building. As Fee says, "for Paul the 'gold, silver and precious stones' represent what

2. M. D. Hooker, "Hard Sayings", 21, in Garland, *1 Corinthians,* 108.
3. Garland, *1 Corinthians,* 107.
4. Garland, *1 Corinthians,* 108.

is compatible with the foundation, the gospel of Jesus Christ and him crucified."[5]

The building is a temple of God in which the Spirit of God dwells (3:16). Once more, the trinitarian nature of Paul's mission is clear: only what is built on *Christ* can be a temple of *God*, inhabited by the *Spirit* of God. Later, when Paul says, "the one who prophesies speaks to people for their *upbuilding*" (1 Cor 14:3), he is clearly referring to the building enterprise of chapter 3. Prophesying must therefore be speech that *integrates the church into Christ*.

Apostolic Authenticity as Authority

By overaligning themselves with particular leaders ("'I follow Paul', or 'I follow Apollos,'" 1:12), the Corinthians are missing the point: "For all things are yours, whether Paul or Apollos or Cephas . . . all are yours, and you are Christ's, and Christ is God's" (1 Cor 3:21–23). David Garland quotes Robertson and Plummer: "*The church is not the property of the Apostles. Apostles are ministers of the church.*"[6] You do not belong to these leaders, Paul is saying, but rather *they* belong to you, and you belong to Christ. Apostles and teachers are "servants of Christ and *stewards of the mysteries* of God" (1 Cor 4:1; italics mine). In this phrase, Boring claims, "Paul incidentally gives a description of Christian prophets."[7]

Paul's apostolic authority is validated by his authentic self-sacrificial service of the church. His message is entirely focused around the message of Christ, and his life is fully consistent with that message. This is why he deserves to be taken seriously when he says, "I urge you, then, be imitators of me" (1 Cor 4:16).

Thiselton claims that the term "apostle"

> carries with it two complementary aspects in the NT: on one side, objective witness that an event has occurred; on the other side, a participatory, self-involving act of nailing one's colors to the mast, of staking one's life or life-style on what is witnessed as true.[8]

---

5. Fee, *First Epistle to the Corinthians*, 140.

6. Robertson and Plummer, *First Epistle to the Corinthians*, 72, in Garland, 124; italics mine.

7. Boring, *Sayings of the Risen Jesus*, 32.

8. *FEC*, 66.

Part Two — The Prophets at Corinth

This has echoes of the Old Testament description of prophets as "men of God."

Paul is our model and pattern, which means that we are to preach as he did, teach as he did, live as he did, and *prophesy* as he did, that is, with Christ-exalting (which is to say, Spirit-taught) speech. The implication is that the speech of congregational prophets, even if it does not carry the authoritative weight of its apostolic counterpart, is nevertheless to follow its pattern faithfully both in purpose and core content.

Chapter 8

The Pneumatics (1 Cor 12)

> Now concerning spiritual gifts, brothers, I do not want you to be uninformed. You know that when you were pagans you were led astray to mute idols, however you were led. Therefore I want you to understand that no one speaking in the Spirit of God ever says "Jesus is accursed!" and no one can say, "Jesus is Lord" except in the Holy Spirit. (1 Cor 12:1–3)

THIS CHAPTER SUMMARIZES AND extends Gillespie's discussion of 1 Corinthians 12.[1]

Gifts or People? (1 Cor 12:1)

First Corinthians 12 begins with the phrase, "Now concerning spiritual gifts" ("*Peri de tōn pneumatikōn*"). Paul does not use the more familiar term for "spiritual gifts" here—"*charismata*" (lit. "grace things" or "grace gifts")—although he does use that term from 12:4, and throughout the rest of the chapter. *Pneumatika* is picked up again in 14:1 ("earnestly desire *ta pneumatika*"). This raises the question of how the two terms relate: the near-universal translation of both terms as "spiritual gifts" simply assumes the terms are entirely synonymous.

A further issue is that, since in the Greek the plural genitive has the same form for both the neuter and masculine genders (*-ōn*), the phrase that opens the chapter could equally mean either "concerning spiritual *things*

---

1. See Gillespie, *First Theologians*, 65–128.

PART TWO—THE PROPHETS AT CORINTH

(or *gifts*)" or "concerning spiritual *people*." The distinction may not be critical, but the main English translations opt for the former.

So the questions raised are:

- Is the section about spiritual *gifts* (or things) or spiritual *people*?
- How do the *pneumatika* relate to the *charismata*?

On the first issue, if the opening phrase of 12:1 is a response to a Corinthian question, what might that question have been? As Gillespie says, it is not at all clear why so general a question as "What about spiritual gifts?" should be answered with such a specific discussion of tongues and prophecy in 1 Corinthians 14.[2]

If, on the other hand, we read the opening phrase of chapter 12 as "Concerning spiritual *people*," then, considering 14:37 ("If anyone thinks he is a prophet or spiritual [*pneumatikos*]"),[3] according to Gillespie, Paul would be ending the discussion where he began, and the two verses would form an *inclusio* uniting the entire intervening discussion.[4] Gillespie also considers that Paul's emphatic use of "no one" twice in 12:3 signals that the emphasis is on people rather than gifts.[5]

Comment

In 12:1, we seem to have a response to a Corinthian question along the lines of, "How are we to recognize the spiritual person?" Paul responds by saying that all speech that acknowledges Christ as Lord is Spirit-enabled—all Christians are people of the Spirit.

Whilst it makes sense in the immediate context of 12:1–3 to read the opening of 1 Corinthians 12:1 as referring to people (and it also ties the opening of the section to its conclusion in 14:37), such a reading seems to

---

2. Gillespie, *First Theologians*, 69.

3. Fee observes that the phrase "If anyone thinks" occurs twice elsewhere in the letter: (3:18; 8:2). It is thus found in each of the three main sections of the letter (chs. 1–4; 8–10; 12–14) and marks discussion of three crucial Corinthian terms ("wisdom," "knowledge," and "spiritual"). In each case, "Paul is zeroing in on the Corinthians' perspective as to their own spirituality. They do indeed think of themselves as 'the wise' (3:18) and as 'having knowledge' (8:2), probably in both cases because they also think of themselves as being *pneumatikoi*" (Fee, *First Epistle to the Corinthians*, 11).

4. Gillespie, *First Theologians*, 75.

5. Gillespie, *First Theologians*, 95.

sit less happily with the rest of chapter 12, and indeed with clear references to *pneumatika* as spiritual gifts in chapter 14. Might it not therefore be possible that the Corinthian question was as ambiguous as Paul's answer? Perhaps they simply asked about *tōn pneumatikōn* ambiguously because they were equally interested in *both* spiritual gifts *and* spiritual people, leaving Paul to respond to both questions.

Pagan Behavior (1 Cor 12:2)

> You know that when you were pagans you were led astray to mute idols, however you were led. (1 Cor 12:2)

David Aune thinks that here Paul is "in all probability referring to pagan religious experiences of possession trance."[6] Fee agrees,[7] but Grudem argues that the phrase "however you were led" (12:2) refers not to religious trance, but to participation in a religious procession or parade.[8]

If these pre-Christian Corinthians were under the power of some kind of religious possession, what kind of speech might they have been uttering at the time? The reference to "mute idols" or "dumb idols" need not suggest that their participation was entirely silent: the same word ("*aphōnos*") is used in 1 Corinthians 14:10, where it describes human languages as not "*meaningless*."[9] AG offers the definition "*incapable of conveying meaning.*"[10] Perhaps we can conclude that since these idols were literally speechless, their worshippers engaged in speech-forms that were either *incoherent babbling* or amounted to no more than *meaningless nonsense*.

The Christomorphic Criterion (1 Cor 12:3)

> Therefore I want you to understand that no one speaking in the Spirit of God ever says "Jesus is accursed!" and no one can say, "Jesus is Lord" except in the Holy Spirit. (1 Cor 12:3)

---

6. Aune, *Prophecy in Early Christianity*, 257.
7. Fee, *First Epistle to the Corinthians*, 576–77.
8. Grudem, in *FEC*, 912.
9. Conzelmann, *1 Corinthians*, 206.
10. *AG*, 127.

Part Two—The Prophets at Corinth

The first part of this verse is mysterious: who, claiming to be speaking in the Spirit, would ever say "Jesus is accursed?" Thiselton catalogues no fewer than twelve possible explanations for this phrase. One widely accepted possibility is that "Jesus is accursed" is simply a hypothetical remark, the opposite of "Jesus is Lord."[11] Another possible reading is that this represents the rejection of Jesus found in Jewish circles (Acts 7:54–60): "They could ... declare Jesus accursed as one who was crucified."[12] A further possibility might be that Paul is using a *reductio ad absurdum* argument to demonstrate that not all speech *about* Jesus is Spirit-enabled: Spirit-enabled speech must both talk accurately about him *and exalt him*.

Whatever the meaning of the first half of the verse, the meaning of the second is clear enough: the fact that no one can say "Jesus is Lord" (and mean it) except by the Spirit suggests that *all* Christ-exalting speech is Spirit-empowered, and therefore all Christians are in *some* sense *pneumatikoi* (although, remembering 1 Corinthians 3:1, this cannot be the whole picture). In one phrase, Paul demolishes any Corinthian notion of "a pneumatic elite,"[13] and he continues to do so throughout the subsequent verses (particularly in verse 7: "To each is given the manifestation of the Spirit for the common good").

Spirit-enabled speech, according to Gillespie, is christomorphic. If the Corinthians judged prophetic speech by how miraculous it appeared (perhaps even valuing tongues above intelligent speech), Paul challenges such a view in 1 Corinthians 12:3 by making it clear that any assessment of the spirituality of speech is to be made primarily on the basis of its Christ-shaped *content*.

Gillespie proposes a schematic paraphrase that highlights the logic connecting 12:2 with 12:3, as follows:

> *Premise*: You know that evidences of ecstasy are an unreliable criterion of authentic divine inspiration because in your pagan past they led you to the dumb idols (v. 2).
>
> *Conclusion*: Therefore (*dio*) the genuineness of all prophetic utterances must be judged on the basis of their *material content alone* (v. 3).[14]

---

11. *FEC*, 920–21.
12. Garland, *1 Corinthians*, 571.
13. Eichholz, 19, in Gillespie, *First Theologians*, 115.
14. Gillespie, *First Theologians*, 83; italics mine.

The Pneumatics (1 Cor 12)

Garland objects to this point: "'Jesus is Lord' is the basic confession made by every Christian and is not a prophetic utterance . . . The confession is a validating sign that one is a Christian, not a touchstone to gauge authentic prophetic speech."[15] However, Gillespie had anticipated this objection: "If it is a confession of loyalty to the Lord Jesus, it is equally a confession of faith in the one who is Lord . . . As such it expresses the gospel to which it corresponds."[16] The way to recognize the authentic voice of the Spirit is by the fact that "the Spirit is, so to speak, *tethered to Jesus*."[17] So "Prophetic utterance genuinely inspired by the Spirit is thus a form of self-testimony provided by the crucified earthly Jesus now raised from the dead and exalted."[18]

We can agree with Garland that 1 Corinthians 12:3 describes the confession by which any Christian is to be recognized. But Gillespie argues that it also offers the standard by which prophetic speech is to be assessed: if one agrees with Gillespie that Paul has already made this case compellingly in chapter 2, one might be inclined to accept his reasoning in chapter 12.

Pneumatika and *Charismata*

How are the terms *pneumatika* and *charismata* related? E. Earle Ellis suggests it is a mistake to equate the two terms completely. He points to Romans 1:11, in which Paul says he wishes to visit Rome to impart "some spiritual gift." Here Paul combines both terms: "*charisma pneumatikon*," that is, he uses *pneumatikon* to qualify *charisma*. From this, Ellis concludes:

> That is, *charisma* can be used of any or all the gifts while *pneumatikon* appears to be restricted to gifts of inspired perception, verbal proclamation and/or its interpretation. Thus in 1 Corinthians 9:11, the "spiritual things" that Paul "sowed" among the Corinthians are defined in the following context as the gospel message. Similarly, in 1 Corinthians 12:1, the "spiritual" gifts (or persons) are connected directly with "speaking" *en pneumati*; when, in 1 Corinthians 12:4ff, other charisms come into consideration, the expression broadens.[19]

---

15. Garland, *1 Corinthians*, 567.
16. Gillespie, *First Theologians*, 88.
17. Gillespie, *First Theologians*, 88; italics mine.
18. Gillespie, *First Theologians*, 89.
19. Ellis, *Prophecy & Hermeneutic*, 24.

Part Two—The prophets at Corinth

Ellis notes the similarity between 1 Corinthians 12:31 ("earnestly desire the higher *charismata*") and 1 Corinthians 14:1 ("earnestly desire the *pneumatika*"), and therefore equates *pneumatika* with the higher *charismata*.[20] Most commentators seem to agree that the phrase "higher gifts" refers to the first three gifts listed in 12:28—apostles, prophets, and teachers—which are given the priorities "first... second... third." Paul also explicitly names prophecy as "higher" (*meizōn*) than tongues in 14:5. So Ellis would restrict *pneumatika* to the gifts of apostleship, prophecy, and teaching.

Gillespie agrees that *pneumatika* refers to speaking in the Spirit, but argues that it is *Corinthian jargon*: he suggests that the Corinthians were indiscriminately identifying both prophecy and tongues as "speaking in the Spirit,"[21] and this explains why Paul is so careful to disaggregate the two. He thus demurs at Robinson's suggestion that the Corinthians were guilty of completely equating *pneumatika* with tongues.[22]

Fee's position on this is perhaps a little unclear: on the one hand, he suggests that *pneumatika* are "utterances inspired by the Spirit";[23] on the other hand, he says, "When the emphasis is on the manifestation, the 'gift' as such, Paul speaks of *charismata*; when the emphasis is on the Spirit, he speaks of *pneumatika*."[24]

In what sense are these gifts "higher?" Gillespie moves toward his definition of prophecy when he says,

> God has ordered the Spirit's work in the church around those activities that mediate the inspired intelligible word. These *charismata* are "greater" not in the sense of *higher* but in the sense of *essential*. In his development of the analogy of the body, which rightly stresses the variety of its organs (vv. 15–20) and their interdependency (vv. 21–26), the apostle does not mention that some parts of the body are *vital organs*. That fact implicitly comes to expression in the concluding injunction ["But earnestly desire the higher gifts" v. 31] ... Prophecy is the most essential gift to which a believer might aspire *because it mediates the gospel to the church in intelligible speech*.[25]

---

20. Ellis, *Prophecy & Hermeneutic*, 24.
21. Gillespie, *First Theologians*, 73.
22. D. W. B. Robinson, "Charismata Versus Pneumatika", 51, in Gillespie, *First Theologians*, 71.
23. Fee, *First Epistle to the Corinthians*, 654.
24. Fee, *First Epistle to the Corinthians*, 576.
25. Gillespie, *First Theologians*, 126; last italics mine.

The Pneumatics (1 Cor 12)

Conclusion

It seems likely that when Paul talks of *pneumatika,* he means not just "spiritual gifts" but the gifts of *speaking in the Spirit.* Of course, when Paul speaks in the Spirit he does so with apostolic authority. Nevertheless, all Christians are capable of speech that exalts Christ through the right use of his word, and such speech is only possible by the enabling of the Spirit (1 Cor 12:3). In this sense, we can say that all Christians are capable of Spirit-inspired (or Spirit-enabled) speech, without any suggestion that they can speak infallibly.

If *pneumatika* means "gifts of Spirit-enabled speech," does it include the gift of speaking in tongues? If, given the similarity between 1 Corinthians 12:31 and 1 Corinthians 14:1, we take *pneumatika* to map precisely to the *higher charismata,* it cannot include tongues, because tongues is not a "higher" gift (1 Cor 14:5).[26] That would imply that Paul, who has spent such effort to locate the Spirit-taught speech around the message of Christ (1 Cor 2, 12), does not consider tongues to be a *pneumatikon,* since only *interpreted* tongues could satisfy that criterion. Paul also stresses that tongues speech originates from "*my* spirit" rather than more directly from the *Holy Spirit* (1 Cor 14:14–15).

This all suggests a rather close mapping of *pneumatika* to the gifts of *prophecy and teaching* (including the apostolic versions of those gifts). However, there is an important contraindication in 1 Corinthians 14:1, and we will consider that passage more closely in chapter 11.

---

26. See Gillespie, *First Theologians,* 130.

Chapter 9

Vagueness, Uncertainty, and Error (1 Cor 13:9–12)

CAN PROPHECIES EVER CONSIST of impressions or pictures that impress themselves on the prophet's mind? Might these sometimes be rather vague so that the prophet himself does not have a clear understanding of their meaning, or even whether he has received a revelation at all?

One text that may appear to argue in favor of such speech concerns the partial nature of prophecy:

> For we know in part and we prophesy in part, but when the perfect comes, the partial will pass away. When I was a child, I spoke like a child, I thought like a child, I reasoned like a child. When I became a man, I gave up childish ways. For now we see in a mirror dimly, but then face to face. Now I know in part; then I shall know fully, even as I have been fully known. (1 Cor 13:9–12)

Grudem comments,

> Prophecy is imperfect, i) because it gives only a glimpse of the subjects it treats ('in part,' v. 9); ii) because the prophet himself only receives some kind of indirect revelation, and a limited one at that ('we see in a mirror,' v. 12); and iii) because what the prophet does receive is often difficult for him to understand or interpret ('dimly,' v. 12).[1]

---

1. *GP*, 102.

Vagueness, Uncertainty, and Error (1 Cor 13:9–12)

He concludes: "Apparently . . . the prophet *may not always understand* with complete clarity just what has been revealed to him, and at times *may not even be sure* that he has received a revelation."[2]

Grudem appears to be drawn to the notion of prophecy that has little meaning to the prophet himself, but which nevertheless somehow meets with a responsive chord from his hearers. Thus, he says, "Although there is no explicit statement that a prophet understood what he was saying, it is clear that the hearers understood."[3] This leads him to assert that revelations "probably took the form of words, thoughts, or mental pictures that suddenly impressed themselves forcefully on the mind of the prophet."[4]

Comment

The word "dimly" translates the Greek "*en ainigmati*" (in a puzzle, riddle, or enigma). The Septuagint uses the same phrase in describing how God speaks more clearly to Moses than to other prophets: "With him I speak mouth to mouth, clearly, and not *in riddles*" (Num 12:8). As Fee says, "God spoke with Moses directly ('mouth to mouth'), not as to the other prophets, to whom he spoke through visions or dreams."[5] However, as we have seen, prophetic "dreams" were really night visions, and these visions often involved an embodied encounter with the Lord. So there was nothing vague about them! Although only Moses met God face to face, the other Old Testament prophets nevertheless had visions of God in which he spoke in the clearest and most unmistakable terms, even supervising *every word* they wrote.

We can agree that in certain aspects the messages of prophets were not always clear:

- Old Testament prophets had only a vague notion of the Christ of whom they spoke. But they were nevertheless aware that they were prophesying for future generations (1 Pet 1:10–12).
- In some cases, a prophet may not always have been aware that he was prophesying. As Carson says, "it is not obvious that when, for instance, Paul was explaining his itinerary to the Corinthians in his

2. *GP*, 102.
3. *GP*, 105.
4. *GP*, 110.
5. Fee, *First Epistle to the Corinthians*, 647 n42; italics mine.

Part Two—The prophets at Corinth

second canonical letter to them he was *psychologically* aware of a revelatory process operating that extended to the words he was dictating."[6]

- Prophecy that is laden with symbolism (as in Daniel and Ezekiel, for example) is hard to understand.

These all seem to be rather special cases and probably have little relevance to the prophesying that Paul earnestly desires for the Corinthians. In verse 12, the ESV and RSV choose "dimly," but the NIV has "For now we see only a reflection as in a mirror." As Grudem himself recognizes,

> The mirror imagery suggests both *indirectness* and *incompleteness* (one does not see everything, but only those things within the borders of the mirror) . . . But it need not suggest that the image is distorted—mirrors in antiquity could have rather high standards of clarity.[7]

Fee agrees, staing that "Corinth was famous as the producer of some of the finest bronze mirrors in antiquity."[8] Fee also suggests that it is likely then that, with the mirror image,

> the emphasis is not on the *quality* of the seeing . . . but to [sic] the *indirect nature* of looking into a mirror as opposed to seeing someone face to face . . . In our own culture the comparable metaphor would be the difference between seeing a photograph and seeing someone in person. As good as a picture is, it is simply not the real thing.[9]

Since a mirror gives a very accurate reflection of reality, and a photograph a very accurate representation it, we should be wary of making too much of the word some translate as "dimly." Prophecy is indeed *partial* revelation (v. 9), but it is accurate revelation nevertheless. We should not miss the fact that Paul even includes his own prophecy when he says, "*We* see in part." Even Pauline Scripture, despite its perfection, is but a partial description of divine things, not the full reality of them.

Grudem says that the prophet *may not always understand* with complete clarity just what has been revealed to him. But this statement runs counter to Paul's statement that the prophecy he commends is not only

---

6. Carson, *Showing the Spirit*, 99.
7. GP, 101.
8. Fee, *First Epistle to the Corinthians*, 647–48.
9. Fee, *First Epistle to the Corinthians*, 648.

Vagueness, Uncertainty, and Error (1 Cor 13:9–12)

intelligible to the *hearer*, but also involves the active engagement of the mind of the *prophet* (1 Cor 14:19). Prophecy that is unintelligible to the prophet runs the risk of being equally unintelligible to the hearer! In that case, it could not qualify as prophecy, since it would fail the edification test of 1 Corinthians 14:3.

As for Grudem's claim that prophecy might consist of "words, thoughts, or mental pictures that suddenly impressed themselves forcefully on the mind of the prophet," this is just fanciful. There are no New Testament examples of pictures impressing themselves on people, forcefully or otherwise. Indeed, any picture is inherently highly ambiguous, which is why God invariably communicates with his prophets *in words*, even when there are also visions.

There is a danger here that prophecy is effectively reduced to tongues ("*glossified?*"); that is, prophecy is assumed, like tongues, to be produced without the active engagement of the speaker's mind (14:14), its use of images is ambiguous and therefore unenlightening ("mysteries in the Spirit," 14:2), it requires interpretation, and so on. But Paul's primary concern in writing the chapter is to draw a sharp distinction between tongues and prophecy for a congregation which was failing to distinguish them, and we should exclude pictures on similar grounds. We should be very wary of putting together what God has divided.

Chapter 10

Prophecy as Loving Speech (1 Cor 14)

Prophecy as an Expression of Love

In 1 Corinthians 13, Paul starts to describe the "more excellent way" of love promised in 1 Corinthians 12:31. In chapter 14, he does not abandon his discussion of love, but rather he describes the exercise of tongues and prophecy *in love*, that is, how prophecy is loving speech. Indeed, all the gifts of God—the *charismata*—being expressions of God's grace, are also to be expressions of our love in meeting the needs of others.

Tongues and Prophecy

The entire chapter of 1 Corinthians 14 is a comprehensive contrast between tongues and prophecy, in which Paul examines the effects of each. The conclusion is that the gift of tongues fails the "loving speech test" and the gift of prophecy passes it.

The summary below brings out this contrast in 1 Corinthians 14:

Prophecy as Loving Speech (1 Cor 14)

Tongues	**Prophecy**
Is addressed to God (v. 2)	Is addressed to people (v. 3)
Is unintelligible (v. 2)	Builds up, etc., because it is intelligible (v. 3)
If I speak in a tongue there is *no benefit* to the hearer because it is unintelligible (vv. 6–11) Only interpreted tongues are intelligible (vv. 13, 16)	So seek gifts that *build up* the church (using intelligible speech) (v. 12)
If I pray in a tongue, my mind is unproductive (i.e., because it is not engaged) (v. 14)	In church I would rather speak five words with my mind so as to instruct (v. 19)
Don't be children in your *thinking* (v. 20)	But be mature in your *thinking* (v. 20)
Speaking in tongues does not lead people to a believing response (vv. 21–22)	But prophecy does lead to a believing response (v. 22)
That is why if all speak in tongues, a visitor will call you mad (v. 23)	But if all prophesy, a visitor will be convicted and judged, and will repent and worship God (vv. 24–25)

Having stated his preference, in church, to *pray* with his mind and *sing* with his mind (v. 15), Paul says, "in church I would rather speak five words with my mind" (v. 19). Paul must surely have in mind the great contrast between tongues and prophecy which he describes both before and after in this chapter; and the commands "Brothers, do not be children in your thinking. Be infants in evil, but in your thinking be mature" (1 Cor 14:20) shine like a beacon over the rest of the chapter.

It might be objected that verses 13–19 is mainly about the contrast between *uninterpreted* and *interpreted* tongues, rather than that between tongues and prophecy. Indeed, Fee says, "The entire section deals with tongues; prophecy is not mentioned" but he adds, "*although perhaps it is alluded to at the end* (v. 19)."[1] Fee's last phrase seems correct: when Paul says, "in church I would rather speak five words in order to instruct" (v. 19), the link back to prophecy is clear since he has already told us that prophecy *builds up* (in v. 3), and that building up the church requires the active engagement of a speaker's mind (v. 19).

Almost every commentator captures the point Paul is making that prophecy is *intelligible* speech (that is, speech the hearer understands). But

---

1. Fee, *First Epistle to the Corinthians*, 668; italics mine.

many miss the fact that in verse 19, Paul is talking not just about the *hearer's* mind being actively engaged in the process, but the *speaker's* also: "speak five words with *my* mind." So he is talking not just about *intelligible* speech, but about *intelligent* speech.

In verses 20–25, Paul applies what he has just said about himself to his Corinthian listeners: in their meetings they are to use their minds just as he does (v. 20). He then looks at the contrasting effects on a visitor of being exposed to tongues and to prophecy. The effect of witnessing tongues is that the visitor thinks the speakers are out of their minds (v. 23). On the other hand, the effects of being exposed to prophecy are powerfully edifying. Why? Again, *because the minds of both the speaker and the listener have been engaged.* It would be a very odd digression if verses 19–20 had nothing *at all* to do with prophecy, and nothing short of perverse if Paul actively believed that prophecy somehow bypassed the intellect: indeed, that would be the very opposite of the apparent meaning. Thiselton agrees:

> So strong is Paul's emphasis on the use of mental reflection and control that it is inconceivable (in our view) that most writers are correct to assume that prophecy is necessarily or uniformly "spontaneous." True, spontaneous prophecy may occur; but to insist that is always or necessarily so is to fail to do justice to the text before us.[2]

If any doubt still remains that Paul's emphasis on the mind has to do with his views on prophecy, consider these two verses:

> I would rather speak five words with my mind in order to *instruct* others (v. 19)

> For you can all prophesy one by one, so that all may *learn* and all be encouraged (v. 31)

Instructing and learning must surely be counterparts of the same act.

---

2. *FEC*, 1076–77.

CHAPTER 11

The Missing Contrast of 1 Corinthians 14:1

> Pursue love, and earnestly desire the spiritual gifts, especially that you may prophesy (1 Cor 14:1).

THIS VERSE, OFTEN SOMEWHAT neglected by commentators, may well hold the key to a proper understanding both of the *pneumatika* and of prophecy.

In attempting to understand this verse, we should first note that the phrase translated *"especially* that you may prophesy" (*"mallon de hina propheteuēte"*) is repeated verbatim in 14:5, where it is translated, "but *even more* to prophesy" (ESV), or "but *I would rather* have you prophesy" (NIV). So, in 14:5, a preference is expressed for one of two contrasting items (tongues rather than prophecy), but in verse 1, the two items under discussion—spiritual gifts and prophecy—do not appear to be contrasting: for prophecy must be a spiritual gift.

According to *AG*, *"mallon de"* ("but rather" or "or rather") "introduces an expression or thought that supplements and thereby corrects what has preceded."[1] According to *LS*, it is used "to correct a statement already made."[2] On this basis, translating *"mallon de"* as "especially" seems questionable, for *what is being corrected?* If Paul had wished to be so emphatic, he could easily have used the superlative *"malista"* (as he frequently does elsewhere), rather than the comparative (*"mallon"*).

---

1. *AG*, 490.
2. *LS*, 861.

Part Two—The Prophets at Corinth

The corrective force is quite clear in Pauline uses of *"mallon de"* elsewhere:

- "But now that you have come to know God, *or rather* to be known by God." (Gal 4:9)
- "Who is to condemn? Christ Jesus is the one who died—*more than that*, who was raised—who is at the right hand of God, who indeed is interceding for us." (Rom 8:34)

So the question remains: in 1 Corinthians 14:1 *what is Paul correcting*? There seem to be two possibilities . . .

A More Precise Term

"Prophecy" is clearly a member of the class *pneumatika*, which must include other gifts. Paul would then be restating with greater precision what he has already said. This is aligned with Fee's understanding: "The 'correction' in the present case is toward *specifying with greater exactness the point of the preceding imperative*."[3]

We agree. It seems possible, however, that *pneumatika* may be only a *slightly* broader term than "prophesying," inasmuch as it may *include the gift of tongues*. So Paul, wishing to exclude tongues from his commendation, uses a slightly more specific term: ". . . *in particular*, that you may *prophesy*."

A Preferred or Explained Term

There is another possible reading. The phrase *"mallon de"* commonly introduces a preferred or more accurate way of saying what has just been said. So "prophecy" may map *precisely* onto *pneumatika* (which would therefore mean it *excludes* tongues), but simply be Paul's preferred term here, perhaps because the Corinthians have such a distorted view of the meaning of *pneumatika*. Thus,

> Pursue love, and earnestly desire the gifts of Spirit-inspired speech, or *to put it more clearly*, that you may prophesy.

This reading seems plausible in light of Paul's focus on correcting faulty Corinthian conceptions of spirituality. As we have seen elsewhere in the letter,

---

3. Fee, *First Epistle to the Corinthians*, 655n11; italics mine.

the term *pneumatika* seems to be familiar to, but distorted by, the Corinthians, and Paul might here be realigning their understanding of that word with what may have been a less ambiguous term: "*prophecy*." This would match Gillespie's reading of 14:37.[4] The reading also makes good sense of 1 Corinthians 14:37: "If anyone thinks that he is a prophet, or *pneumatikos*." Here the two terms would be synonymous.

Conclusion on *mallon de*

Both of these readings have merit. However, we prefer the first, meaning that "prophecy" is only a slightly more precise term than *pneumatika*, the latter being a term that *includes tongues*. Paul then corrects himself in order to exclude tongues. We therefore propose a translation such as

> Pursue love, and earnestly desire the gifts of Spirit-enabled speech, or *more specifically* (since that would include tongues) that you may prophesy.

This reading would support our developing proposition that *all Spirit-enabled speech apart from tongues constitutes prophesying*.

Pneumatika and *pneumatikos* in 1 Corinthians 2 and 1 Corinthians 14

One remaining issue, however, concerns how we are to relate the terms *pneumatika* and *pneumatikos* in 1 Corinthians 14 to the same terms in 1 Corinthians 2.

The adjective *pneumatikos* does not map completely onto the English word "spiritual." The Greek seems to be more intensive. So, for example:

- "Spiritual songs" (Col 3:16) probably means "Spirit-inspired songs"
- "Spiritual food" and "spiritual rock" (1 Cor 10:3–4), mean "heavenly" or "supernatural"
- "Spiritual person" (1 Cor 3:1) means both "spiritually mature" and "Spirit-filled" (1 Cor 2:15; Gal 6:1)

With this in mind, how are we to view Paul's comment that "If anyone thinks that he is a prophet, or spiritual, he should acknowledge that the

---

4. Gillespie, *First Theologians*, 76.

things I am writing to you are a command of the Lord" (1 Cor 14:37)? Paul is talking about people who seem to have an inflated view of their own speech gifts (v. 36), and this suggests that *pneumatikos here* means "having a gift of spiritual speech" (which is consistent with our understanding of *pneumatika*).

Turning to 1 Corinthians 2, if *pneumatikois* in 2:13 is taken as masculine ("to those who are spiritual"), as it clearly is in 3:1, then it would be parallel with *en tois teleois*, "among the mature" (2:2). Opting for this reading, Ellis concludes,

> As they are in 1 Corinthians 14, the pneumatics here (1) are distinguished from the believers generally. (2) They are *both the recipients and the mediators of revelation,* "the wisdom of God in a mystery," wisdom that had been hidden.[5]

Ellis is suggesting that "*pneumatikoi*" is Paul's designation for mature believers who receive revelation (in 1 Corinthians 2) and pass it on to others (in 1 Corinthians 14) as "prophets."[6]

So for Paul the *pneumatika* seems to consist broadly of the Spirit-inspired, Bible-related speech gifts, which he would expect all mature, spiritual Christians (*hoi pneumatikoi* of 1 Corinthians 3:1) to be actively practicing. The Corinthians were certainly familiar with the term *pneumatika*, but it appears to have become closely aligned in their thinking with tongues and disconnected both from the message of Christ and from their understanding of prophecy.

---

5. Ellis, *Prophecy & Hermeneutic*, 25; italics mine.

6. Such a reading suggests that in 1 Corinthians 2, when Paul talks of imparting wisdom "*among* the mature" rather than "*to* the mature" (2:6), and says "*we* impart" not "*I* impart" (2:13), he may be referring to the same practice of *group prophesying* that he describes later in 1 Corinthians 14:29–32, with himself as the chief among several participants.

CHAPTER 12

A Definition of Prophecy? (1 Cor 14:3)

> The one who prophesies speaks to people for their upbuilding (*oikodomē*) and encouragement (*paraklēsis*) and consolation (*paramythia*). (1 Cor 14:3)

IN 1 CORINTHIANS 8:1, Paul establishes the connection between love and upbuilding: "knowledge puffs up, but *love builds up*" (see also Ephesians 4:16: "the body . . . builds itself up in love"), and in 1 Corinthians 14:3 we see that prophecy has the same effect. In other words, prophecy, rightly understood and exercised, involves an expression of loving self-sacrifice for the edification of others (just a we saw in 1 Corinthians 3–4). The other functions of prophecy listed in verse 3—"exhortation" and "consolation"— also emphasize the compassionate and relational nature of the gift. In this chapter, we examine each of these three functions of prophecy and ask whether the verse might offer practically a *definition* of prophecy.

A Functional Definition?

Gillespie quotes Reiling, who says that 14:3 "sounds like a functional definition of prophecy," and "there is no other statement in the New Testament which comes closer to a definition than this," although Reiling also thinks this is "deceptive" since the effect of "upbuilding" is not limited to prophecy.[1]

---

1. Reiling, "Prophecy, the Spirit and the Church", 69, in Gillespie, *First Theologians*, 141.

Part Two—The prophets at Corinth

Grudem does not see 14:3 as a definition of prophecy at all, but entirely as a description of its effects. He notes that upbuilding is also a feature of church discipline (2 Cor 10:8; 13:9), not offending others by what we eat (Rom 14:19), self-denial for the benefit of others (Rom 15:2), and acting in love (1 Cor 8:1): "When the church comes together, any legitimate speech activity can result in edification: a hymn, a teaching, a revelation, a tongue, an interpretation—all give 'edification' (1 Cor 14:26)."[2] Therefore, "prophecy cannot be distinguished from other speech activities simply by means of its functions, for there is no one function that will serve as a distinguishing characteristic."[3]

However, Grudem seems to throw in the towel a little prematurely here. The fact that none of these characteristics is unique to prophecy does not mean they tell us nothing at all about the nature of the gift. Indeed, the fact that characteristics are shared by various activities may well suggest how those activities are related: a hymn teaches, teaching is to be an expression of love, and so on. Furthermore, when Paul says "love builds up" (1 Cor 8:1), he is not only saying that upbuilding is an *effect* of love ("love people and they will be built up"); he is also saying that upbuilding is an *expression* or example of love ("building people up is a loving thing to do"). Likewise, in 14:3, acts of upbuilding, exhortation, and consolation may be expressions or examples of prophetic speech. So Paul *may* be saying that practically *any speech* that achieves these goals is prophesying just as any speech that builds people up is loving and is teaching. This point may be suggested in the Greek, which reads literally, "He that prophesies *speaks upbuilding* and exhortation and consolation."

Gillespie would agree: in response to Grudem's comment that prophecy is not the only activity that edifies, he says, "At issue is not whether prophecy *alone* builds up the church, which is manifestly not the case. The question is *how* prophecy as the inspired word of the Spirit contributes to this end."[4] In other words, once we understand how Spirit-inspired edification and exhortation occur in Scripture, we may have a clearer idea of the nature of prophecy. So we should now explore that issue.

---

2. *GP*, 126.
3. *GP*, 127.
4. Gillespie, *First Theologians*, 142.

A Definition of Prophecy? (1 Cor 14:3)

Upbuilding—*oikodomē*

The Corinthians seem to have developed an unhealthy obsession with the gift of tongues, possibly seeing it as the highest form of Spirit-inspired speech, and Paul points out the shortcomings of such a view throughout 1 Corinthians 14. His key message to them is: "since you are eager for manifestations of the Spirit, strive to excel in building up the church" (1 Cor 14:12). In other words, "You want gifts that show the Spirit. *But building up the church is the most spiritual thing you can do.*"

The emphasis on building up the church is relentless in this chapter:

- The one who prophesies speaks to people for their *upbuilding* (v. 2)
- The one who prophesies *builds up* the church (v. 4)
- Without interpretation, the church won't be *built up* (v. 5)
- Excel in *building up* the church (v. 12)
- The other person is not being *built up* (v. 17)
- Let all things be done for *building up* (v. 26)

Building the church is clearly fundamental to Paul's apostolic task: "According to the grace of God given to me, like a skilled master builder, I laid a foundation, and someone else is building upon it" (1 Cor 3:10); and of course, such upbuilding is also the key concern of Christ himself (Matt 16:18).

Paul talks about "our authority, which the Lord gave for building you up" (2 Cor 10:8; cf. 13:10). Gillespie quotes John Howard Schütz: "Paul does not think of authority as anything other than the authority granted him in his commission to preach the gospel."[5] Gillespie notes that "Vielhauer infers from these texts that *oikodomē* is a technical designation of the apostolic task which . . . is *fulfilled by preaching*."[6] Gillespie comments, "Essential is the notion that *oikodomē* and the proclamation of the gospel are both *functionally* and *materially* related."[7] Prophesying "effects *oikodomē* . . . through an articulation of the one gospel that *alone* creates and builds up the church."[8] We see this connection between gospel proclamation and *oikodomē* in, for example, Paul's statement that it is his "ambition to

---

5. Schütz, *Paul*, 224–25, in Gillespie, *First Theologians*, 142.
6. Vielhauer, *Oikodome*, 86–87, in Gillespie, *First Theologians*, 142.
7. Gillespie, *First Theologians*, 142.
8. Gillespie, *First Theologians*, 142; italics mine.

preach the gospel, not where Christ has already been named, lest I *build* on someone else's foundation" (Rom 15:20).

Of course, *oikodomē* is not restricted to the initial proclamation of the gospel, but also includes all kinds of Christ-centered, Christ-forming biblical speech-acts "for *building up* the body of Christ . . . until we all attain . . . to mature manhood" (Eph 4:12–13). Such maturity is evidenced by *doctrinal stability*: "so that we may no longer be children, tossed to and fro by the waves and carried about by every wind of doctrine, by human cunning, by craftiness in deceitful schemes" (Eph 4:14).

At the end of 2 Corinthians, referring back to all he has said in the letter, Paul concludes: "It is in the sight of God that we have been speaking in Christ, and *all for your upbuilding*, beloved" (2 Cor 12:19). So Paul's letter has been focused entirely on the upbuilding of the church. But Paul doesn't just teach doctrine; he also lovingly encourages the Corinthians to faithful discipleship by sharing his heart, describing his own experiences in the service of Christ, and exhorting them to similarly faithful discipleship. Thiselton is one of the few commentators to capture this life-on-life quality in prophetic speech when he says that prophecy takes place "in the context of interpersonal relations" (Thiselton, FEC, 1094).

Exhortation—*paraklēsis*

Paraklēsis is often translated as "encouragement," although "exhortation" would be more accurate: Thiselton defines it as "a varied range of . . . speech-acts which plead, encourage, challenge, brace, console, provide comfort *on the basis of . . . covenant promises*."[9] He notes that the verb and noun occur some 109 times in the New Testament, and he quotes J. Thomas: "On the basis of statistics alone *parakaleō* and *paraklēsis* are among the most important terms for speaking and influencing in the NT."[10]

There is a very tight association between *paraklēsis* and prophecy. Joseph the Levite was given the Aramaic name by which we know him—Barnabas (*bar naḇyā,*), which means "Son of the *prophet*." But Luke explains this as meaning "Son of *encouragement*" (Acts 4:36) in Greek. This strongly suggests that in Luke's mind prophecy and exhortation are *virtually synonymous*.

---

9. *FEC*, 1088; italics mine.
10. Thomas, J., "*Paraklēsis*," EDNT, 3:23, in *FEC*, 1088.

A Definition of Prophecy? (1 Cor 14:3)

The church at Jerusalem sent prophets to Antioch on three occasions, and on two of these visits *paraklēsis* is mentioned. For example, Barnabas "*exhorted* them all to remain faithful to the Lord with steadfast purpose" (Acts 11:23), and Judas and Silas "who were themselves prophets, *encouraged* and strengthened the brothers with many words" (Acts 15:32).

How is *paraklēsis* effected? Thiselton notes that, "scripture remains the definitive source for *paraklēsis* (cf. Rom: 15:4–5)."[11] There is also the *paraklēsis* of the letter from the Jerusalem Council (Acts 15:31), and the *paraklēsis* of the words of the prophets who explained it, the latter deriving from the former, in what we would surely call "preaching" (see Acts 15:32 in light of 15:27). Likewise, in 2 Timothy 4:2 ("preach the word . . . reprove, rebuke, and exhort"), the text of Scripture provides the basis for exhortation.

It is no surprise, therefore, to see that there is also a close connection between teaching and *paraklēsis*, with *paraklēsis* being a key goal of teaching:

- "I appeal to you, brothers, bear with my word of exhortation, for I have written to you briefly" (Heb 13:22).
- "He must hold firmly to the trustworthy message as it has been taught, so that he can encourage others by sound doctrine and refute those who oppose it" (Titus 1:9, NIV).
- In 1 Thessalonians 2:2–3, the declaration of the gospel (v. 2) is described as "our *paraklēsis*" in verse 3. Gillespie says, "Here missionary preaching is designated without qualification as *paraklēsis*."[12] The two are also associated in 1 Thessalonians 2:9–12 and 1 Thessalonians 3:1–3.
- "Therefore encourage one another with these words" (1 Thess 4:18) refers to encouragement that comes from consideration of the return of Christ.

The inescapable conclusion here is that the *paraklēsis* undertaken by the prophets here involves communicating Scripture with the goal of forming people into the likeness of Christ. In summary, "Through exhortation

---

11. *FEC*, 1090.
12. Gillespie, *First Theologians*, 145.

as theological and ethical exposition of the confessed gospel, faith is strengthened."[13]

Our conclusion is that the terms "prophecy" and "*paraklēsis*" which appear to be synonymous for Luke (Acts 4:36), were probably so for Paul as well.

Paraklēsis as Confrontation

The English word "encouragement" is undoubtedly gentler and narrower than *paraklēsis*, which can imply anything from gentle encouragement to sharp rebuke.

Boring makes a similar point in his discussion of the book of Revelation:

> The Apocalypse is throughout a prophetic rebuke of immorality and unfaithfulness and a pronouncement of Judgment upon those who do not repent (e.g., 2:23; 3:10; 13:10; 16:6; 22:12, 18–19) . . . The legal connotation of *paraklēsis* is important here, for the Paraclete functions as a *prosecuting attorney*, rather than counsel for the defense, as the agent of the heavenly court who presses the case against the unbelieving world before the eschatological judge. By realizing the future eschatological Judgment, the Paraclete reproves or exposes the unbelieving world.[14]

Meira Kensky agrees:

> The forensic role of the Johannine Paraclete goes beyond that of defense counsel or advocate. The role as envisioned in [John]16:7–11 is one of a *prosecuting attorney* . . . His job is to convict the world, to prove that it is guilty in the matters of sin, justice and Judgment. On the other hand, the previous passages envision the Paraclete as the one who provides comfort, consolation, one who teaches, and represents the disciples in their ongoing trials. The Johannine Paraclete, therefore, seems to fill both of these forensic roles . . . The Paraclete will function as a defense counsel for the disciples . . . But this very assistance . . . is an *offensive* role against the world in the cosmic lawsuit.[15]

---

13. Gillespie, *First Theologians*, 148.
14. Boring, *Sayings of the Risen Jesus*, 117; italics mine.
15. Kensky, *Trying Man, Trying God*, 232; italics mine.

A Definition of Prophecy? (1 Cor 14:3)

Kensky is surely correct to say that, in relation to unbelievers, the Paraclete acts as a prosecuting attorney: "And when he comes, he will convict the world concerning sin and righteousness and judgment" (John 16:8). But wherever believers sin willfully, the Spirit, through the words of prophets, can be similarly confrontational. The important point here is that the work of the Paraclete entirely matches—because it enables—that of the prophet, since both speak on behalf of God. The Paraclete enables *paraklēsis*, and all such speech may, on that basis, be termed "prophetic."

Consolation—*paramythia*

Paramythia means "*encouragement, esp. comfort, consolation,*"[16] and is explicitly related by Paul to love (Phil 2:1). Thiselton says, "Malherbe identifies the term closely with . . . *pastoral care.*"[17] *Paramythia* is broadly similar to *paraklēsis*, but seems to describe an exclusively positive approach, in contrast to the sometimes more confrontational *paraklēsis*: we are told, for example, to "encourage [*paramytheisthe*] the fainthearted" (1 Thess 5:14). It seems to be the verbal equivalent of an arm around the shoulder, and is thus offered to those in mourning (John 11:19, 31). In other words, it communicates God's love, and is particularly appropriate to Christians suffering persecution.

What is the content of Christian consolation? Gillespie highlights the gospel content of consolation by quoting Stählin: "All the comfort which the apostle (1 Thess 2:12), the prophets (1 Cor 14:3) and Christians themselves (1 Thess 5:14; Phil 2:1) give is drawn from the Gospel."[18]

More specifically, the content of this consolation is *the eschatological promises of God*: "for this light momentary affliction is preparing for us an eternal weight of glory beyond all comparison" (2 Cor 4:17). It is clear that consolation not only sympathizes with those who suffer for the gospel, but also reminds them that their suffering is necessary, and of the eternal reward awaiting them. Its message is that "through many tribulations we must enter the kingdom of God" (Acts 14:22).

---

16. *AG*, 626.
17. *FEC*, 1089.
18. Stählin, "*paramutheomai*" 823, in Gillespie, *First Theologians*, 149.

Part Two—The prophets at Corinth

Conclusion

The three effects of prophecy listed in 1 Corinthians 14:3 are common, even technical, Pauline descriptions of his teaching and disciplemaking ministry. This suggests that they are not merely characteristics of prophetic speech, they are expressions of it, and that *any* speech that achieves these outcomes, following the biblical pattern, may be called prophesying: just as any speech that builds people up in Christ may be described as teaching or as an expression of love.

We saw how each of these three goals is achieved in the New Testament. In short:

- The church is *built up* in Christ by communication that focuses on the gospel message of Christ, and which explains Christian doctrine.
- The church is *exhorted* by Scripture, as the gospel is expounded, explained, and applied, in the context of interpersonal relationships.
- The church is *consoled* by the promises of Scripture, particularly the *eschatological* promises of the gospel.

There is ample evidence here of the *gospel and biblical content* of prophetic speech, for there is simply no other way by which the church may be edified, exhorted, and consoled.

There is a striking parallel between these three elements and the typical teaching activity of Paul and Barnabas: we hear that they travelled through Lystra, Iconium, and Antioch "strengthening the souls of the disciples [*upbuilding*], encouraging them to continue in the faith [*exhortation*], and saying that through many tribulations we must enter the kingdom of God [*consolation*]" (Acts 14:22).

If we see people designated as prophets (Paul and Barnabas) engaged in what is for them a typical activity which closely matches what we know to be the characteristics of prophecy, we must surely assume that what they are doing is their *typical prophesying*. In other words, the preaching and teaching ministry Paul and Barnabas carried out as they travelled around, in public and from house to house, was their prophesying.

Finally, the fact that the rare word *propheteia* is so tightly associated with the much more common term *paraklēsis* (in Acts 4:36; 11:23; 14:22; 15:32), implies a broader meaning to *propheteia* than is often suspected, and helps explain the apparent scarcity of the prophecy word-group in the New Testament: *it is often simply called something else.*

Chapter 13

Revealing Secrets (1 Cor 14:24–25)

> But if all prophesy, and an unbeliever or outsider enters, he is convicted by all, he is called to account by all, the secrets of his heart are disclosed (*phaneron genetai*), and so, falling on his face, he will worship God and declare that God is really among you. (1 Cor 14:24–25)

EXPLAINING THIS TEXT, GRUDEM says, "In this case, those who prophesy make a public disclosure of the secrets of a visitor's heart (v25a) . . . And apparently *everyone who prophesies* contributes to this act of conviction and investigation."[1]

In other words, Grudem is saying that the prophets *miraculously perceive*, and then *publicly announce*, the secret sins of an individual unbeliever who is visiting the church. Thus he sees a similarity with the story of the Samaritan woman at the well in John 4, in which the woman's secret past is laid bare by the words of Jesus. Grudem asserts,

> Verse 25 *must mean* that specific mention of one or more of his [the outsider's] particular, individual sins is made in the prophecies.
>
> According to Grudem, This is true because of the meaning of the word used and because of the context. The word for "disclosed" or "become manifest" is the Greek term *phaneros*. Both this word (eighteen times in the New Testament) and its related verb, *phaneroō* (forty-nine times in the New Testament) always refer to a public, external manifestation and are never used of

---

1. *GP*, 114.

private or secret communication of information or of the internal working of God in a person's mind or heart.[2]

Comment

Grudem seems to believe that a hapless visitor will have his secret sins publicly exposed and announced by multiple members of the congregation in what Garland calls "gang evangelism."[3] That would be ungentle at best, and rather grotesque at worst. Would such an activity really be likely to cause the visitor to fall to his knees and worship God? Would it not be far more likely to cause him to flee the building in horror?

Does Paul really expect the Corinthian prophets to know the inner thoughts of others? Surely not. Paul seems to deny the possibility of such a thing: "For who knows a person's thoughts except the spirit of that person, which is in him" (1 Cor 2:11)? Although Jesus is indeed able to see the secret sins of the Samaritan woman at the well in John 4, he does not declare them to others—indeed, Jesus sent his disciples away expressly so that he might speak to the woman *in private*.

Deciphering an Activity from a Description of its Effects

In the passage, Paul has just been talking about the *effect* on the outsider of being exposed to multiple people speaking tongues: "Will they not say that you are out of your minds" (14:23)? Then he turns to look at prophecy and considers the *various effects* on the outsider of exposure to prophecy (he is convicted, called to account, etc.). So when he says, "the secrets of their hearts are disclosed" (14:25), Paul is talking about an *effect on the outsider*, not about the activity of the prophets. In fact, Paul tells us little about the content of the prophetic speech here—we have to work that out from his account of its effects.

What we do know is that the unbeliever is not the primary audience of prophecy—it is targeted at the believing congregation (14:22); but nevertheless, the content of the prophecy is so gospel-centered that the unbeliever, *eavesdropping* as it were on in-house Christian communication, is led to repentance, as often happens in preaching today.

---

2. *GP*, 152–53; italics mine.
3. Garland, *1 Corinthians*, 652.

Revealing Secrets (1 Cor 14:24–25)

A Double Disclosure

Grudem argues that public disclosure *must* be implied with *phaneroō* and *phaneros*, and that they are never used "of the internal working of God in a person's mind or heart."[4]

However, I would suggest that there is both a public *and* a private disclosure here. The prophet does indeed make a public disclosure, but he or she does not accuse specific members of the congregation of specific sins that could only be known by miraculous revelation; rather, as the prophet speaks, he carefully explains the gospel and *publicly discloses the sinfulness of sin*. The hearer senses that his deepest thoughts have been accurately portrayed in the prophet's message, and thinks to himself, "*He is describing me!*" So there is a double disclosure here: a general, public disclosure of sin in the prophet's message, and a private disclosure in which the listener's own sinfulness is made apparent to himself.

This passage has clear echoes of other passages describing the last judgment:

- For nothing is hidden except to be made manifest (*phaneroō*); nor is anything secret except to come to light (*phaneron*) (Mark 4:22).
- For nothing is hidden that will not be made manifest (*phaneron genestai*), nor is anything secret that will not be known and come to light (*phaneron*) (Luke 8:17).
- Each one's work will become manifest (*phaneron genestai*), for the Day will disclose it (*apokalyptō*) (1 Cor 3:13).
- Therefore do not pronounce judgment before the time, before the Lord comes, who will bring to light the things now hidden in darkness and will disclose (*phaneroō*) the purposes of the heart (1 Cor 4:5).

Indeed, one day, at the judgment, our secret sins and the quality of all our works will indeed be publicly revealed before God's heavenly court. But such insight belongs to God alone, and to that day: for now the disclosure of sin is partial at best.

Scripture is key in effecting this revelation: "For the word of God is living and active . . . discerning the thoughts and intentions of the heart. And no creature is hidden from his sight, but all are naked and exposed to the eyes of him to whom we must give account" (Heb 4:12–13). This

---

4. GP, 153.

strongly suggests that the prophets described in 1 Corinthians 14:24–25 are *explaining and applying Scripture.*

In summary, as prophets preach Christ, they bring people before the holiness of God and they reveal the sinfulness of sin. But they do not miraculously discern the sins of particular individuals, nor do they announce these sins publicly to others.

The Description of a Conversion

> "falling on his face he will worship God and declare that God is really among you" (1 Cor 14:25).

Fee says, "The final result of such exposure before God is *conversion*, which is what Paul's language unmistakably intends."[5] Thiselton reminds us that the act of prostration was, in the Old Testament and the first century, a sign of devotion, before high-ranking persons or divine beings, especially when one approached with a petition (eg Matt 2:11; Rev 5:14).[6] Yes, this person is thoroughly converted.

What has led to this? We are told, "he is convicted by all, he is called to account by all" (*elenketai hupo pantōn, anakrinetai hupo pantōn*). The key verbs here are:

- *elenkō*: Bring to light, expose, convict, or convince someone of something.
- *anakrinō*: Question, examine, judge, call to account.

It is hard to ignore the resonance here with the work of the Holy Spirit described by Jesus: "And when he comes he will *convict* [*elenkō*] the world concerning sin and righteousness and judgment" (John 16:8; cf. John 8:46; Acts 6:10; Titus 2:15).

So in this passage we see *conviction of sin, coming under judgment, repentance, confessing faith, and prostration before God in submission and worship.* In other words, we see a thorough, end-to-end depiction of conversion. As Thiselton says, "the words of the prophets bring home the truth

---

5. Fee, *First Epistle to the Corinthians*, 687; italics mine.
6. See *FEC*, 1130.

of the gospel in such a way that the hearer 'stands under' the verdict of the cross (cf. 1:18-25)."[7]

The prophetic speech here *must* include Scripture because it is only the word of God that shows the causes and effects of sin for what they are (as we have seen in Hebrews 4:12); and the whole act is a supernatural work of the Spirit, who alone can bring conviction and awareness of impending judgment (John 16:8). Thus Hill says, "Paul demonstrates his desire to affirm the missionary function of the word, even in the case of the prophetic word spoken in worship."[8]

We conclude (with Hill,[9] Gillespie,[10] Garland,[11] Thiselton[12]) that this verse strongly indicates that prophecy here includes a clear explanation of the gospel message, resulting in conversion. As Thiselton says, "Both the church and the world stand under a prophetic announcement of Judgment and grace in the mode of warning and promise, as indeed was the case in the OT."[13]

Paul's Rejection of Miraculous Signs

If a sinner could routinely be converted by a miraculous disclosure of his secret thoughts—even if that just makes a key contribution to his conversion—*the cross would be emptied of its power* (1 Cor 1:19). As we have said, Paul specifically eschewed signs in his gospel preaching: "Jews demand signs . . . but we preach Christ crucified" (1 Cor 1:22-23). Paul "decided to know nothing among you except Jesus Christ and him crucified" (1 Cor 2:2). His sole focus was Christ and the cross; and this alone is up to the task. Only the Holy Spirit, working through the gospel message, shows me my sin and converts me.

---

7. *FEC*, 1128.

8. Hill, "Christian Prophets as Teachers or Instructors in the Church" in Panagopoulos, *Prophetic Vocation*, 112.

9. *New Testament Prophecy*, 124-25.

10. Gillespie, *First Theologians*, 157.

11. Garland, *1 Corinthians*, 652.

12. *FEC*, 1128.

13. *FEC*, 1128-29.

Part Two — The Prophets at Corinth

Conclusion

The man in 1 Corinthians 14:24–25 falls on his face, worships God, and declares, "God is *really* among you" not because he has witnessed a miracle, but because he has been exposed to the gospel and *converted*.

In the formal addresses, there must have been discussion of sin, and perhaps even particular congregational sins known to the prophet (such as Paul highlights in 1 Corinthians 5), but this text and this context do not require miraculous perception of the sins of individuals.

So in this chapter we have seen further strong evidence for our proposition that,

- The role of New Testament prophets (as of apostles) involved the receipt and faithful communication of Christ-centered biblical wisdom.

What is not clear, however, is whether this activity matches the preaching we might engage in today, or whether, as the cessationist would argue, it carried an *additional level of Spirit inspiration* long since lost to us. But so far we have seen no evidence for this in 1 Corinthians 14.

CHAPTER 14

Judging and Fallibility (1 Cor 14:29)

> Two or three prophets should speak, and the others should weigh carefully what is said. And if a revelation comes to someone who is sitting down, the first speaker should stop. (1 Cor 14:29–30 NIV)

IS PROPHECY TODAY AN admixture of truth and error that needs careful sifting? If prophets do speak error, does that make them false prophets? Grudem believes that prophecy today does indeed contain much that is false, but that this does not necessarily mean that those who speak it are false prophets. As we have already seen, Grudem's main conclusion from his examination of prophecy in 1 Corinthians 14 is that the prophets at Corinth "did *not speak with a divine authority of actual words* and were not thought by others to speak with an absolute divine authority."[1]

Grudem does not believe that prophesying in the New Testament was similar to gospel preaching today, yet his argument here does little to threaten (and much to support) such a position; his main intended target is the view that all prophecy is the infallible word of God. He believes that 1 Corinthians 14:29 does not describe fully authoritative, Scripture-quality prophetic speech, but rather a lower-grade, fallible form of prophecy that continues today.

Grudem's more detailed conclusions from this passage are as follows:

1. *GP*, 69; italics mine.

Part Two—The Prophets at Corinth

1. Paul is referring to the evaluation of *prophecies*, not of prophets. This means that one can utter a prophecy containing errors without necessarily being a false prophet.

2. Prophecy had to be "*sifted*," which implies that each prophecy contained true and false elements within it.

3. Prophecy was assessed by the whole congregation (often silently), with each person drawing his or her own conclusions.

4. Prophecy could be *interrupted*, and therefore must not have been thought to be the very words of God.

5. Prophecy is *spontaneous* here and therefore must always be spontaneous today.

We argue that these points have some merit, especially insofar as they could be describing preaching, but they are *over-conclusions*; that is, they exclude other possible meanings prematurely. Taken together, particularly when poorly understood, these readings also hold a serious danger: they open the floodgates to allow people today to present as prophetic, unchallenged and with impunity, *any vague extra-biblical thought and impression that might pop into their heads*. Can such low-grade speech *really* be what Paul has in mind for Corinth—and for us?

We will address these views over the course of the next two chapters. But first, we need to understand them more fully.

Accepted Prophets

Grudem argues that Paul is not discussing *visiting* prophets, unknown to the congregation. Rather,

> in 1 Corinthians 14, Paul is talking about a meeting of those who are *already accepted* in the fellowship of the church ("When you come together," v. 26, RSV; 'earnestly desire to prophesy' v. 39, RSV) ... In such a case, it would be very unlikely that they would be "judged" and declared "true" prophets again and again, every time they spoke, month after month.[2]

Grudem therefore argues that a different sort of evaluation must be in view: "the *evaluation of the actual prophecies* of those already accepted by the

---

2. *GP*, 58; italics mine.

Judging and Fallibility (1 Cor 14:29)

congregation."³ We can agree with Grudem that this is indeed the most likely scenario being described, although the language does not altogether exclude other possibilities.

Next, Grudem claims that in this text members of the congregation are assessing (often silently) *which bits* of the prophecy are true or false, rather than declaring the prophecy as a whole to be true or false:

> We can conclude that 1 Corinthians 14:29 indicates that the whole congregation would listen and evaluate what was said by the prophet, forming opinions about it, and some would perhaps discuss it publicly. Each prophecy might have *true and false elements* in it, and those would be *sifted* and evaluated for what they were.⁴

Grudem uses an argument from context and an examination of the Greek word *diakrinō* ("weigh" in ESV, "weigh carefully" in NIV) to conclude that *each prophecy might have both true and false elements in it*. This is in contrast with the process of judging prophets described in the Old Testament, in which it was a heinous crime to make any utterance claiming falsely to be from God (Deut 18:20).

How are we to explain this contrast? Grudem says that it can be explained "only if there is a difference in the kind of speech envisioned by the Old Testament and that in 1 Corinthians 14."⁵ The Old Testament prophet "was in a position of speaking with God's *absolute authority*," whereas in the New Testament, the prophets "*must not* have been thought to speak with divine authority attaching to their actual words. Their prophecies were subject to evaluation and questioning at every point."⁶

Grudem also considers that the text refers to a judgment made *by the whole congregation*: "but they would not judge the prophet *himself* to be true or false"⁷ because such a declaration by a large group that a prophet was either true or false would be inappropriate without a voting process. Rather, "the congregation would simply evaluate the prophecy and form opinions about it."⁸ This suggests to him that the assessment might often be made privately and perhaps *not expressed vocally*.

3. *GP*, 59.
4. *GP*, 59; italics mine.
5. *GP*, 62.
6. *GP*, 62; italics mine.
7. *GP*, 59.
8. *GP*, 62.

Part Two — The Prophets at Corinth

Diakrinō: Sifting, Evaluating, Judging

Grudem considers the word *diakrinō* (translated "weigh" in v. 29) and claims that "it very frequently carries the idea of separating, distinguishing, or making careful distinctions among related things or ideas."[9] He claims that it would therefore be an appropriate term to describe a process of distinguishing the true elements within a particular speech from the false ones.

But is this correct? The word *diakrinō* has a wide range of meanings. Translations include "evaluate" (NLT), "pass judgment" (NASB), and "judge" (AV). According to *AG*, it can also mean "separate," "make a distinction," "differentiate," or "distinguish between." However, as Jonathan Bertin points out, when it has these meanings "the *different categories are typically identified explicitly*"[10] as in distinguishing "between us and them" (Acts 15:9), or "good from evil" (Heb 5:14).

Grudem quotes Philo for two examples of the word that refer to *sifting*. But both texts explicitly identify what is being distinguished—fine flour from the commoner sort,[11] and bran from chaff.[12] However, in 1 Corinthians 14:29 there are *no named objects*.[13] The absence of named objects suggests the more likely meanings are, "judge," "judge correctly," "pass judgment," or "render a decision." *LS* adds, "to settle, decide, *of judges*."[14] Indeed, *AG* specifies the meaning of *"pass judgment"* for this verse.

These meanings are suggestive of a definitive judgment *made vocally*.[15] This is significant, because it implies that Paul may here be requiring a *vocal assessment* of any prophetic utterance (probably, as we shall see later, by other *prophets*).[16] Grudem acknowledges that verbal evaluation "would

9. *GP*, 59.

10. Bertin, "Syntactical and Exegetical Analysis," 86; italics mine.

11. Philo, *De Mutatione Nominum*, 249.

12. Philo, *De Iosepho*, 113.

13. Nevertheless, "sifting" seems to have gained wide traction as a reading of 1 Corinthians 14:29—even Carson (Carson, 95) and Thiselton (Thiselton, *FEC*, 1140) have been drawn to it. On the other hand, Fee, noting the similarity with "distinguishing between spirits" (1 Cor 12:10), suggests it refers to assessing "whether the prophecy itself truly conforms to the Spirit of God" (Fee, *First Epistle to the Corinthians*, 693).

14. *LS*, 296.

15. A similar usage in Zechariah 3:7 LXX, must refer to a *spoken* judgment (see also Lev 24:12 LXX).

16. Fee would agree: he suggests that the command to let two or three prophets speak is not one that limits the number of speakers, but one that requires *verbal evaluation* of

have been appropriate, at least *sometimes*,"[17] but doesn't always absolutely require it. But I think we can safely say that if a prophecy was considered to contain error, there must surely always have been some vocal challenge.

Of course, if *diakrinō* means "pass judgment" here, we are really no wiser as to whether the discussion concerns *which bits* of the prophecy are true or false, or whether the prophecy *as a whole* is true or false. So although the context might incline us to prefer one reading over the other, on purely lexical grounds both readings must remain equally possible.

Grudem argues that if Paul had meant to refer to a judgment as to whether a prophet was a true or false prophet (or, presumably, whether a prophecy as a whole was true or false), he would have used *krinō* rather than *diakrinō*. He claims, "This [*krinō*] is the term the New Testament prefers when speaking of judgments where there are only two possibilities, such as guilty or not guilty, right or wrong, true or false."[18]

But is there any evidence for this contention? Not really. Grudem himself points out that in the New Testament, *diakrinō* is used in various passages to describe what is clearly a binary judgment:

- Distinguishing between Jewish and gentile believers (Acts 15:9)
- "What distinguishes you [from other people]?" (1 Cor 4:7)

To these we could add

- Discrimination between rich and poor (Jas 2:3–4).

These are all clearly binary judgments made about individuals. Furthermore, consider the use of the corresponding noun *diakrisis* ("distinguishing" or "differentiation"). In 1 Corinthians 12:10 (NIV), we read about "distinguishing [*diakrisis*] between spirits." This clearly refers to determining whether what is at work is a good or an evil spirit—in other words, a binary judgment again. Grudem himself recognizes this, since he defines the distinguishing of spirits in binary terms as "the ability to recognize the influence of the Holy Spirit or of demonic spirits in a person."[19] So he seems to be saying that the *diakrisis* of spirits involves a binary judgment, but the *diakrisis* of prophecy does not.

---

prophecy *after every two or three prophecies* (Fee, *First Epistle to the Corinthians*, 693, italics mine).

17. *GP*, 60; italics mine.
18. *GP*, 60.
19. *GP*, 55.

Part Two—The Prophets at Corinth

Grudem points to 1 Corinthians 6:2–6 where Paul uses both *krinō* (2–3, 6) and *diakrinō* (5). So, for example, "I say this to shame you. Is it possible that there is nobody among you wise enough to judge [*diakrinō*] a dispute between believers? But instead, one brother takes another to court [*krinō*]—and this in front of unbelievers!" (1 Cor 6:5–6 NIV).

Grudem comments,

> Paul may consciously be distinguishing formal legal judgments outside the church (for which he uses *krinō*) from more informal decisions inside the church (for which he uses *diakrinō*). Within the church, it is less likely that one party will be declared "guilty" or the other "not guilty" and more likely that a careful evaluation will find *some fault on both sides*.[20]

Aside from the dubious assertion that the church is likely to make judgments that are less binary than those made by the world, the suggestion that a *nuanced* judgment is implied by *diakrinō* is without warrant. If we ask what force the prepositional prefix *dia-* brings to the verb *krinō*, according to *LS*,[21] it adds the notion of "completion," "to the end," "utterly," "thoroughly," and "out and out."[22] One definition for *diakrinō* in *AG* is "judge correctly."[23] So the point that Paul is making seems to be one of *thoroughness* or *correctness*.

Paul makes a similar point in another text which again uses both verbs: "But if we judged ourselves *truly* [*diakrinō*], we would not be judged [by God] [*krinō*]" (1 Cor 11:31). Here the sense of the word is perhaps at its clearest, and the implication is clearly one of thoroughness and accuracy: "if we did a *proper job of judging* ourselves, we would not be judged by God." Indeed, Grudem himself understands this verse as meaning "If we (*correctly*) evaluated ourselves."[24] We also see this meaning clearly when Jesus remonstrates with the Pharisees and Sadducees: "You know how to interpret (*diakrinō*) the appearance of the sky, but you cannot interpret the

---

20. *GP*, 60; italics mine.

21. *LS* is the standard lexicon of classical Greek and should be used cautiously when considering New Testament texts. Sadly, however, *AG* (the standard lexicon of New Testament Greek) does not include in its definitions of prefixes the meanings they bring to composites.

22. *LS*, 289.

23. *AG*, 184.

24. *GP*, 60; italics mine.

Judging and Fallibility (1 Cor 14:29)

signs of the times" (Matt 16:3). In other words, "You know how to interpret the appearance of the sky *correctly*."

So our conclusions from our study of the word *diakrinō* are that

- It is likely (but not certain) to be referring to an assessment made *vocally* rather than to one made silently.
- It is referring to a *thorough* assessment, but it could be referring to assessing the prophecy *as a whole* or to assessing the good and bad elements *within a single prophecy*. In short, this verse does not necessarily imply that Corinthian prophesying contained a mixture of both truth and error (as Grudem expects with impressions, or as we would expect in preaching).

Testing Prophecies but Not Prophets (1 Thess 5:19–22)

> Do not quench the Spirit. Do not despise prophecies, but test everything; hold fast what is good. Abstain from every form of evil. (1 Thess 5:19–22 ESV)

In this passage, Grudem again argues that it is the *prophecies* that are evaluated or judged—*not the prophets*:

> We should notice here that Paul does not say "test all persons," or "test all prophets," but rather (literally), "Test all things" . . . Paul's command rather puts this kind of prophecy in the same category as the prophecies in Corinth, where every *prophecy*, but not every prophet, was tested.[25]

In 1 Thessalonians 5:19–22, Paul is saying that prophecies are neither to be accepted uncritically nor dismissed out of hand. It is often tempting to "despise" prophecy since, unlike false prophecy, true prophecy can contain sharp confrontation and rebuke, which can be hard to bear.

The ESV ("test all *things*") seems preferable to the NIV ("test *them* all") since "prophesies" (*prophēteias*) is feminine, but "all" (*panta*) is neuter, meaning "all things" or "everything." Had Paul intended to refer narrowly only to prophecies, he could have done so. So whilst "everything" here certainly includes prophecies, it has wider implications, as suggested by the words that immediately follow: "hold fast to what is good. Abstain from

---

25. *GP*, 85; italics his.

every form of evil" (v. 21). We are to test *everything*, and this must include prophets as well as prophecies.

Paul uses the same word for "test" (*dokimadzō*) elsewhere: "Test yourselves" (2 Cor 13:5), as does John: "Test the spirits to see whether they are of God" (1 John 4:1). So prophecies, people, and spirits are all embraced by the generic command to "test *everything*."

As we have seen, Grudem believes that 1 Corinthians 14:29 is only about "the evaluation of true prophets (genuine Christian believers speaking under the influence of the Holy Spirit)."[26] He acknowledges the possibility of outsiders coming in who were false prophets but believes that these would have been detected by those with the ability to discern spirits (1 Cor 12:10), and that "these false prophets would have betrayed themselves by their *blatantly aberrant doctrine* (1 Cor 12:3, 1 John 4:2–3)."[27] However, if only those guilty of "blatantly aberrant doctrine" were false prophets, there would be little need for the gift of discerning spirits. Indeed, there are plenty of examples of false prophets in Scripture who do not preach blatantly aberrant doctrine: the fact that the false prophets of Matthew 7:15–20 are described as wolves in sheep's clothing implies great subtlety in their error. Subtlety and deceptiveness are clearly key to the success of false prophecy (see also 2 Pet 2:1).

Testing against Scripture

Against what criteria are prophecies to be judged? Grudem rightly sees the role of Scripture here: "the criterion for evaluation of public speech in the churches seems always to have been conformity to Scripture or received teaching (Acts 17:11; 1 Cor 14:37–38; Gal 1:8; 1 John 4:2–3, 6)."[28]

Dokimazō ("test") in 1 Thessalonians 5:21 implies careful examination and, since the word is used of the testing of gold with fire (e.g., in 1 Cor 3:13, 1 Pet 1:7), it suggests testing against the refining fire *of Scripture* (Jer 23:29).

In 1 Corinthians 14:29, the term *diakrinō* ("weigh") also has clear hints of assessing against Scripture. Thus, the writer of Hebrews laments, "you need someone to teach you again the basic principles of the oracles of God" (Heb 5:12). His hearers are "unskilled in the word of righteousness"

26. *GP*, 61.
27. *GP*, 61.
28. *GP*, 61.

Judging and Fallibility (1 Cor 14:29)

(meaning Scripture), and their powers of discernment (*diakrisis*) have not been trained by "constant practice" (Heb 5:14). This must be referring to the practice of testing things against Scripture. Indeed, in the assessment of prophecy in 1 Corinthians 14:29, there may be a parallel with the examining (*anakrinō*) of the Scriptures such as that commended in the Bereans in Acts 17:11.

So it seems beyond doubt that any assessment of prophetic insight must have included an examination *against Scripture* (as in Acts 15:15).

Conclusion

We agree with Grudem that the congregational prophesying described in this text seems unlike the authoritative prophesying we see in the Old Testament; it is hard to imagine Isaiah having his speeches judged by a panel of prophets, such as that described in 1 Corinthians 14:29. But it would be equally hard to imagine Paul submitting himself to similar congregational scrutiny. The lesson must be that apostolic prophesying is surely more authoritative than its congregational counterpart, and that congregational prophesying must operate within the bounds established by apostolic doctrine.

Yet again, however, there is nothing in this text that is inconsistent with Spirit-enabled (albeit fallible) preaching of a kind that could be expected today (although Paul seems to expect two or three sermons in any meeting). If this is the case, then although congregational prophesying is never perfect, it should not contain significant error, and the fact that a speaker may occasionally say things that are not strictly accurate biblically does not necessarily mark him out as a false prophet.

Chapter 15

Spontaneity and Interruption (1 Cor 14:30)

> Let two or three prophets speak, and let the others weigh what is said. If a revelation is made to another sitting there, let the first be silent. (1 Cor 14:29–30)

Interruption

FIRST CORINTHIANS 14:30 SEEMS to some to describe a situation in which, while one prophet is speaking, a second prophet signals that he has something to say and the first gives way. According to Grudem, the first prophet "does not finish his prophecy but *immediately* sits down."[1] His prophecy would thus be interrupted.

Perhaps the first speaker might resume his speech after the interruption? Grudem rejects this possibility: "it would make much more sense for the second prophet to wait, instead of rudely interrupting the first prophet and make him give his speech in two parts."[2] Grudem concludes that "The remainder of the first prophet's prophecy would be *intentionally neglected*, and probably *never heard* by the church."[3]

---

1. *GP*, 62; italics mine.
2. *GP*, 62.
3. *GP*, 64; italics mine.

Spontaneity and Interruption (1 Cor 14:30)

This is an important comment because it implies that no prophecy is so precious that it cannot afford to be lost. New Testament congregational prophets therefore cannot have been speaking *fully authoritative* words from God; rather they spoke "*merely human words* to report something that God had brought to mind."[4] This would mark a transformation of prophecy in the New Testament, since it is hard to imagine an Old Testament prophet such as Isaiah being interrupted by another prophet (although, yet again, this view would be consistent with an understanding of prophecy as gospel preaching).

Comment—The Bigger Picture

In approaching a complex passage such as this, it may help to start with the bigger picture of what Paul is saying and consider what concerns he is addressing. Paul's main concerns in the wider context are that:

- "you can all prophesy one by one" (v. 31). Everyone who wishes to speak (perhaps only among those so gifted or designated) should be given an opportunity to do so.
- "all things should be done decently and in order" (v. 40). In this process, decorum and courtesy should prevail.

So, in broad terms, this must be what Paul is saying in verses 29–30 too. On this basis, a rather rude interruption (with, at worst, one person effectively shutting down the speech of another) is unlikely to be what Paul has in mind.

Next, it is worth noting the parallels and contrasts with the verses on tongues that immediately precede these verses. We can highlight these as follows (mixing a few translations):

Tongues (vv. 27–28)	Prophecy (vv. 29–30)
If any speak in a tongue,	*As for prophets* (my paraphrase),
let there be only two or at most three,	*let two or three speak,*
and each in turn, and let someone interpret.	*and let the others weigh what is said.*
But if there is no one to interpret,	*If a revelation comes to another sitting there,*
let each of them keep silent in church and speak to himself and to God.	*the first speaker should stop.*

---

4. *GP*, 63; italics mine.

Comparing these verses in this way suggests (no more than this for now) that:

- The assessment of prophecy might be *vocal* just as interpretation is insisted upon with tongues.
- The phrase "the first speaker should stop" in verse 30 could also mean "should *keep quiet*," as it does in the context of tongues in verse 28.

In fact, there seems to be good evidence for both these conclusions, as we will see shortly.

Who Does the Judging?

First, we should ask, who are "the others" who carefully weigh what the prophets say? Grudem believes this refers to *all the members of the congregation* as they listen, arguing (following Godet) that if Paul had wanted to say, "the other prophets" he would have said "*hoi loipoi*" rather than "*hoi alloi*."[5] But this is too narrow a reading of the word *alloi*, which can manifestly mean not just "others of a *different* type" but also "others of the *same* type" (see Matt 13:5, 21; 21:33).

While it is of course likely that Paul expects the whole congregation to be silently assessing the prophecies they hear, in this passage he does seem more likely to be talking about an activity *of the prophets*. Thiselton agrees with this view, although he adds "but . . . it would be surprising if *teachers*, let alone *apostles*, were excluded."[6]

Having discussed the case of those speaking in tongues, Paul says literally, "*But in the case of prophets*, let two or three speak, and let the others (*alloi*) pass judgment; but if revelation is made to another (*allō*) sitting by, the first should stop." The word order suggests that *alloi* probably refers to prophets beyond the two or three given leave to speak. The word is then repeated—*allō* ("to another")—which certainly refers to another prophet. This suggests that the first occurrence of the pronoun also refers to the plural noun *prophētai*.

First, in verse 28, Paul talks about what tongues-speakers should do when there is no interpreter (namely, keep quiet); then here he talks about what prophets should do when they are not exercising their gift (namely,

5. *GP*, 56.
6. *FEC*, 1141.

assess what the other prophets are saying). There is an implication here that those gifted in prophesying also have the gift of discernment. The gift of discernment certainly has wider application than solely to prophecy, but nevertheless, when it comes to prophecy, who better to exercise the gift of discernment than other prophets?

Interruption?

> Let two or three prophets speak, and let the others weigh what is said. If a revelation is made to another sitting there, let the first be silent (1 Cor 14:29–30).

One common understanding of verse 30 is, "If, while one prophet is speaking, another prophet has a revelation (on something completely different), the first prophet should stop speaking."

Even if this passage does describe an interruption, there are some important caveats to be made.

Interruption Would Need to be Relevant

It is clear that the person doing the interrupting is not operating in a vacuum when he has his moment of revelation—he has been *weighing what was being said*: "the others should *weigh carefully* what is said. And if a revelation comes to someone who is sitting down . . ." (1 Cor 14:29–30). *The interrupting revelation is therefore very likely to be a reaction or response to what has been said.* Thiselton quotes a phrase from Gadamer about "the to-and-fro of dialogical sharing,"[7] and suggests that the revelation that comes to the second speaker may refer to a realization given by God "that the first speaker has begun to indulge in *self-deception, distraction or sheer error*" or the second speaker may have some wisdom that enables him "*to take the theme forward* more imaginatively, accurately or deeply than the first."[8]

The text could also be describing speech given *during the process of evaluating* the speech of the first prophet; in other words, "the others should weigh what is said, and when any of them has a comment to make on what has been said . . ."

---

7. *FEC*, 1142.
8. *FEC*, 1092; italics his.

Part Two—The Prophets at Corinth

Interruption Need Not Be Immediate

Grudem's idea that a prophet who is speaking then "*immediately* sits down" when another prophet indicates that he has something to say is surely a caricature of what Paul is saying. Grudem appears to contradict his initial view later when he says, "the second prophet apparently did not suddenly burst into speech but rather signaled that he was ready to prophesy and then *waited for the first to stop.*"[9] This does seem more reasonable: the first prophet might then not be interrupted at all, but allowed to wind up his prophecy; so *nothing necessarily need be lost.*

Another possibility is that Paul may be advocating something like our practice today in conferences, business meetings, and debates in Parliament, whereby one speaker gives way to allow a relevant contribution or a question from those listening. In such contexts there is never any sense in which the first speech is curtailed or lost, because permitting an interruption does not prevent one from resuming the discourse later.

In other words, verse 30 could mean:

> "If, while one person is speaking, one of the other prophets listening has a revelation (i.e., a comment to make *on what has been said*), the speaker should *give way.*"

There is also at least one further possible reading of this verse: the revelation that comes to one of the other prophets could come *after* the assessment of the first prophet. In other words, "One prophet should speak, and other prophets should then *discuss his prophecy.*[10] Then, if revelation comes to another prophet, the first prophet should *let him have his turn.*"

Both of these readings are supported by the fact that *sigaō* can mean "stop speaking," "keep silent," and "refrain from speaking" (thus in verse 34 we read that women are to "keep silent" in church). Again, none of these readings require that a prophet is ever *curtailed*, and they are all also fully consistent with Paul's concern to allow everyone to prophesy one by one and to preserve decency and order.

---

9. *GP*, 105; italics mine.

10. It makes sense that the assessment would be made after *each* prophecy, rather than after two or three prophecies (as Fee suggests). If the assessment is only made after two or three prophecies, the use of the word "first" in verse 30 becomes awkward. But the textual evidence is not decisive.

Spontaneity and Interruption (1 Cor 14:30)

Spontaneity

Grudem says that in 1 Corinthians 14:30,

> The thought that occurs to a prophet is pictured as coming to him *quite spontaneously*, for it comes while the first speaker is talking. So this prophecy does not seem to be a sermon or lesson that had been prepared beforehand; it comes rather at the prompting of the Holy Spirit.[11]

Although some of the speech here is indeed spontaneous, it may be only the assessing comments rather than the prophecy that are spontaneous or impromptu: the prophecy itself may have been prepared beforehand. But even if there is spontaneous prophecy here, it certainly need not mean that *all* prophecy must *always* be spontaneous.[12] The only situation described here may be that in which a person receives a revelation *while someone else is speaking*. If several people arrive at the meeting, each indicating that they have some message to bring, they would presumably speak in turn, and perhaps agree an order at the outset.[13]

Conclusion

Our conclusions from 1 Corinthians 14:30 are as follows:

- The text is describing speeches by various prophets, and discussion of those speeches by other prophets.
- The text need not mean that one prophet could interrupt another prophet, or do so with an irrelevant comment, or that part of a prophet's speech was necessarily lost.
- Although there may be a spontaneous element in some of the prophesying here, this does not mean that *all* prophecy is *always* necessarily spontaneous.

Perhaps the key phrase explaining the process appears in verse 31: "For you can all prophesy *one at a time* [*kath' hena*]." That is the core principle here—the importance of order, inclusion, and humility so that each person

---

11. *GP*, 96.

12. Moses was not speaking spontaneously when he warned Pharaoh of the plagues: see Exodus 7:15; 8:1, 20; 9:1, 13; 10:1.

13. See also, Turner, *Holy Spirit and Spiritual Gifts*, 199.

wishing to speak should have an opportunity to do so. Paul is clearly seeking to guard against the domination of the platform by one person or by a few: no one person has a monopoly on biblical truth, and prophetic truth often emerges through discussion and dialogue. That is surely a principle that could be more heeded in our church services today.

Chapter 16

Impression and Revelation (1 Cor 14:30)

> And if a revelation comes to someone who is sitting down, the first speaker should stop (1 Cor 14:30).

WHEN WE LOOKED AT Old Testament prophets, we saw that they received their messages through *revelation* (e.g., 1 Sam 3:7, 21; Isa 22:14, Amos 3:7). First Corinthians 14:30 makes it clear that New Testament prophets also reported revelations. But the question is, what does Paul mean by "revelation" ("*apokalypsis*")?

Grudem believes that *apokalypsis* refers to *nonrational impressions*:

> Whereas the teacher or preacher would only be able to obtain information about the specific spiritual concerns of the people from observation or conversation, the prophet would have in addition the ability to know about specific needs through "revelation."[1]

This is to view "revelation" as entirely divorced from observation and the working of wisdom, but simply as "something God brings to mind,"[2] and prophecy then as "merely human words to report something that God had brought to mind."[3] So it can be, according to Grudem,

---

1. *GP*, 128.
2. *GP*, 95.
3. *GP*, 63, cf. 100, 142, 219, 220, 225, 320.

- "words, thoughts, or mental pictures that suddenly impressed themselves forcefully on the mind of the prophet"[4]
- "something which *arouses awe and wonder* in people because of its apparent contradiction of normal laws of natural human or physical behavior"[5]
- "a public disclosure of the secrets of a visitor's heart"[6]

Such an understanding excludes from revelation anything which involves the engagement of human wisdom. But by that measure we would have to say that none of the writings of Paul are prophetic, nor indeed any of the New Testament.

The Mind of the Prophet

Grudem seems to see a complete disjunction between the work of the mind and the work of the Spirit. Thus he quotes Dennis and Rita Bennett approvingly:

> in preaching, the intellect, training and skill, background and education are involved and inspired by the Holy Spirit. The sermon . . . comes from the inspired intellect. Prophecy, on the other hand, means that the person is bringing the words the Lord gives directly; it is from the spirit, *not the intellect*.[7]

Such a sharp dualistic contrast between the working of the Holy Spirit and the human mind is a *category error* (a concept we explore in chapter 27), and it fails to take account of the evidence for the active engagement of the prophet's mind in 1 Corinthians 14:14–20. As we suggested in our introduction to 1 Corinthians 14, the whole chapter is a comprehensive contrast between tongues and prophecy (including interpreted tongues), both being gifts of the Holy Spirit, but the former, when not interpreted, is unintelligible and involves the operation of *the human spirit* (1 Cor 14:14), while the latter is clearly intelligible and involves the operation of *the human mind* (1 Cor 14:19).

By suggesting that prophets utter mere impressions, Grudem is in effect advocating that, rather than engaging our minds, we should speak

---

4. *GP*, 110.
5. *GP*, 109.
6. *GP*, 114.
7. Dennis and Rita Bennett, 108–109, in *GP*, 121; italics mine.

Impression and Revelation (1 Cor 14:30)

from the human imagination; but such practice is strongly condemned in Scripture (Ezek 13:2; Jer 23:26), and the polar opposite of what Paul says about prophecy in 1 Corinthians 14.

Revelation

Grudem rightly maintains that all prophecy consists of a revelation plus a report of that revelation:

- "Prophecy must be based on a 'revelation' from God"[8]
- "If there is no such revelation, there is no prophecy"[9]
- "A report of the revelation is necessary for a prophecy"[10]

In short,

> *Prophecy = Revelation + Report*

This is not in the least contentious; but the all-important questions are,

- What constitutes a revelation *of the type required for a prophecy*?
- With what authority is the report given—an absolute authority of words, or are the words *merely human*, as Grudem suggests?

Grudem believes that prophecy in Corinth (and prophecy today) consists of a miraculous revelation combined with a fallible, nonmiraculous report.

Two Types of Revelation

It is important to note that in Scripture *apokalypsis* can describe both *original* and *derived* insights:

1. *Original, miraculous insights,* which we might call *new-to-the-world revelations.* They would include, for example, the insight Jesus had into the heart of the woman at the well in John 4:19, the predictions of Agabus, and much of the book of Revelation. Grudem gives other examples in Acts 11:28, 21:10–11, and Luke 7:39.

2. *Derived, biblical insights,* which we might call *new-to-the-person revelations.* These are the *realizations* gained when we study Scripture,

---

[8]. GP, 95.
[9]. GP, 116.
[10]. GP, 117.

such as the insights God gives growing Christians into themselves, into his purposes, and into into particular circumstances (e.g., Matt 11:27; Rom 1:18; Eph 1:17; Phil 3:15).

The distinction between these two forms of revelation is not clear-cut: as we have already suggested, even when apostles did receive original revelations (such as the vision of Peter in Acts 10), their interpretation of those revelations was also at least partly derived from Scripture. Thus, Paul talks of "the mystery hidden for long ages past, but now revealed and made known *through the prophetic writings*" (Rom 16:25–26, NIV).

While Grudem is willing to acknowledge a wide semantic field for the word "revelation," he does not allow a correspondingly wide semantic field for the word "prophecy." That is, he says that prophecy is the report of a revelation—but he doesn't consider whether reports of *any kind* of revelation might constitute prophecy. So although he is well aware that there are different kinds of revelation, he only ever quotes examples of what we have called *derived* revelation to make the point that reports of revelation are not normally given in the very words of God, but not *at all* to inform his understanding of the prophetic gift. Thus he says, for example, "it would not be possible to think that every time a believer gained new insight into his privileges as a Christian and reported it to a friend, the actual words of that speech would have been thought to be God's very words."[11] To which we must respond, "No, *but might it constitute prophecy?*"

Instead Grudem assumes that prophetic speech must involve spontaneous promptings that are not derived from Scripture: "Paul is simply referring to something God may suddenly bring to mind, or something that God impresses upon someone's heart or thoughts in such a way that the person has a sense that it is from God."[12] He draws this conclusion despite the fact that none of the texts he quotes on the subject of revelation either requires or implies such a reading, whereas it is beyond question that the term "revelation" does indeed include *all* spiritual understanding.

It does indeed seem likely that the "revelations" shared by the prophets at Corinth are precisely such biblically derived spiritual understandings or realizations. In other words, what is described in 1 Corinthians 14:30 may well be broadly similar to what happens in church home groups today, when individuals share spiritual insights. When one Christian shares with a Christian friend something that has struck her recently from Scripture,

---

11. *GP*, 65.
12. *GP*, 320.

Impression and Revelation (1 Cor 14:30)

she might say, "God showed me this the other day . . ." If she does so, she is using the language of *revelation*. This may well be what Paul has in view in 1 Corinthians 14:30.

Teaching and Prophecy

If prophecy were simply "the report of a revelation," teaching might overlap with prophecy. But Grudem says, "'teaching' is based not on a 'revelation' but on Scripture, and generally results from conscious reflection and preparation."[13] So why study Scripture if not to gain revelation from it? Again, Grudem's view of prophecy consists only of *original* revelation, and he seems to ignore *derived* biblical revelation altogether. By contrast, David Hill suggests, "Undoubtedly, this discovery of the 'meaning' of Scripture belonged to the prophetic charism: at least part of the ministry of prophets in the New Testament was the interpretation of the Old."[14]

Indeed, according to Ellis,

> there is no clear distinction in Judaism or in the primitive church between the teaching of a prophet and of a teacher. Likewise, the false prophets in the church teach (1 John 2:22, 26f; 4:1ff.), and the false teachers in the church correspond to the false prophets in the Old Covenant (2 Pet 2:1).[15]

But Grudem says of Ellis,

> E. Earle Ellis sees exposition and interpretation of Scripture as a function of Christian prophets in Acts. However, he can show no examples where the person expounding Scripture is doing so specifically *in the role of a prophet* and not in the role of a teacher or apostle or evangelist. Everyone expounding Scripture in Acts has one of these other roles. So the argument is not really persuasive.[16]

Now I believe Ellis does indeed give examples of precisely what Grudem is asking for—exposition of Scripture by men acting in the role of prophets; we will see this clearly in chapter 21, when we explore Acts 15, and in particular Acts 15:32.

Following this argument, one wonders on what basis the apostles can *ever* be said to evangelize or teach—since they surely do everything "in the

---

13. *GP*, 118.
14. Hill, *New Testament Prophecy*, 100.
15. Ellis, *Prophecy & Hermeneutic*, 140–41.
16. *GP*, 135; italics mine.

role" of apostles! Grudem views apostleship and prophecy as occupying entirely distinct categories, even though he reads Ephesians 2:20 as referring to the "apostle-prophets" or "apostles *who are also prophets.*"[17]

For Grudem, then, there is a complete disjunction between the gifts of prophecy and teaching, with prophecy communicating new-to-the-world truth, and teaching communicating previously-revealed truth. So he does not see prophecy simply as Spirit-inspired speech, but rather as *merely human words reporting a spontaneously-received original* (as opposed to derived) *impression* (as opposed to biblical wisdom). This means that he does not believe that teaching can itself be prophetic—only that it might *include* prophecy. Grudem does agree that prophecies might include Scripture quotations and applications, perhaps even frequently, but insists, "it is important to emphasize that where such exposition was based on preparation and reflection instead of a spontaneous revelation, the New Testament would call it 'teaching' and not prophecy."[18]

On the other hand, if all Paul's writing can be termed "prophecy" then it must be *both* prophecy *and* teaching. Indeed, all teaching in churches today would then aspire to the "prophetic," and to declare a sermon "prophetic" would simply be a way of saying that one believes it to be Spirit-enabled.

In Grudem's view, preparation and reflection would play no part at all in yielding revelation; so the careful Bible message given by a preacher on a Sunday morning would not then come to him in any sense by revelation, nor when he speaks would his congregation receive revelation.

I wonder if Grudem would accept that Peter's sermon in Acts 2—clearly an example of *teaching*, which specifically applies the prophecy of Joel to the events of Pentecost—is also an act of *prophecy*. Christopher Forbes certainly does not: "To describe Peter's speech in Acts 2 as *prophetēia* is simply tendentious."[19]

But Peter's speech here seems to pass the prophecy test under virtually any possible definition: it announces a mystery revealed by God; it is revelation reported spontaneously; it takes an Old Testament prophecy and partially rewrites it; it includes prediction (Acts 2:38, 39) and a denunciation of contemporary culture (Acts 2:40). If that were not enough it is also, of course, Scripture, and so the very word of God. *Just what test for prophecy could this sermon conceivably fail?*

---

17. GP, 340; italics mine.
18. GP, 136.
19. Forbes, *Prophecy and Inspired Speech*, 235.

Impression and Revelation (1 Cor 14:30)

An Authoritative Report?

It seems very possible that Paul was expecting the Corinthian prophets to share insights from Scripture, exactly as we might today.

Of course, in one sense, such *derived* insights are never given in God's very words (in that sense, we can grant that they are merely human). But when people exhort one another using Scripture, they are exposing each other to the prophetic power of God's word, a prophetic power that does indeed come *in the very words of God* and brings revelation. (We explore this further in chapter 25.)

Conclusion

We see in Scripture examples of revelations that are highly *original* and are invariably reported as the very words of God. There is no doubt that these speech acts constitute prophecy.

But we are also familiar from our own experience with examples of revelation *derived from Scripture*, whereby individuals come to understand something about God, themselves, their culture or their church from Scripture and report it to others; it happens in every good sermon, and in every good Bible discussion in a home group. We suspect that this kind of reporting is what Paul is commending in 1 Corinthians 14, and it could be described under the broad heading of the *Spirit-enabled ministry of God's word*.

On the other hand, the idea that prophecy consists only of *spontaneous impressions* dislocates it from work of the Holy Spirit, because it seeks to loosen it from the word of God, the gospel of Christ, prayer, and the human mind. But the Spirit and the word of God are not to be separated. God's words, as Moltmann says, are carried on the breath of the Spirit:

> The Father utters his eternal Word in the eternal breathing out of his Spirit. There is in God no Word without the Spirit, and no Spirit without the Word. In this respect the uttering of the Word and the issuing of the Spirit belong indissolubly together.[20]

"What therefore God has joined together, let not man separate" (Matt 19:6).

---

20. Moltmann, *Trinity and the Kingdom*, 169–70.

Chapter 17

Women Prophets (1 Cor 14:34–35)

> The women should keep silent in the churches. For they are not permitted to speak, but should be in submission, as the Law also says. If there is anything they desire to learn, let them ask their husbands at home. For it is shameful for a woman to speak in church. (1 Cor 14:34–35)

Women Prophesying

PAUL ALLOWS WOMEN TO prophesy: "But every wife who prays or prophesies with her head uncovered dishonors her head" (1 Cor 11:5). On the other hand, he also says: "The women should keep silent in the churches. For they are not permitted to speak" (1 Cor 14:34).

Grudem claims that in this latter verse, "the type of speech in view . . . *is only speech that assumes authority over the men of the congregation.*"[1] He reasons that this only makes sense if "the type of prophecy done by women at Corinth did not involve authoritative speech, that is, speech that assumed the right to enforce obedience or belief."[2]

Yet again, this is taken by Grudem as an indication that the prophets at Corinth did not speak with "a divine authority of actual words."[3]

---

1. *GP*, 68; italics mine.
2. *GP*, 68.
3. *GP*, 69.

Women Prophets (1 Cor 14:34–35)

Women Evaluating Prophecy

The phrase "women should keep silence" should be read, according to Grudem, as meaning "the women should keep silence *during the evaluation of prophecies*."[4] Carson agrees;[5] on the other hand, Fee,[6] and a number of others[7] doubt the authenticity of 14:34–35.

Comment

One key to understanding 1 Corinthians 14:34 may lie in the fact that the word for "women" ("*gunaikēs*") could equally be translated as "wives" (as in 1 Corinthians 11:5). This meaning seems to be indicated by the injunction in verse 35 that these women are to ask their "husbands at home."[8] The command that they "keep silent" in verse 34 would then indicate that they are to refrain from making judgments about any prophetic utterances from *their own husbands*, and the "submission" would be only to their husbands. There is another possible reading, which is that the command to keep silent may refer to refraining from constantly intervening with questions (cf. verse 35). Thiselton admits both of these readings.[9] In either case, the text is not necessarily a general injunction against women either prophesying themselves or evaluating the prophecy of men who are not their husbands.

Elsewhere, Paul says that he does not allow women to teach men: "I do not permit a woman to teach or to assume authority over a man" (1 Tim 2:12). To teach, according to Grudem, is to exercise "a *de facto* leadership and authority":

> But New Testament church prophecy had no such authority. Those who prophesied did not tell the church how to interpret and apply Scripture to life. They did not proclaim the doctrinal and ethical standards by which the church was guided . . . Prophets in New Testament churches rather reported in their own words something which, it seemed to them, God had forcefully brought to mind

---

4. *GP*, 191; italics mine.
5. Carson, *Exegetical Fallacies*, 40–41.
6. Fee, *First Epistle to the Corinthians*, 699–708.
7. See, for example, Garland, *1 Corinthians*, 665, n17.
8. Garland, *1 Corinthians*, 667.
9. *FEC*, 1152–53.

Part Two—The Prophets at Corinth

... Prophecies were subordinate to the authoritative *teaching* of Scripture.[10]

Teaching was "based on the written Word of God," but prophets rather spoke "in their own words something which, it seemed to them, God had forcefully brought to mind."[11]

This may solve one problem, but it runs headlong into another: if prophecy is not as authoritative as teaching, why does Paul list teaching *below* prophecy in what appears to be a prioritized list in 1 Corinthians 12:28? Grudem acknowledges this difficulty: "Someone may object that the ordering of gifts in 1 Corinthians 12:28 . . . indicates that prophets had greater authority than teachers in the church."[12] His explanation: "However the list in 1 Corinthians 12:28 is not an ordering according to authority . . . [It] should be understood . . . as a listing according to *value in edifying the church*."[13]

So Grudem is saying that prophecy has a greater *value in edifying* the church than teaching, but somehow less *authority*: "Teaching . . . is always based on an explanation and/or application of Scripture or received apostolic doctrine . . . That is why teaching has so much more authority for governing the congregation."[14]

This seems to be a distinction without a difference. What is authority in the church if not an authority to build up? Indeed, Paul talks of "the authority the Lord gave us for building you up" (2 Cor 10:8, cf. 13:10). There is no other authority.

Support for Grudem here seems thin on the ground. Fee talks of an ordering of "precedence . . . in the founding and building up of the local assembly."[15] Thiselton reports Chrysostom's view that "the terms 'first' and 'secondly' are not used by Paul at random but in order . . . to point out the more honorable and the inferior."[16]

The conclusion must be that Paul considers prophecy to be a higher gift than teaching. Grudem's view does seem confused on this point: on the one hand, he says, "teaching has so much more authority for governing

10. *GP*, 121–22.
11. *GP*, 122.
12. *GP*, 122.
13. *GP*, 122; italics mine. See also, 53.
14. *GP*, 123.
15. Fee, *First Epistle to the Corinthians*, 620.
16. Chrysostom, *Homilies on First Corinthians*, 32:2, in *FEC*, 1015.

the congregation,"[17] and yet on the other he can say, "Prophecy, then, is superior to the other gifts."[18]

Grudem wants us to accept his version of prophecy—spontaneous, impressionistic, fallible, low authority—but quite rightly acknowledges that this would be hard to prioritize above teaching. However, Paul's version of prophecy is indisputably placed *above* teaching. This is a clear indication that Grudem's view of the nature of prophecy differs significantly from Paul's. However, Paul's ordering of the gifts would indeed be appropriate under the notion of prophecy as *Spirit-enabled preaching*. On this reading, *contra* Grudem, no limit on the authority of prophecy given by women need be implied by 1 Corinthians 14:34, and the injunction on women to be silent may refer only to the evaluation of prophecies *from their own husbands*.

So Why are Women Allowed to Prophesy but Not to Teach?

What, finally, are we to make of texts that appear to say that women are not to teach (1 Tim 2:12) but may prophesy (1 Cor 11:5)?

First, some believe that in 1 Timothy 2:12, Paul is not forbidding women to teach, but only to exercise an *autocratic* authority over men.[19] If we agree with this view, then the issue dematerializes: women may teach and women may prophesy.

On the other hand, for those who believe that Paul does indeed forbid women to teach in 1 Timothy 2:12, the issue remains. They may however wish to maintain that, since Paul expects several individuals to prophesy in any church service (1 Cor 14:29), he may only be prohibiting women from taking a position of overall leadership in the church, or perhaps from offering the main, formal teaching address. This seems to be, in practice, how many churches operate today, that is, denying women the position of overall church leadership, and so not allowing them to give the main teaching address, which has a magisterial function, but welcoming speech contributions of other kinds to the service.

Whatever the case, it does seem likely that in Corinth women were free to contribute to congregational proceedings by taking part in group prophesying.

17. *GP*, 123.
18. *GP*, 128.
19. See, e.g., Marshall, *Acts*, 454–60.

PART THREE
AGABUS

Chapter 18

Agabus and the Disciples at Tyre

> Now in these days prophets came down from Jerusalem to Antioch. And one of them named Agabus stood up and foretold by the Spirit that there would be a great famine over all the world (this took place in the days of Claudius). So the disciples determined, every one according to his ability, to send relief to the brothers living in Judea. And they did so, sending it to the elders by the hand of Barnabas and Saul. (Acts 11:27–30)

INTRODUCTION

GRUDEM COMMENTS,

> When Luke says that Agabus foretold "by the Spirit" ... this construction ... allows room for a large degree of personal influence by the human person himself ... A degree of imprecision is also suggested by the word translated "foretold" (Greek *sēmainō*, "signified, indicated") ... and we may conclude that absolute divine authority is neither required nor ruled out by this description ... In fact, the vagueness attaching to the expressions "signified, foretold" and "through the Spirit" would seem to suggest—but only *suggest*—some lesser kind of authority.[1]

Later, in Acts 21:10–11, Agabus introduces a prophecy with the words, "Thus says the Holy Spirit." According to Grudem, "'Thus says the Holy

---

1. *GP*, 71–72.

Spirit' means here *not that the very words* of the prophecy were from the Holy Spirit but *only that the content generally* had been revealed by the Spirit."[2]

This conclusion has major implications. If correct, it would add weight to Grudem's claim that prophecy today *need not be strictly accurate and may contain error*. But is such a conclusion warranted from this text?

Comment

The preface "thus says the Holy Spirit," echoing as it does the Old Testament prophetic preface "thus says the Lord," is clearly a claim to be speaking the words of God. Looking at the letters to the churches in Revelation 2 and 3, we see that they consist of prophecy reported in the first person as the *very words* of Jesus. But they also include the repeated phrase "He who has an ear, let him hear *what the Spirit says* to the churches" (Rev 2:7, 11, 17, 29; 3:6, 13, 22). So what the Spirit says to the church and what Jesus says to the church are identical, and equally authoritative. Indeed, to suggest a distinction between the two would be to risk an assault on the Trinity. There is no hint here or anywhere else of any vagueness in the phrase "by the Spirit" (*dia tou pneumatou*).

There is indeed extrabiblical evidence of the word *sēmainō* ("indicate [beforehand]") being used of prophetic speech "that simply gives a vague indication of what is to happen."[3] But the key question for us is, how is the word used in the New Testament? The answer again is that there is never a hint of vagueness in the use of *sēmainō*:

- The revelation of Jesus Christ, which God gave him to show to his servants the things that must soon take place. He *made it known* by sending his angel to his servant John. (Rev 1:1)
- He said this to *show* by what kind of death he was going to die. (John 12:33; see also 18:32; 21:19)
- For it seems to me unreasonable, in sending a prisoner, not to *indicate* the charges against him. (Acts 25:27)

---

2. *GP*, 82; italics mine.
3. *AG*, 755.

The related noun *sēmeion* ("the sign or distinguishing mark by which something is known," "a sign consisting of a wonder or a miracle"[4]) appears sixty-six times in the New Testament and never has any connotation of vagueness, but only of *meaningful significance*. The text of Acts 11:27–30 could not be clearer:

1. Agabus miraculously predicted a catastrophic famine.

2. When the disciples heard him, they all took radical and appropriate action (which demonstrates that they accepted the prediction unconditionally).

3. Subsequently there was a famine, which Luke associates with the prediction.

To cast doubt on the level of authority in this predictive prophecy is surely to miss the point Luke is conveying. There may be evidence elsewhere of prophecy in the New Testament that contains error, but there is none here.

The Disciples at Tyre: Prophecy Paul Disobeys (Acts 21:4)

Grudem claims that the prophecy of the disciples at Tyre in Acts 21:4 also contains an error. Paul lands at Tyre and Luke reports that, "having sought out the disciples, we stayed there for seven days. And *through the Spirit* they were telling Paul not to go on to Jerusalem" (Acts 21:4). Paul ignores their command. Grudem says,

> It is significant because Paul simply disobeyed their words, something he would not have done if he had thought that they were speaking the very words of God . . . Suppose that some of the Christians at Tyre had had some kind of 'revelation' . . . about the suffering Paul would face at Jerusalem. Then it would have been natural for them to couple their subsequent prophecy (their report of this revelation) with their own (erroneous) interpretation, and thus warn Paul not to go.[5]

Grudem summarizes the prophecy of the disciples at Tyre as "an unreliable human response to revelation from the Holy Spirit."[6] Again, Grudem believes that speech made "through the Spirit" allows the possibility of error.

---

4. *AG*, 755.
5. *GP*, 75–76.
6. *GP*, 77.

Part Three—Agabus

In summary, he concludes, "this passage indicates a type of prophecy which was not thought by Paul to possess absolute divine authority."[7]

Comment

It is clear that Paul had "resolved in the Spirit" to go to Jerusalem in Acts 19:21, and he was going "bound" or "constrained" by the Spirit: "And now, behold, I am going to Jerusalem, constrained by the Spirit, not knowing what will happen to me there, except that the Holy Spirit testifies to me in every city that imprisonment and afflictions await me" (Acts 20:22–23).

The apparent contradiction is that, on the one hand (in Acts 21:4), the disciples at Tyre tell Paul *not* to go to Jerusalem through the Spirit, and on the other hand, in Acts 19:21, Paul is constrained *to* go to Jerusalem by the same Spirit.

How are we to resolve this contradiction? This does indeed seem to be, as Grudem says, an "unreliable human response to revelation from the Holy Spirit."[8] Marshall agrees, "The simplest solution is that the Christians at Tyre were led by the Spirit to foresee suffering for Paul at Jerusalem, and therefore *of their own accord* they urged him not to go."[9]

I think Grudem is essentially correct here, but the key point is surely that, if it was indeed "an unreliable human response to revelation from the Holy Spirit," *it was not made in the Spirit*. Paul considered their warning as well-meaning advice, rather than as the voice of God. So when Luke says, "through the Spirit they were telling Paul not to go on to Jerusalem," what he actually means may be, "through the Spirit they were aware of the suffering facing Paul, and therefore told him not to go." Luke's report is then a contraction or summary of this longer thought. So, despite what the verse appears to be saying, the advice itself *was not from the Spirit*.

Marshall makes a further point: "The disciples of Tyre may not have been well-informed on the finer points of predestination and could have thought it was possible to say to Paul, 'If this is what is going to happen to you, don't go.'"[10]

It goes without saying that the voice of the Spirit can be misinterpreted; this seems to be what happens here.

7. GP, 76.
8. GP, 77.
9. Marshall, *Acts*, 338–39; italics mine.
10. Marshall, *Acts*, 339.

CHAPTER 19

Agabus Predicts the Arrest of Paul

THE ISSUE

THE QUESTION POSED IS, was Agabus mistaken in some aspects of his prophecy in Acts 21? Grudem believes the prophecy of Agabus contains "two small mistakes."[1] Carson agrees: "I can think of no reported Old Testament prophet whose prophecies are so wrong on the details."[2]

In the prophecy in question, Agabus takes Paul's belt, ties his own hands and feet, and says: "Thus says the Holy Spirit, 'This is how the Jews at Jerusalem will bind the man who owns this belt and deliver him into the hands of the Gentiles'" (Acts 21:11). The fulfillment is found chiefly in Acts 21:27–36.

Why Does It Matter?

This question is significant because if Agabus's prophecy can be demonstrated to contain error, it would support the notion that New Testament prophets were fallible, and that prophecy today might also contain within it a mixture of both truth and error. On a reading of prophecy as inspired preaching this is unobjectionable, but this speech of Agabus is certainly not conventional preaching, and includes the preface, "Thus says the Holy Spirit..."

1. *GP*, 77.

2. Carson, *Showing the Spirit*, 98

PART THREE—AGABUS

In this chapter we argue that it is unlikely that this prophecy contains errors.

The Theory

According to Grudem,[3] the two supposed "errors" in Agabus's prophecy are:

- The Jews *did not bind Paul*—the Romans did.
- The Jews *did not deliver Paul* into the hands of the Romans—the Romans took him by force.

EVIDENCE FOR THE THEORY

The Jews Did Not Bind Paul

Grudem says "Luke tells us twice that it was not the Jews but the Romans who *bound* Paul."[4] He refers to Acts 21:33 and Acts 22:29, both of which refer to the Romans binding Paul.

The Jews Did Not "Deliver" Paul to the Romans

Agabus prophesied that the Jews would "deliver" (*paradidōmi*) Paul into the hands of the gentiles. Grudem says,

> Essential to the sense of this word is the idea of *actively, consciously, willingly* "delivering, giving over, handing over" something or someone to someone (or something) else—this is the case in all of the other 119 instances of its use in the New Testament . . . None of the other 119 instances of the word in the New Testament lacks the idea of an action that is *consciously, intentionally* done by the one doing the "delivering."[5]

According to Grudem, the Jews "do not 'deliver' Paul over to the hands of the gentiles. Rather than intentionally 'giving Paul over' to the hands of the gentiles . . . they tried to kill him themselves (Acts 21:31). He had to be

---

3. *GP*, 78.
4. *GP*, 78.
5. *GP*, 78; italics mine.

Agabus Predicts the Arrest of Paul

forcibly *rescued from* the Jews by the Roman tribune and his soldiers (Acts 21:32–33)."[6] Sam Storms goes even further, claiming that the Jews "stubbornly refused" to turn Paul over to the Romans.[7]

THE THEORY EXAMINED

Did the Jews "Deliver" Paul to the Romans?

> When the rioters saw the commander and his soldiers, they stopped beating Paul. The commander came up and arrested him and ordered him to be bound with two chains. (Acts 21:32b, 33)

Grudem claims that Paul had to be "forcibly rescued" from the Jews.[8] But although the Romans certainly did arrest Paul, there is simply no indication in the text of any resistance on the part of the Jews.

Grudem believes that, since the Romans arrested Paul (*epilambanomai*, "take hold of"), the Jews therefore did not hand him over to the Romans. But the two are not at all incompatible: the word *paradidōmi* is used extensively in Scripture to describe Judas delivering Jesus into the hands of the Romans (see, e.g., Matt 20:19, 26:2; Mark 10:33; Luke 18:32, 24:7), and yet we have no issue with accepting that the Romans also actively arrested Jesus.

There seem to be three possible scenarios, all of which are equally plausible explanations of the Roman arrest of Paul:

1. The Romans approached and *forcibly wrested* Paul from the hands of the Jews. Under this scenario, Paul was not "handed over," Grudem is correct and the prophecy of Agabus does indeed contain an error.

2. The Romans approached and demanded that Paul be handed over. The Jews complied, and handed Paul over, actively and consciously (either willingly or unwillingly), precisely as predicted by Agabus.

3. As the Romans approached, the Jews abandoned Paul to them, like vultures abandoning their prey before an approaching lion. On this reading, the Jews *surrendered* or *abandoned* or *delivered up* Paul to the Romans, whether bidden or unbidden.

---

6. *GP*, 79.
7. Storms, "A Third Wave Conclusion," 322.
8. *GP*, 79.

Part Three — Agabus

We will now see that the Greek word for "deliver" or "hand over" (*paradidōmi*) certainly allows for either of the last two readings above.

Paradidōmi

To repeat Grudem's lexical understanding of the word *paradidōmi*: "Essential to the sense of this word is actively, consciously, willingly 'delivering, giving over, handing over' something or someone to someone (or something) else."[9] Here Grudem overstates the level of activity implied or required by the word *paradidōmi*. After all, Judas is described as "handing over" Jesus *with a kiss*; and if I *allow* something to be taken, that is, if I *surrender* it, my involvement need not be active at all. Nor does the compliance need to be willing: when someone comes into a bank and says, "*Hand over the cash!*" the response may be *active* and *conscious*, but not at all *willing*.

The word *paradidōmi* certainly has these meanings in Greek: thus, Moisés Silva says its meaning includes "*deliver up*" and the corresponding noun (*paradōsis*) can mean "*surrender*."[10] We see this meaning in, for example:

- "and if I *deliver up* my body to be burned, but have not love, I gain nothing." (1 Cor 13:3)
- "Christ loved the church and *gave himself up* for her." (Eph 5:25)
- "the Son of God, who loved me and *gave himself up* for me." (Gal 2:20)

Jesus passively *allowed himself* to be arrested and killed: that is, he did not actively turn himself in, but neither did he resist arrest. We conclude that Paul may not have been actively "delivered" to the Romans, but he may well have been "delivered *up*" to them.

So Grudem's statement that "*paradidōmi*" always involves *active and willing* delivery (like a postman delivering a letter) in all instances of the word in the New Testament is not accurate. He seems not to have considered the notion of *surrendering, abandoning*, or *delivering up* in the definition of *paradidōmi*. The text could certainly describe a scenario under which the Romans approached, ordered the Jews away, and the Jews withdrew, abandoning Paul to them.

---

9. GP, 78.
10. Silva, *New International Dictionary*, 3:622.

3. Did the Jews Bind Paul?

The fact that the Romans bound Paul with two chains (21:33) has led many to assume that this must be the partial or inaccurate fulfillment of the prophecy by Agabus that he would be bound hand and foot *by the Jews* (21:11). But it is possible that there was an additional, unrecorded binding by the Jews prior to the Roman arrest. This could also have been carried out with Paul's own belt, precisely as demonstrated by Agabus.

There are a number of textual and circumstantial indications that Paul may have been bound in this way by the Jews:

1. Acts 28:17 describes the passing of Paul from Jewish to Roman hands ("I was delivered *as a prisoner*"). This suggests that Paul was *already* a prisoner when he was handed over. By etymology (admittedly a poor guide), the word for "prisoner" (*desmios*) implies "bound."

2. Binding would have facilitated the subsequent actions of *dragging* (21:30), *beating* (21:32), and *killing* (21:30).

3. Then, as now, arrests routinely involved binding. We see it both here (21:33) and, for example, in the arrest of Jesus (John 18:12).

4. The same word—*epilambanomai* ("lay hold of")—is used to describe both Paul's seizure by the Jews (21:30) and his arrest by the Romans (21:33), which suggests a parity between the two events. ("Arrest" is one of the more minor meanings of the word *epilambanomai*.) Since there was a binding in the Roman arrest, there is likely to have been a binding in the Jewish arrest too.

5. When the tribune Claudius Lysias later describes the arrest of Paul by the Jews (23:27), he uses a word with much stronger connotations of "arresting"—*syllambanō* (as in, e.g., Matt 26:55; Acts 1:16). The tribune says that when he came across Paul, he *had been arrested by the Jews*. Since Roman arrests routinely involved binding, Claudius Lysias may also be implying binding here too. Paul himself then uses the same word in describing the event to Agrippa (Acts 26:21).

It therefore seems at least plausible that something along the following lines occurred:

1. The Jews arrested Paul in the Temple (v. 30) by binding his hands behind his back, probably with his own belt.

2. They then "dragged him" (v. 30) out of the temple, by the belt.

3. Once outside, in order to immobilize him on the ground, they used the same belt to bind his feet also, so that they could "beat" (v. 32) him more effectively, and then "kill him" (v. 31).

Some commentators seek to defend the prophecy of Agabus by suggesting that, even if the Jews did not bind Paul, since their actions *led to* his binding, they bear a level of responsibility for it, and are therefore guilty of it. Kenneth Gentry points to several passages that assert that the Jews crucified Christ (Acts 2:22–23; 3:13–15; 5:30; 7:52; 1 Thess 2:14–15), although we know the Romans were the more direct agents of it. Gentry claims this offers a strong parallel to the prophecy of Agabus: just as the Jews were guilty of crucifying Jesus inasmuch they *handed him over* to be crucified, in the same way the Jews were guilty of binding Paul inasmuch as they *handed him over* to be bound. He argues that to accuse Agabus of error is to employ "an overly literal hermeneutic."[11] I am not entirely persuaded by this argument: the fact that Agabus uses Paul's belt to make the point that he would be bound hand and foot implies to me that Paul's own belt would be used in the process.

We have touched briefly on Paul's report on these events in Acts 28:17. We consider that report in more detail in an addendum to this chapter.

An Objection Answered

If the Jews did bind Paul, why, one might ask, did Luke not record it more explicitly? There seem to be two possible answers to that question:

- It may simply not have been one of Luke's narrative priorities to confirm in detail the reliability of a respected prophet whose credentials he had already firmly established (Acts 11:28).

- It is possible that Luke had not ascertained from Paul the fine detail of the arrest, and so, as an historian wedded to accuracy, he could not report it.

---

11. Gentry, *Charismatic Gift of Prophecy*, 43. See also Peterson, *Acts of the Apostles*, 580–81, and Bock, *Acts,* 638.

Conclusion

In summary, the thesis that there are clear errors in the prophecy of Agabus fails because it assumes too narrow a semantic range in the use of the word *paradidōmi*, and it fails to examine the evidence for the Jewish arrest of Paul in sufficient detail.

Our view is that the prophecy of Agabus does not contain errors. The fact that his prediction is introduced with the phrase "Thus says the Holy Spirit," which is so clearly an echo of the Old Testament prophetic preface "Thus says the Lord," taken with the evidence we have seen, is for me decisive.

My suggestion of a binding by the Jews may appear somewhat speculative. But it does mean, I think, that we cannot conclude unequivocally that Agabus was wrong, and that therefore when Grudem says of Agabus, "On these two key elements he is *just a bit wrong*,"[12] Grudem is in fact just a bit wrong himself.

The accuracy of Agabus's prophecy is not the only important question surrounding this prediction; another is whether Paul was right to ignore it. My preferred reading is that it was a gracious warning from God, much as an airline pilot might forewarn his passengers of turbulence ahead. It was a reminder to Paul of what he knew well already—that his suffering was part of God's plan (Acts 9:16; 20:23). As such, this prediction has the same purpose as Agabus's prediction of a famine in Acts 11:28; it was not given so that Christians might avoid suffering altogether, but that they might be prepared for it.

Addendum: Further Comments on Acts 28:17

We have already referred to Paul's own report of his arrest. He says, "Brothers, though I had done nothing against our people or the customs of our fathers, yet I was delivered as a prisoner from Jerusalem into the hands of the Romans" (Acts 28:17). The Greek is, "*desmios ex Ierosolumōn paredothēn eis tas cheiras tōn Romaiōn.*"

This text is slightly difficult both to translate and to tie to the actual events.[13] Some suggest that the phrase *ex Ierosolumōn* could be describing

---

12. *GP*, 79.

13. One minor question is whether *ex Ierosolumō* is to be read adjectivally, as a genitive describing the noun *desmios* ("I was delivered as a prisoner *of* Jerusalem into the

Part Three—Agabus

the rescue of Paul from the hands of the Jews by the Roman tribune Lysias. So it would mean:

> I was delivered (handed over) as a prisoner from the *power* of Jerusalem (i.e., the Jews) into the *power* of the Romans.

On the other hand, others, including Grudem, propose that since Paul was already in Roman hands before he left the city, the sentence does not describe the Jewish handling of Paul at all, but rather means:

> I was delivered as a prisoner (under Roman arrest) from the *city* of Jerusalem into the *hands* of the Romans.

On this possibility, we would have to ask whether the fact that Paul was handed over by one group of Romans into the hands of another group of Romans is really a point worth making. Grudem says that it refers to the passage of Paul "into the jurisdiction and processes of the Roman judicial system."[14] But can the phrase "*into the hands of* the Romans" really mean this since Paul is already *in the hands of* the Romans? Surely not.

On the meaning of the preposition "*ek*" ("from," "out of"), *AG* points to its use to denote "*from someone's power*" (e.g., John 10:39 "he escaped from their grasp"), and reports examples such as "from the hands of." On that basis, a reading along the lines of "*from the power of Jerusalem*" looks reasonable.

AG also allows that the word "Jerusalem" can legitimately refer not simply to the geographical location, but also to "the people of Jerusalem." *AG* refers to Acts 21:31 (also 21:30) when "the whole city of Jerusalem was in uproar," which could be precisely what Paul was referring to here (see also Matt 23:37, "O Jerusalem, Jerusalem . . ."). So a reading along the lines of "*from the power of the people of Jerusalem*" looks plausible.

Such a reading is also reasonable in the context of the whole sentence: "Brothers, *though I had done nothing against our people or the customs of our fathers*, yet I was delivered as a prisoner from Jerusalem into the hands of the Romans." The sentence conveys Paul's sense of betrayal that although he had done nothing against his people, yet they had handed him over to the Romans.

---

hands of the Romans") or whether it is to be read as qualifying the verb *paredothēn* "(I was delivered as a prisoner *from* Jerusalem into the hands of the Romans"). On balance, the latter reading seems preferable.

14. *GP*, 310.

Agabus Predicts the Arrest of Paul

Furthermore, since the second half of the phrase explicitly describes a movement *into* the power of the Romans, there is a meaningful contrast if the sentence is read as describing a movement from one set of hands to another; and the notion in *paradidōmi* of handing *over* appropriately describes a passing from one power to another. So a translation along these lines seems to be the happiest:

> I was delivered (handed over) as a prisoner from the power of Jerusalem into the power of the Romans.

Why does all this matter? Well, on this reading we would have Paul's own testimony that he had indeed been *"handed over"* (actively and consciously) to the Romans; it would clinch the debate about the reliability of Agabus on that score. Also, this reiterates the fact that Paul was a prisoner of the Jews when he was handed over and, as we pointed out earlier, this suggests that he had been *bound by the Jews*.

Chapter 20

Does Agabus Model Prophecy for Today?

Normative and Exceptional Prophecy

IF YOU WERE TO write a very brief history of the twentieth century, what events would you include? The two World Wars certainly. The moon landings? The assassination of Kennedy? You could produce a detailed and accurate history of the *striking events* of the century, but it would not give a very accurate picture of daily life: a reader might easily assume, for example, that the whole century was a daily stream of universal violence. This is because the normal practice of historians is to narrate not the most *typical* events in the period they cover, but the most *remarkable*. All historical narrative is necessarily selective and is therefore an interpretation of events rather than a straightforward record of them.

When we read of the amazing events of the Old Testament, we therefore need to be able to distinguish the extraordinary from the ordinary. Was daily life in Old Testament times an endless stream of miracles? By no means. Equally, when we read the book of Acts in the New Testament, we need to be very careful how we use it to construct a mental picture of typical New Testament church life, and normative behavior. For example, when he records Philip being transported miraculously to Azotus (Acts 8:40), Luke is describing a truly remarkable event, not a typical Christian mode of travel.

Does Agabus Model Prophecy for Today?

By the same token, Agabus made two remarkable predictions, at least one of which was introduced with the phrase, "Thus says the Holy Spirit." But did he make similar predictions when he prophesied *normally*? Probably not. You might read a story in a newspaper about a doctor who performs a tracheotomy in the street with a penknife; but doctors do not *routinely* carry out such operations. Similarly, to imagine that prophecy *routinely* involves making predictions such as those made by Agabus would be to *confuse the normative and the exceptional*. To use another example, a policeman may occasionally drive at high speed, but that does not make him a racing driver. The point is, we cannot always understand someone's role simply by looking at a single activity: we need a broader picture.

To gain a broader picture of the role of Agabus, we need to remember that there were three missions by prophets to Antioch:

1. The mission of Barnabas (Acts 11:22–26), who "exhorted [*parakaleō*] them all to remain faithful to the Lord with steadfast purpose" (Acts 11:23).
2. The visit of a group of prophets which included Agabus (who foretold a worldwide famine) (Acts 11:27–30).
3. The mission of Judas and Silas, the purpose of which was to explain the letter from the Jerusalem Council, and during which they "encouraged [*parakaleō*] and strengthened the brothers with many words" (Acts 15:32).

In other words, when a new gentile church needed to be strengthened and established in the faith, those sent were invariably prophets. Considering these three missions to Antioch, it seems clear that the role of these prophets was to contribute to the spiritual welfare of a fast-growing church, and that the predictions of Agabus, although a component of this contribution, were exceptional events.

But the question we need to answer next is, should we *ever* expect to see predictions such as those of Agabus today?

Prediction that Cements the Jewish-Gentile Bond

Our answer to this question will depend on our understanding of the nature of Agabus's predictions. If we see them simply as random acts of divine

Part Three—Agabus

grace, we may well be drawn to expect such predictions today. But there seems to be more to them than that.

Gaffin, for example, draws attention to what he calls the "covenantal-historical character"[1] of the predictions of Agabus. We know that the revelation of the mystery of gentile inclusion in the church came not just to apostles, but also to prophets (Eph 3:4–6). Gaffin sees the predictions of Agabus as actively promoting this declared unity between Jews and gentiles in the church. Thus,

> In the one instance (Acts 11:28) prophecy is directed toward cementing the newly-established foundational bond of fellowship within the church between Jew and gentile. Prophecy functions to induce the Greeks at Antioch (v. 27; cf. v. 20) to contribute famine relief for their (Jewish) brothers in Judea (vv. 29f.). In other words, this prophecy is directly related to an important aspect of the mystery revealed in Christ (cf. Eph. 3:6). In another instance (Acts 21:10f.), prophecy concerns the unfolding of Paul's apostolic ministry to the gentiles (cf. 20:23).[2]

For Gaffin, the predictions of Agabus are certainly not random acts of grace; indeed, he maintains, "Scripture leaves no place for privatized, localized revelations for specific individual needs and circumstances. The appeal to the predictions of Agabus to support such a notion is particularly inappropriate."[3]

The Eschatological Character of the Predictions of Agabus

In the case of Agabus's prediction of a famine in Acts 11, we might ask, why would the prediction of a *worldwide* famine result in action targeted specifically at Palestine?

Bock claims that there was not a single global famine, but a series of localized famines over five different years of the reign of Claudius.[4] In the unreported detail of his speech, Agabus may have singled out a specific famine in Judea, which took place in AD 44–48.[5] On the other hand, a pre-

---

1. Gaffin, *Perspectives on Pentecost*, 99.
2. Gaffin, *Perspectives on Pentecost*, 99.
3. Gaffin, *Perspectives on Pentecost*, 98–99.
4. Bock, *Acts*, 417.
5. Bock, *Acts*, 418.

diction of general famine may naturally have moved the church to concern for its poorest, most vulnerable members.

But Aune goes further and suggests that there are *eschatological* aspects to this prediction:

> While Agabus predicts a *worldwide* famine, the famine which occurred in AD 47/8 seems to have been limited to Palestine. On that basis, then, it appears that Agabus emphasized the universality of the famine in the expectation that it would constitute *a sign of the inauguration of the end of the age*. Luke has, in effect, removed the eschatological features of the prediction of Agabus.[6]

We will examine the eschatological nature of prophecy further, including this example, a little later. For now, we should point out that both of Agabus's recorded predictions—of famine and of the persecution of Paul—are specific applications of eschatological events promised by Jesus—namely that in the last days there would be famines (Matt 24:7), and persecution of Christians (Matt 24:9–10). So the predictions of Agabus appear to be *Spirit-given revelations* of incidences of promised End Times events. Just as Old Testament prophets predicted particular instances of the blessings and curses announced by Moses (such as exile and drought), so Agabus seems to have foreseen specific instances of the evidences of the end times announced by Jesus.

If this is what Agabus is doing, his activities would parallel those of suitably gifted preachers and thinkers today who declare material evidences in our culture of signs of the end times, however miraculously or otherwise they might do so.

If you find any merit either in the covenantal-historical reading or in the eschatological reading of these predictions, you must conclude that the predictions of Agabus are so remarkable that they cannot serve as a model for "privatized, localized revelations" today. However, by the same token, neither can they preclude them; indeed, it could be argued that "privatized revelations" are precisely what we seek each time we open the Bible, and ask God to speak to us through it.

---

6. Aune, *Prophecy in Early Christianity*, 265; italics mine.

PART FOUR
SYNTHESIS

Chapter 21

Foundational and Congregational Prophecy

> The mystery of Christ, which was not made known to the sons of men in other generations as it has now been revealed to his holy apostles and prophets by the Spirit. This mystery is that the gentiles are fellow heirs, members of the same body, and partakers of the promise in Christ Jesus through the gospel. (Eph 3:4–6)

Revelation to Prophets?

ACCORDING TO EPHESIANS 3:4–5, both the apostles and prophets received the revelation of the mystery of Christ. However, as we saw earlier in our study of Ephesians 2:20, Grudem believes that the apostles and prophets are the same group ("apostle-prophets"), and he justifies this view at least partly on the grounds that "the prophets in the New Testament *did not* receive the revelation that the gentiles were to be included in the New Testament church on an equal standing with Jewish believers."[1]

What then could Paul be referring to in the Ephesians passage? To understand how prophets *did* in fact receive the revelation of gospel mysteries, we need to consider the Council of Jerusalem, the key meeting at which gentile inclusion in the church was discussed and decided. We know

---

1. *GP*, 335; italics mine.

Part Four—Synthesis

that the meeting involved "the apostles and the elders" (Acts 15:6). But did prophets also have a role to play here?

They certainly did. The prophet Barnabas was actively involved in the meeting along with Paul (Acts 15:12). Furthermore, after the council made its conclusions, the apostles and elders chose the prophets Judas and Silas to communicate their decision to the church in Antioch. These two are described as "men *from among them*" and as "leading men" (Acts 15:22), which suggests that Judas and Silas may well also have participated in the council's deliberations. As Ellis says, "Probably they [Judas and Silas] were chosen because they had already established an influential role in establishing (or proclaiming) the biblical rationale upon which the provisions of the Decree were justified."[2]

On this reading, prophets did indeed receive the foundational revelation that the gentiles are fellow heirs of the gospel, as indicated in Ephesians 3:5, although they were perhaps not its *first* recipients. For that we would need to look to the apostles Peter and Paul and the earlier visions they each received.

Prophets had a key role not only in perceiving or receiving spiritual truth, but also in *communicating* it. We are told that Judas and Silas were sent to Antioch in support of Paul and Barnabas (Acts 15:22), bearing an important letter from the Jerusalem council concerning its decisions about gentile believers. Their task was to reiterate and reinforce the contents of this letter—to tell people "the *same things* by word of mouth" (Acts 15:27).

Acts 15:32 reads literally, "Judas and Silas, *also being prophets themselves*, encouraged [*parakaleō*] and strengthened the brothers with many words." The word "also" ("*kai*") may refer to the fact that their companions Paul and Barnabas were prophets.[3] So it would mean, "Judas and Silas, being *likewise* prophets themselves."

This phrase binds the prophetic gift of Judas and Silas to their ability to fulfill their commission; that is, they were able to encourage *because* they were prophets. This strongly suggests that their encouraging *was* their prophesying. In other words, the encouragement offered by the letter itself (v. 31) and the encouragement given by the prophets (v. 32) were closely related. The prophetic gift enabled Judas and Silas to tell people "the same things" as the letter, that is, to explain its contents (and presumably its implications) clearly, authoritatively, and encouragingly. As Ellis says,

2. Ellis, *Prophecy & Hermeneutic*, 138.
3. See Sandnes, *Paul*, 3.

> It is very likely that the fact that Judas and Silas were prophets is the basis of their ministry of *paraklēsis*. The clause should then be translated 'since they themselves also were prophets'... In Luke's thought *paraklēsis* is one way in which the Christian prophets exercise their ministry and, in this context, is a form of prophecy.[4]

This activity was a theological endeavor; it was unquestionably consistent with their role as prophets, and seems to have been synonymous with it. They were, as Gillespie says, *"the first theologians of the church."*[5] Thus, a firm connection is established between prophetic ministry and the exhortation of the church through the exposition of Scripture—Scripture here being both the letter from the council, and the text from Amos 9:11–12 that proved decisive in the council discussions (see Acts 15:16–17).

Any objection to this point would have to argue that the prophetic activity of Judas and Silas was purely incidental to their main task. But there is simply no evidence of that here.

To summarize what we have suggested so far:

1. When the apostles needed newly formed doctrine to be explained in detail to the church at Antioch, they turned to four people, all of whom were prophets.

2. Judas and Silas were able to encourage and strengthen the church *because they were prophets* (Acts 15:32).

3. In fulfillment of this mission, these prophets used "many words" (v. 32) to communicate the "same things" (v. 27) as the contents of the council letter, and this activity had the effect of encouraging and strengthening the brethren (v. 32). (Using "many words" to say "the same things" might be an accurate, albeit telling, description of expository preaching today!)

4. The prophetic gifting seems thus to have consisted in their ability to explain and apply apostolic revelation (that is, Scripture) clearly and effectively.

On this reading, we have yet more strong evidence that prophesying involved the communication of gospel revelation. Grudem argues that "no prophecy in New Testament churches is ever said to consist of the

---

4. Ellis, *Prophecy & Hermeneutic*, 132.
5. Gillespie, *First Theologians*, 263; italics mine.

interpretation and application of texts of Old Testament Scripture."[6] On the evidence of Acts 15, we have to disagree.

Prophecy as Both Communicating and Effecting Revelation

The events of Acts 15 not only impact our understanding of prophecy, they also impact our understanding of the nature of revelation. For God's revelation that gentiles were to be included in the church, and that salvation is by grace rather than keeping the law, was not the result of spontaneous revelation and a single event, but came through a gradual, developing understanding:

- Peter had a vision (Acts 10:10–16).
- He did not immediately understand this vision, but subsequent events led him to realize that gentiles could become Christians (Acts 10:34–35).
- He reported this to the other leaders in Jerusalem, and they came to accept what he said (Acts 11:18).
- There was still the question of whether gentiles should be circumcised and required to keep the law. At the Council of Jerusalem (Acts 15), the apostles and elders, including prophets, debated the matter and James made a decisive contribution, referring to Amos. His proposal was accepted.
- A decision was made by the apostles and elders, endorsed by the whole church, to send a mission to Antioch to communicate the council's decision, and a letter was written.
- The prophets Paul, Barnabas, Judas, and Silas communicated the council's letter and explained it clearly.
- The result was that the church was encouraged and strengthened.

The point is that revelation comes to the church through this entire sequence of events. What is more, apostles and prophets play a role at every step. So revelation is not to be viewed simply as a miraculous event, such as the initial vision that Peter received, but as also involving the entire subsequent process of discussion and examining Scripture. The complete

6. *GP*, 120.

revelation is then communicated to others through clear exegesis and application: so prophecy both receives and effects revelation.

Conclusion

In Ephesians 2:20 and 3:5 Paul may be remembering the role played by prophets a few years earlier in explaining the implications of the apostolic letter to gentile believers (Acts 15:22–32). Their prophetic gift seems to have confirmed to them, and enabled them to confirm and explain to others, the doctrine of gentile inclusion. They were, "together with the apostles, the hermeneuts of the foundational message of Christ crucified and raised from the dead."[7]

The preaching gift of Silas and Judas appears to be the same preaching gift we often see exercised today. It is conceivable that their prophesying was somehow miraculous, but there is no evidence of miracle here.

---

7. Gillespie, *First Theologians*, 199; italics mine.

CHAPTER 22

Prophecy as *Paraklēsis* and Hermeneutics

ÉDOUARD COTHENET SAYS, "IT is striking that the notions of prophecy, *paraklēsis*, and the interpretation of Scripture are tightly associated in the New Testament."[1]

In other words, Cothenet sees these terms as orbiting each other in a triangular relationship:

Prophecy

Paraklēsis   Interpretation of Scripture

Figure 2

In the course of this study we have come across evidence for each of these three relationships. It might therefore be helpful to summarize this evidence briefly, adding a few further examples from Cothenet.

---

1. Cothenet, "Les prophètes chrétiens comme exégètes," 81. All quotations from Cothenet's text are my own translations.

Prophecy as *Paraklēsis* and Hermeneutics

1. *Paraklēsis* and Prophecy

- Luke translates the Aramaic "Barnabas," which means "Son of the *prophet*" (*bar nabyā,*), as meaning "Son of *encouragement*" (Acts 4:36).
- Prophecy effects *paraklēsis* (1 Cor 14:3).
- The *paraklēsis* given by the prophets Barnabas, Judas, and Silas (Acts 11:23, 15:32).
- The book of Revelation is both prophecy and *paraklēsis*. It is encouragement to live in the light of future events.

2. *Paraklēsis* and the Interpretation of Scripture

- Thiselton notes that, "scripture remains the definitive source for *paraklēsis*," pointing to Romans 15:4 ("the *paraklēsis* of Scriptures").[2]
- The *paraklēsis* of the letter from the Jerusalem Council (Acts 15:31) is supported by the *paraklēsis* of the words of the prophets explaining it, the latter deriving from the former, in what we would call "preaching" (see Acts 15:32 in light of 15:27).
- In 2 Timothy 4:2, the text of Scripture seems to provide the basis for exhortation, "preach the word . . . reprove, rebuke, and exhort."
- "When he arrives at Antioch . . . Paul is invited to give some words of encouragement (*paraklēsis*) (Act 13:15). His sermon consists of a messianic interpretation of the history of Israel."[3]
- "The letter to the Hebrews, which is a thorough hermeneutical treatise, is described by its author as a 'word of encouragement' (Heb 13:22)."[4]
- The Paraclete reminds the disciples of the words of Jesus (John 14:26), and thereby contributes to the creation of Scripture.[5]
- In the book of Revelation, "in order to strengthen believers in tribulation, [John] is concerned to show them the fulfilment of the mystery of God, according to the announcement made formerly by the prophets

---

2. *FEC*, 1090.
3. Cothenet, "Les prophètes chrétiens comme exégètes," 80.
4. Cothenet, "Les prophètes chrétiens comme exégètes," 80.
5. See Cothenet, "Les prophètes chrétiens comme exégètes," 81.

(10:7). They are therefore to await the hour of God's judgment with confidence."[6]

- Cothenet considers *parakalein* in LXX as a translation of the Hebrew *niham* ("comfort"), especially in the second book of Isaiah: "Comfort, comfort my people, says your God" (Isa 40:1). Prophetic *paraklēsis* involves reminding people of the ancient promises of God, with a view to facing the future with confidence (Isa 51:2–3).[7]

Given this evidence, it is little surprise that there is also a tight association between *paraklēsis* and teaching, with *paraklēsis* being the key goal of sound teaching, and sound teaching a source of *paraklēsis*:

- We noted the parallel between the three *effects* of prophesying in 1 Corinthians 14:3, and the three *activities* of prophetic ministry in Acts 14:22, which clearly involve teaching.
- "He must hold firmly to the trustworthy message as it has been taught, so that he can *encourage others by sound doctrine* and refute those who oppose it" (Titus 1:9 NIV).
- In 1 Thessalonians 2:2–3, the declaration of the gospel (v. 2) is described as "our exhortation" (*paraklēsis*) in verse 3. "Here missionary preaching is designated without qualification as *paraklēsis*."[8] The two are also associated in 1 Thessalonians 2:9–12 and 1 Thessalonians 3:1–3.
- "Therefore encourage one another with these words" (1 Thess 4:18) refers to encouragement that comes from consideration of the return of Christ.

3. Prophecy and the Interpretation of Scripture

- The prophetic blessing of Zachariah (Luke 1:67–79) "takes up a number of Old Testament texts."[9]

---

6. Cothenet, "Les prophètes chrétiens comme exégètes," 81.
7. See Cothenet, "Les prophètes chrétiens comme exégètes," 82–83.
8. Gillespie, *First Theologians*, 145.
9. Cothenet, "Les prophètes chrétiens comme exégètes," 79.

- "Revelation presents itself explicitly as a 'book of prophecy' (Rev 1:3, 22:7, 10, 18, 19), and is saturated with Old Testament citations and allusions . . . So one can see in Revelation 'a clear translation of Old Testament prophecies in the light of the New Testament.'"[10] (ibid., 81).

- Scriptures are a key source of prophetic revelation. Thus Paul says, "the mystery hidden for long ages past, but now revealed and made known *through the prophetic writings*" (Rom 16:25-26 NIV).

- In determining the validity of prophetic revelation, James seeks confirmation from the prophecy of Amos (Acts 15:16).[11]

Conclusions

There seems little doubt that, as Cothenet maintains, there is a tight correlation between prophesying, the interpretation of Scripture, and exhortation. Some conclusions drawn by Cothenet:

- "Instructed by the Spirit, Paul can thus unveil to mature Christians the deep meaning of the wisdom of God, just as the risen Christ unveiled the meaning of the Law and the Prophets to the disciples on the Emmaus road and to the eleven (Luke 24:25-27, 46)."[12]

- "The originality of Christian exegesis . . . lies in the fact that its starting point is not a text but the Christ event. Convinced that Christ is the definitive Amen of God to his own promises (cf. 2 Cor 1:20, cf. Heb 1:1), and convinced of the presence of the Son of Man in the midst of his Church (Rev 1:12f.), the Christian prophets search the Scriptures for indications . . . of the unsearchable riches of his mystery (cf. Ephesians 2:7; Col 2:3)."[13]

A definition of prophecy in line with Cothenet's position might be as follows: *New Testament prophecy builds and exhorts the church by the Spirit-empowered interpretation of Old Testament Scripture in light of the Christ event.*

---

10. L. Cerfaux–J. Cambier, *L'Apocalypse de S. Jean lue aux chrétiens*, Paris, 1955, 89, in Cothenet, "Les prophètes chrétiens comme exégètes," 105.

11. Cothenet, "Les prophètes chrétiens comme exégètes," 105.

12. Cothenet, "Les prophètes chrétiens comme exégètes," 95-96.

13. Cothenet, "Les prophètes chrétiens comme exégètes," 104-5.

PART FOUR—SYNTHESIS

Rereading Texts in the Light of *Paraklēsis*

Once *paraklēsis* gains its rightful prominence in our understanding of prophecy, we will find our readings of certain texts challenged. For example, what is it that makes the book of Revelation "prophecy?" Revelation is surely described as "prophecy" not primarily because it predicts future events, but because it encourages the church to live *in the light of eschatological events*; it is encouragement to be steadfast through tribulation because of the end that is to come (Rev 2–3).

This is why John describes prophecy as something that is to be *"kept"* (Rev 22:7)—that is, *obeyed* (as in John 14:21; 1 John 2:4, 3:24), which would make no sense if John simply had prediction in mind. Prophecy is encouragement to live now in the light of promised kingdom realities.

Consider two examples of speech clearly labeled as "prophecy" in 1 Timothy, which are often assumed to involve predictions:

> This charge I entrust to you, Timothy, my child, in accordance with the prophecies previously made about you, that by them you may wage the good warfare. (1 Tim 1:18)

> Do not neglect the gift you have, which was given you by prophecy when the council of elders laid their hands on you. (1 Tim 4:14)

If prophecy is primarily concerned with *paraklēsis* rather than with prediction, Paul could be referring in both these texts simply to an exhortation given to Timothy at his commissioning. Since *paraklēsis* is concerned with exhortation based on the promises of God in 1 Timothy 1:18, Paul could be encouraging Timothy to wage war using some particular Scripture promises given to him at that time (apparently by Paul himself—see 2 Tim 1:6).[14] So Paul may simply be reminding Timothy of *what he was commissioned to do*.

An understanding of prophecy as *paraklēsis* also helps with our understanding of Paul's command "Do not despise prophecies" (lit. "reject with contempt") (1 Thess 5:20). As we have already suggested, the reason prophecy is likely to be treated with contempt appears to be because *paraklēsis* often involves *rebuke*, and rebuke can be hard to take (see Prov 13:1; 15:12).

---

14. The text may be referring to a prayer made "over" Timothy, rather than simply "about" him (see *epi*, *AG*, 288: III, ζ) as in James 5:14.

Finally, when Matthew says, "For all the prophets and the law prophesied until John" (Matt 11:13), in what sense can the law be said to "prophesy?" The law could never predict, but in the mouths of prophets, it could *exhort*.

CHAPTER 23

The Doctrinal Content of Prophecy (Rom 12:6)

> Having gifts that differ according to the grace given to us, let us use them: if prophecy, in proportion to our faith . . . (Rom 12:6)

WE HAVE SEEN MANY indications in the New Testament that prophecy was a theological enterprise and often had doctrinal content. We saw this, for example, in 1 Corinthians 2, in Paul's description of his practice of explaining the Spirit-revealed mystery of the gospel; we saw it in 1 Corinthians 14:3, in which prophecy results in upbuilding and encouragement, and in 1 Corinthians 14:24, 25, when we saw the impact of prophecy on the unbeliever; we saw it in Acts 15, in the prophesying of Judas and Silas. We also see a further indication of it in Romans 12:6.

There are two main ways in which the phrase "in proportion to our faith" (*kata tēn analogian tēs pisteōs*) is understood. We should note that the pronoun "our" is not in the text: it says literally "the faith," which can mean simply "faith." Some see the text as referring to "*the* faith," i.e., "the faith *which* we believe" (sometimes referred to by theologians as "*fides quae creditur*"), others see it as "faith," or "the faith *by which* we believe" ("*fides qua creditur*"). The former is the objective body of belief which we hold, the latter is our subjective response of faith to that body of belief.

On the latter interpretation, the text would be saying that prophecy is to be proportionate to the depth of the prophet's subjective trust in God. In other words, he is to prophesy only as far as his faith allows. Grudem

The Doctrinal Content of Prophecy (Rom 12:6)

sees both 12:3 and 12:6 as statements about *quantity* of faith; he talks about "greater and lesser degrees of prophetic ability, ranged all along a wide spectrum."[1] However, Ernst Käsemann contends that, "It makes no sense at all to suggest that the prophet must judge himself by his own faith" for that "would open the gates to every abuse and even false teaching."[2]

On the other hand, if the meaning is *the* faith, then the text is saying that prophecy is to be in accordance with orthodox doctrine and practice. This is the meaning of "the faith" in Galatians 1:23, 3:25, and 6:10, Romans 10:8, and Philippians 1:27. If the meaning is "*the* faith," then the point is that "prophetic inspiration can be assessed only by the material content of the utterances."[3] Gillespie quotes Müller: "Prophecy walks in agreement with the faith."[4] Indeed, *AG* translates the Greek here as "in agreement with (or proportion to) the faith."[5]

According to Gillespie, "Romans 12:6 specifies 'the faith' of the gospel as the norm by which the substance of prophecies must be evaluated and *to which they will materially correspond* if they are genuine communications of the Spirit." He concludes: "The logical inference is that, for Paul at least, prophecy was a form of gospel proclamation."[6]

C. E. B. Cranfield seems to suggest a third way. He sees "faith" here as "basic Christian faith" (as in verse 3). "The prophets are . . . to be careful not to utter . . . anything which is incompatible with their believing in Christ."[7] This could be taken to imply that as long as a prophecy is not incompatible with the faith, it need not materially correspond to it. But that, surely would give too much leeway to false prophets.

We agree with Gillespie that the content of prophecies must in some sense "materially correspond" to the faith. But perhaps this need not mean that prophecy must *always* explicitly express the gospel. You are not preaching the gospel when you gently warn someone of a sinful behavior; you may not even mention a verse of Scripture. Yet such speech acts can indeed "walk in agreement with the faith" and are "in proportion to the faith." They correspond to the gospel even if they do not explicitly express it, because they originate from a heart that has been shaped and formed by the gospel.

---

1. *GP*, 176.
2. Käsemann, *Commentary on Romans*, 341, in Gillespie, *First Theologians*, 59.
3. Gillespie, *First Theologians*, 59.
4. Müller, *Prophetie und Predigt*, 187, in Gillespie, *First Theologians*, 61.
5. *AG*, 56.
6. Gillespie, *First Theologians*, 63; italics mine.
7. Cranfield, *Romans*, 304–5.

Chapter 24

Addressing Perceived Need

Confronting Sin

PARAKLĒSIS CAN BE EFFECTIVE only if it corresponds to the spiritual needs of those it seeks to help. Prophecy therefore seems often to be marked by a diagnosis of spiritual condition. We saw this, for example, with Micah: "But as for me, I am filled with power, with the Spirit of the Lord, and with justice and might, to declare to Jacob his transgression and to Israel his sin" (Mic 3:8).

True prophets contend for the faith (Jude 3) by declaring sin and error openly to individuals, communities, cultures, and nations. This is a risky business and always demands courage: a prophet puts his life where his mouth is.

The starting point for good preaching today is sometimes a text or a topic, which is then applied to issues facing particular congregations or cultures. On the other hand, Paul seems to vary his approach, sometimes starting with matters of doctrine (as in Romans) but sometimes also addressing particular sins, with 1 Corinthians being a prime example of the latter approach. But Paul's perception of the sins of the Corinthians is never miraculous: he simply responds to what he has heard from or about them.

Addressing Perceived Need

The Letters to the Seven Churches

The letters to the seven churches in Revelation 2–3, like 1 Corinthians, are pin-sharp diagnoses of the spiritual condition of particular churches. Again, there is little in these perceptions that is obviously miraculous, but they are nonetheless deeply telling and Spirit-given.

These letters seem to follow a standard pattern, with each letter including:

- An address to the angel of a particular church
- An assertion to be the words of Christ
- A brief description of Christ which captures some aspect of the fuller description of him given earlier in Revelation 1:12–20
- A claim to knowledge of the church in question
- Diagnosis of the spiritual condition of an individual church: acknowledgment of the good in the church, and (in all but one case) one key sin
- A call to repentance (in all but one of the letters)
- A promise (and often a warning)
- An urging that the prophecy, as the voice of the Spirit of God, be taken seriously

As the words of Christ given through John, these letters constitute prophetic speech by any definition. But the repeated pattern here suggests something more: if the risen Christ follows a standard format in his addresses to the churches, might John be outlining a template for future prophetic discourse?

Letter	Sin described	OT reference
Ephesus	Rev 2:4	Jer 2:2
Smyrna	n/a	n/a
Pergamum	Rev 2:14	Num 25:1–3; 31:16
Thyatira	Rev 2:20	1 Kgs 16:31
Sardis	Rev 3:2–4	Isa 64:6
Philadelphia	Rev 3:9	Isa 45:14; 49:23; 60:14
Laodicea	Rev 3:17–18	Hos 12:8; Isa 55:1

Part Four—Synthesis

If these letters are, at least to some extent, such a template, the lessons would seem to be as follows:

- Prophecy often diagnoses the spiritual condition of a specific church, confronting it with Scripture.
- Penetrating though each insight is, it need not amount to *miraculous* knowledge; nevertheless, these observations are clearly Spirit-given.
- Prophecy largely consists of exhortation or consolation.
- Prophecy often includes eschatological promise or warning.
- A call to repentance is frequent, although not universal, in prophecy.

Is what we see here qualitatively different from what Paul does in 1 Corinthians, where he systematically tackles specific issues of which he is aware in that church? I suggest not.

How to Discern Spiritual Condition

How is the prophet to gain such clear-sighted perception of the spiritual condition of others? "The sins of some are obvious" (1 Tim 5:24 NIV), so the perception of sin may be relatively straightforward. But God also reveals understanding of spiritual condition *through prayer* and *through Scripture*. God rebukes his shepherds for failing to gain wisdom simply because they fail to ask him for it: "For the shepherds are stupid and do not inquire of the Lord; therefore they have not prospered, and all their flock is scattered" (Jer 10:21).

The two keys seem to be:

1. Seeking the voice of God in Scripture, because *prophetic wisdom comes through the word of God*: "I have more understanding than all my teachers, for your testimonies are my meditation" (Ps 119:99).
2. Seeking the face of God in prayer, because *prophetic wisdom comes from the presence of God*. God promises to give his wisdom to those who seek his presence: "if they had stood in my council, then they would have proclaimed my words to my people" (Jer 23:22). God promises to deliver the wisdom we need (Jas 1:5).

We should be careful not to suggest, however, that prophetic wisdom is always given immediately in response to a request for it; wisdom is normally developed over time, often through long years of the study of Scripture and prayer.

Does All Prophecy Address Perceived Need?

Although we have seen that prophecy often does address local needs, it need not always do so; it can equally involve bringing a message that is more widely applicable to the church at large, either in a particular time or for *all* time, since the church has a permanent, universal need to be reminded of the gospel of Christ. Prophecy can take a timeless gospel message and makes it a timely one, so that people say, "*He's talking about me!*"

The key point is that prophets are, above all, effective communicators of gospel truth, and they are effective communicators because they are interpreters not just of texts but of people. As Thiselton says, prophesying is "preaching *pastorally contextualized.*"[1]

Calvin's understanding of the gift of prophecy (which we quoted in our Introduction) seems closely aligned with this view, and therefore bears repetition:

> Let us, then, by Prophets . . . understand, first of all, eminent interpreters of Scripture, and farther, persons who are endowed with no common wisdom and dexterity in taking a right view of the present necessity of the Church, that they may speak suitably to it, and in this way be, in a manner, ambassadors to communicate the divine will . . . by applying with dexterity and skill prophecies, threatenings, promises, and the whole doctrine of Scripture, to the present use of the Church.[2]

---

1. *FEC*, 1140.

2. Calvin, *Commentary on the Epistles*, 415–16. Whilst Calvin believed that the gift of prophecy involved interpreting Scripture and making known the will of God, it should be noted that he also believed that it involved these elements to a miraculous extent, and that it has all but ceased. Thus he says, "It is difficult to form a judgment as to gifts and offices of which the Church has been so long deprived, excepting only that there are some traces, or shadows of them still to be seen" (Calvin, *Commentary on the Epistles*, 416).

Chapter 25

Speaking God's Word Today

EARLIER IN OUR STUDY, we described Matthew 28:18–20 as "the ongoing prophetic call to every Christian." We also noted that the one difference from Old Testament prophecy is that the apostles are to speak not "whatever I command you" but "all that I *have* commanded you." In other words, the speech of the New Testament apostles is rooted in the proclamation and exposition of the *already-revealed* message of Christ.

In this chapter, we support our earlier conclusions regarding the hermeneutical or exegetical content of New Testament prophecy with a few further texts.

Can Christians Today Speak the Very Words of God? (1 Pet 4:11)

> If anyone speaks, they should do so as one who speaks the very words of God. (1 Pet 4:11 NIV)

> whoever speaks, as one who speaks oracles of God. (1 Pet 4:11 ESV)

There is a significant ambiguity in this verse, centering on the meaning of the word "*as*" (*hōs*). Grudem uses this verse to demonstrate that those who speak in a church service (teachers, prophets and others) *do not* speak the very words of God. He says:

Speaking God's Word Today

> Peter is not saying that everyone who speaks in the church service . . . is speaking the very words of God. He is rather speaking of the solemnity of purpose and care with which all congregational speech should be uttered—people should speak as carefully as they would *if they were* uttering the very 'oracles of God.'[1]

Such a reading is certainly possible. However, the word "*hōs*" is as ambiguous in Greek as "as" is in English: it can be used as a comparative particle, e.g., "will be saved *as* through fire" (1 Cor 3:15), but it can also describe "an *actual quality*"[2] as in, for example:

> Why am I still being condemned *as* a sinner? (Rom 3:7)

> I could not address you *as* spiritual people. (1 Cor 3:1)

> Be subject for the Lord's sake to every human institution, whether it be to the emperor as supreme, or to governors *as* sent by him. (1 Pet 2:13–14)

In 1 Peter 4:10, Peter says that we are to use our gifts "*as* good stewards of God's grace," and in 4:11, he who serves is to do so "*as* one who serves by the strength that God supplies." Neither of these usages are comparative, but rather are descriptions of the *actual ways* we are to behave. So when, in between these two statements, Peter urges whoever speaks to do so "*as* one who utters oracles of God," it seems very possible that Peter is saying that Christians today *can actually speak from God* (presumably because of the authority of the Scripture they proclaim). Thus, Tim Keller sees this passage as referring to the authoritative communication of biblical truth:

> No Christian should ever claim that his or her teaching is to be treated with the same authority as biblical revelation; nevertheless, Peter makes the powerful, eye-opening claim that Christians who are presenting biblical teaching are not to be simply expressing their own opinion but giving others "the very words of God."[3]

Keller is making a vital point: when a preacher faithfully communicates the word of God today, *God speaks*. God speaks authoritatively today *through his word*.

Our conclusions are that Peter is saying that:

1. *GP*, 86. See also Grudem, *1 Peter*, 183.
2. *AG*, 906.
3. Keller, *Preaching*, 4.

- *All* who speak (particularly in a congregational context) should aim to speak prophetically, by which he means with complete faithfulness to Scripture.

- Whenever we communicate the word of God faithfully today, *God speaks*.

Scripture Is the Language of the Spirit

We tend to think that God spoke to the Old Testament prophets directly, whereas he speaks to us through Scripture. But, as we have already noted, this is simplistic, since God's voice to the Old Testament prophets—even though it was original and miraculous—cannot be entirely separated from God's voice to them *in Scripture*. As men and women of God who meditated on Scripture day and night (Josh 1:8; Ps 1:2), they found that it talked to them, guided their paths, and gave them wisdom (Prov 6:22), so that God's thoughts became their thoughts (see Isa 55:8–9). Old Testament prophets constantly reframe and re-present older biblical texts: God speaks to them afresh through Scripture.

The prophetic exegesis of Scripture, which is clearly demonstrated in the theological discourse of Paul, is no less a feature of the book of Revelation, an example of a completely different genre of prophetic speech. Unlike Paul, who frequently cites Old Testament passages, in Revelation, according to Boring, John *"never once formally cites an Old Testament passage."*[4] And yet,

> In Revelation, 499 . . . usages of Old Testament materials are found, an average of 11.3 per page . . . . Heinrich Kraft hardly overstates the matter when he asserts that for every statement in the Apocalypse the Seer has a Scripture source, which he reinterprets and sets forth afresh in the light of the Christ-event.[5]

Boring explains this as follows:

> The prophet no longer experienced the inspired texts as a *past* voice of the Lord that was to be "applied" to the *present* experience of the congregation. The texts became the vehicle for communicating the present word of the risen Lord. They are thus not

---

4. Boring, *Sayings of the Risen Jesus*, 99; italics mine.
5. Boring, *Sayings of the Risen Jesus*, 98–99.

quoted, but re-presented in new forms and combinations so that neither the past/present distinction nor the subject/object distinction is maintained. The way the Scriptures are used in Revelation indicates a community *intensively occupied* with Scripture.[6]

It is as if Scripture, absorbed deeply into the apostle's consciousness, provides the vocabulary and grammar used by the Spirit to express the miraculous vision John receives. In the book of Revelation, the Spirit speaks afresh through Scripture to deliver original revelatory material. *Scripture is the language the Spirit speaks.*

The Ongoing Prophetic Power of Scripture

God delivered Scripture by the gift of prophecy, and Scripture is the *living* prophetic word of God through which he continues to speak today: "For the word of God is living and active, sharper than any two-edged sword, piercing to the division of soul and of spirit, of joints and of marrow, and discerning the thoughts and intentions of the heart" (Heb 4:12).

This means that words of Scripture have an ongoing power to build, instruct, exhort, challenge, renew, rebuke, and warn (2 Tim 3:16). Scripture both *originated* in revelation and continues to *effect* revelation today: it is not simply God's word to God's people then, but God's word to *us now*. It is through the effective, active, authoritative application of his word to individuals, churches and cultures that God continues to accomplish his divine purposes today: "so shall my word be that goes out from my mouth; it shall not return to me empty, but it shall accomplish that which I purpose, and shall succeed in the thing for which I sent it" (Isa 55:11).

It is primarily through this forming and creative power of Scripture that God speaks and changes the world today. Whenever we are challenged or encouraged by Scripture, we have experienced its creative power, and have received *revelation*. In this sense, those who speak Scripture appropriately, bringing God's words to people today (whatever the context), are acting as God's prophets and are prophesying.

The fact that God is committed to changing the world through his written word has monumental implications for the Christian: it means that we should be committed to knowing it, delighting in it (Jer 15:16; Psa. 1:2), meditating on it, that is, thinking about it with a view to putting it into

---

6. Boring, *Sayings of the Risen Jesus,* 99; italics mine.

practice (Josh 1:8), and proclaiming it to others. Scripture needs to become the language we speak and the lens through which we see and interpret the world around us.

Since our relationship with God is personal, as we understand and apply God's word we are given clear, relevant, personal communication from him day by day. Sadly, however, many Christians today see the biblical text as virtually a dead letter, that is, as no more than a set of principles for living, and this leads them to seek a more personal communication from God elsewhere. For example, on the relationship between Scripture and Christian prophecy, David Watson says,

> Whilst the written word is God's truth for all people at all times, the prophetic word is a particular word, inspired by God, given to a particular person or group of persons, at a particular moment for a particular purpose.[7]

Watson seems to fail to see here that God does indeed address his people *personally* and *particularly* through his written word, as his people understand its meaning and ponder its implications for their lives. Of course, God *can* communicate through any means he chooses, but he communicates chiefly—both generally and particularly—through his living word. If we will approach this word humbly, and with a readiness to obey, we will find that it challenges our thinking and transforms our lives; for it is truly *all we need*: "His divine power has granted to us *all things* that pertain to life and godliness, *through the knowledge of him* who called us to his own glory and excellence, by which he has granted to us *his precious and very great promises*" (2 Pet 1:3–4).

---

7. Watson, *Discipleship*, 136.

CHAPTER 26

Prophecy as Eschatology

PROPHECY AND PREDICTION HAVE always been close bedfellows. The predictive aspects of prophecy, so prominent in the Old Testament, continue in the New. For whenever those who proclaim the gospel declare its eschatological message of judgment and salvation, they are practicing predictive prophecy; for the gospel message is inherently predictive.

We have already examined the eschatological character of the predictions of Agabus, including his prediction of a famine (Acts 11:27–30), and we noted Aune's comment that "Luke has, in effect, removed the eschatological features of the prediction of Agabus."[1]

Boring agrees that New Testament prophecy is far more concerned with eschatology than with foreseeing more mundane future events:

> The support in our sources for the view that Christian prophets predicted the historical future is extremely slight. The author of Revelation does not predict the future in the normal sense of this expression because in this sense the future did not exist for him. The series of catastrophes he announces are not predictions of events *in* history but those which form the end *of* history ... Paul's "predictions" (e.g., 1 Thess 3:4) were an element of his eschatology.[2]

Jesus promised that in the last days there would be false prophets and false christs who would deceive many with great signs and wonders (Matt 24:24), wars, earthquakes, famines (Matt 24:6–7), hatred and persecution

---

1. Aune, *Prophecy in Early Christianity*, 265.
2. Boring, *Sayings of the Risen Jesus*, 120; italics his.

of Christians (Matt 24:9–10), a cooling of Christian love (Matt 24:12), with the gospel being preached to the world before the end (Matt 24:14). Much apostolic prophecy restates and elaborates upon these events. The prime example of eschatological prediction in the New Testament is of course the book of Revelation; indeed, each one of the letters to the seven churches in Revelation 2–3 includes eschatological warnings and promises.

The New Testament epistles reiterate these warnings: we read that the Church is not to be surprised by persecution (2 Tim 3:13; 1 Pet 4:12; 1 John 3:13), is to be aware of the antichrist (2 Thess 2:1–12; 1 John 2:18, 22), and is to be on her guard against the destructive behavior of deceitful teachers (1 Tim 4:1–3; 2 Pet 2:1–3; 2 Tim 3:1–4) and scoffers (2 Pet 3:3–4; Jude 17–18). These are all characteristics of the last days, and New Testament prophets would surely have perceived and highlighted evidences of them in their culture.

Beyond repeating these generic reminders, the Spirit also seems occasionally to warn of *specific instances* of the eschatological events promised by Christ. For example, in Paul's awareness that he faces persecution in every city (Acts 20:23); and both of Agabus's predictions, as we have seen, are related to eschatological events promised by Christ (famine and persecution). In our survey of Old Testament prophecy, we suggested that the prophets were led to predict specific incidences of the blessings and curses set out by Moses in Deuteronomy 28; similarly, in the New Testament, we occasionally see predictions of specific incidences of the signs of the times promised by Jesus (in Matthew 24, for example).

The question that then arises is, might *all* New Testament prophecy include at least some element of eschatology? Does the eschatological future supply the motivational power behind all effective *paraklēsis*? Perhaps it does, though not because eschatology needs to be explicitly discussed in all prophecy (it clearly does not), but inasmuch as all Christian theology is eschatological. More mundane prediction may have had some role to play in Old Testament prophecy, but this seems to be one of the "many ways" in which God spoke *formerly* through the prophets (Heb 1:1), which has now been largely superseded by the eschatological concerns of the New Testament prophets. These are:

1. To declare the gospel of Christ, which includes the fact that our response to Christ is key to determining our eternal destiny.

2. To discern and declare material evidences that we are living in the last days. As Boring says, thinking of John 16:13, "the Spirit-Paraclete will convict the world by declaring the things to come as *already operative.*"[3]

3. To remind the church that the end is imminent: "The revelation of Jesus Christ, which God gave him to show to his servants the things that must *soon* take place" (Rev 1:1).

4. To exhort Christians to live in the light of this; that is, to awaken a foolish and slumbering church which, because her Master is delayed, behaves as if he will never return (Matt 25:5). "Therefore encourage one another with these words," Paul says, after he has described the return of Christ (1 Thess 4:18), and Peter says, "The end of all things is at hand; therefore be alert and of sober mind so that you may pray" (1 Pet 4:7 NIV).

5. To console and comfort the suffering church in the light of the reward to come: "Do not fear what you are about to suffer . . . Be faithful unto death, and I will give you the crown of life" (Rev 2:10).

---

3. Boring, *Sayings of the Risen Jesus,* 131; italics mine.

Chapter 27

Is All Spirit-enabled Speech Prophecy?

WE HAVE SUGGESTED, FOLLOWING Gillespie, that according to Paul in 1 Corinthians 2, Spirit-enabled speech is focused on the message of Christ. It therefore seems possible that prophecy is no more or less than *all Spirit-enabled speech*. In this chapter we explore this possibility further.

Preaching as Exclusively Evangelistic Speech

In the New Testament, the focus of the verb *kēryssō* ("preach") is *entirely* evangelistic; the term is never used as we use it today to describe the exhortation and upbuilding of the Christian community:

> [Preaching] is not religious discourse to a closed group of initiates . . . The current understanding of preaching as biblical exposition and exhortation, while a valid extension of the term, has tended to obscure its primitive meaning.[1]

This explains why Paul uses *kēryssō* four times in 1 Corinthians 1:1—2:4 as he describes his first visit to Corinth, but as soon as he turns to describe how he now addresses them as believers (2:6), he abandons his use of the term.

In the Old Testament, the distinction is not absolutely clear cut. In LXX, *kēryssō* can refer to any shouting and proclaiming (e.g., Gen 41:43; Esth 6:9); but it can also have hints of what we would call "preaching," both

---

1. Mounce, "Preaching," 1023.

Is All Spirit-enabled Speech Prophecy?

to those who are clearly God's people (Mic 3:5) and to those who are not (Jonah 3:2). However, in the great messianic announcements of Isaiah, the sense of preaching as proclaiming God's good news is crystalized: "The Spirit of the Lord God is upon me . . . to bring good news (*euangelidzō*) to the poor . . . to proclaim (*kēryssō*) liberty to the captives" (Isa 61:1).

Prophecy as Speech Addressed to the People of God

If "preaching" becomes the generic New Testament term for addressing a non-Christian audience, is there a corresponding generic term for speech to the assembled church? Is it possible that the only generic term Paul uses—in a way that is consistent with its Old Testament meaning as any Spirit-inspired discourse to Israel—is "*prophesying?*"

Perhaps. After all, "prophecy . . . is not for unbelievers but for believers" (1 Cor 14:22 NIV). Furthermore, when Paul says, "Every man who prays or prophesies with his head covered dishonors his head" (1 Cor 11:4), why does he single out only prayer and prophecy? What is the man to do when he teaches, or shares some encouragement from Scripture? Could it be that the phrase "prays or prophesies" covers virtually *every* form of speech contribution Paul expects from members of the congregation (tongues apart)? In other words, does "prophecy" cover any and all Spirit-inspired, believer-directed speech, including what we call "preaching" today?

There is at least one important contraindication (or perhaps just a qualification) to this theory, which is that not all prophecy is directed at the people of God:

1. Old Testament prophecy can be made *against* God's enemies. Obvious examples are Moses' prophecies to Pharaoh, and Jeremiah's prophecies against Egypt, Assyria, and Babylon.

2. God says of Jeremiah, "I appointed you *a prophet to the nations*" (Jer 1:5).

3. In the New Testament, Paul's prophetic calling was to preach the gospel to the nations (Gal 1:15–16).

The conclusion must be that although prophecy is mainly addressed to the people of God, it is not exclusively so. Nevertheless, since the term "preaching" is only used in the New Testament to describe evangelistic discourse, there is no obvious New Testament word to describe what we call "preaching" today, that is, edifying and exhorting discourse addressed to the gathered church. The word "teaching" is surely inadequate to describe what a good preacher aims for in a sermon today, as he unfolds a text so as to show its vital relevance to life today, and challenges his congregation to live in the light of it.

Perhaps, therefore, we can suggest that wherever speech exhorts and encourages believers powerfully from the Scripture, Paul would describe the effect of this speech as *paraklēsis* and would describe the speech itself as "*propheteia*"—prophecy.

The Polymorphic Nature of Prophecy

> Long ago, at many times and in many ways, God spoke to our fathers by the prophets, but in these last days he has spoken to us by his Son, whom he appointed the heir of all things. (Heb 1:1–2)

According to the writer of Hebrews, God spoke by the Old Testament prophets "at many times and in many ways." The first point to make here is that the Greek ("*polymerōs kai polytropōs*") does not actually refer to time at all: *polymerōs* means "in many ways,"[2] and literally means "having many parts," and *polytropōs* means "in various ways,"[3] literally, "turning many ways." So it would be more accurate to say that Old Testament prophets spoke "*in many and various ways.*"

We have argued that prophecy in both the Old and New Testaments involves God speaking through people using any speech-form he chooses. In the New Testament we have seen that the word covers the scriptural writing of the apostles and Luke, the gospel preaching of Judas, Silas, Barnabas, and Paul, and the Spirit-led oracles of Agabus. So prophecy is *multiform*.

Just as prophecy comes in multiple genres of speech, so it also has different modes of production. On the one hand, we see every evidence in the letters of Paul that prophecy works through human reasoning; on the other hand, in the prophecies of Agabus we see insight that seems not to involve such reasoning. Similarly, the book of Revelation is not simply a reasoned discourse, but the inspired report of an extraordinary vision. God speaks both through and beyond human reasoning, but both forms of speech are

---

2. *AG*, 693.
3. *AG*, 696.

equally Spirit-inspired, and both constitute prophecy. As we suggested earlier in our study (p.26 above), prophecy is *multimodal*.

"Prophecy" should therefore be considered an umbrella term, a polymorphic, polyvalent concept whose precise parameters can only be determined by the context in which the term is used. As Aune says, Christian prophecy "does not readily lend itself to categorical conceptualization," and "*produced no distinctive speech forms which would have been readily identifiable as prophetic speech.*"[4]

In Old Testament times, we saw that prophecy always involved people speaking from God, as his spokesmen and spokeswomen. The term was applied to any and all Spirit-inspired speech, including the songwriting of 1 Chronicles 25, which seems to have been praise and thanksgiving addressed to God rather than discourse to people. The definition of prophecy as *any Spirit-empowered speech* appears to be reinforced in the New Testament. We saw evidence for this in the fact that Peter was happy to equate the praise and proclamation speech of the tongues at Pentecost with prophecy (Acts 2:17), proclaiming it as evidence of the arrival of a new age of the Spirit in which all God's people would be filled with the Spirit.

This again suggests that prophesying may not be a particular activity, like teaching or preaching, but rather the *quality* of a speech-act as Spirit-enabled, which in the New Testament means a speech-act that exalts Christ. On this reading, all good preaching is prophetic, and a sermon might well be described as "prophetic" as a way of acknowledging that God has spoken through it: the eternal word of God has become a particular word for a particular person or group in the present—God's word to people then becomes God's word to *us now*. Without realizing it, our preachers have been prophesying all along! At this point, they might be excused for feeling a touch of self-congratulation, like the character in Molière's play who, on learning the meaning of the word "prose," congratulates himself that he has been speaking it for forty years without realizing it!

Category Errors

Thiselton says that to argue that since prophecy is *sometimes* spontaneous, it must *always* be so, is to make a "category mistake."[5] This useful term was

---

4. Aune, *Prophecy in Early Christianity*, 231; italics his.
5. *FEC*, 1092.

originally proposed by Gilbert Ryle to attack the Cartesian notion that the mind and the body are completely distinct categories, which he calls a "category mistake" or a "category error."[6] Thiselton's point is that the insistence on spontaneity as a qualification for prophecy confuses *a part for the whole* (just as does, for example, too tight an equation between prophecy and prediction).

Category mistakes abound in theology and appear whenever we draw too sharp a distinction between overlapping notions. They appear, for example, in the misconception that faith and reason are entirely contrasting concepts (see how Paul is described as "reasoning" with his audience in Acts 17:2, 17; 18:19), in attempts to distinguish the "natural" from the "supernatural," and in conceptions of the Holy Spirit and the word of God as being entirely distinct (whereas Jesus says, in John 6:63, "The words that I have spoken to you *are* spirit and life"). The widespread understanding that prophecy and teaching are entirely distinct seems likewise to be a category mistake since both overlap in Spirit-enabled preaching.

To insist that all prophesying must be spontaneous is to classify as a generic class what is in fact only a specific genus of that class; it is rather like assuming that all cats must be of the common domestic type, and to ignore the fact that the term may also refer to the class or family of animals that includes tigers, lions, and leopards. It *overconstrains* what prophecy can be.

Perhaps we make such errors because we prefer concrete terms to abstract notions and we are more comfortable with specific members of a class than with higher-level taxonomic terms: for example, everyone knows what a square is, but some struggle to define a quadrilateral. We too often miss the wood for the trees.

---

6. Ryle, Concept of Mind, 17–25. Ryle gives a couple of helpful examples to clarify the meaning of the term "category error":

A visitor, after looking round the colleges and library of Oxford, asks, "But where is the *University*?" The mistake here is to assume that the University is somehow distinct from its component parts. It is to fail to grasp that it is a more abstract notion than a building or a number of buildings.

A boy watching the march-past of an army division, having had pointed out to him such and such battalions, batteries, squadrons, etc., asks when the division is going to appear. "He would be supposing that a division was a counterpart to the units already seen, partly similar to them and partly unlike them . . . The march-past was not a parade of battalions, batteries, squadrons *and* a division; it was a parade of the battalions, batteries and squadrons *of* a division" (Ryle, *Concept of Mind*, 18).

Is All Spirit-enabled Speech Prophecy?

We have proposed that the word "prophecy" refers to *any* speech that is Spirit-enabled, and so, having criticized others, we need to be careful ourselves not to over–constrain the forms prophecy might take: Spirit-enabled preaching is indeed prophesying, but is not the only form of prophesying.

We will need to elaborate on this in our conclusion.

Chapter 28

Conclusion

Prophecy in both the Old and New Testaments involves God speaking though people to reveal his plans and purposes. The primary (but not the sole) purpose of prophecy is to produce Scripture. The literary styles of Scripture are many and varied (historical narrative, songs, wisdom literature, sermons, etc.), and this suggests that prophecy is not to be defined by any particular form or mode of speech; we agree with Aune that, "the distinctive feature of prophetic speech was not so much its content or form, but its supernatural origin."[1] In other words, we suggest, just as all prophecy is Spirit-enabled speech, so *all Spirit-enabled speech (apart from tongues) may be called "prophecy."*

"Prophecy," then, is a broad categorical or umbrella term, whose precise contours can only be determined by the context in which the term is used. To insist that it must always be spontaneous and miraculous (as Grudem does), or infallible and miraculous (as Gaffin does) is therefore to make a category error: it is to confuse a part for the whole.

Given such a breadth of possible forms, it is important for us to ask what form of the gift Paul has in mind when he commends prophesying to the Corinthians (and to us) in 1 Corinthians 14:1. Is he expecting the Corinthians to make miraculous predictions, like Agabus? Or to write praise songs, like Jeduthun? Or to contribute to the canon of Scripture? Or miraculously to discern the sins of others, like Jesus? Or to describe visions of the return of Christ, like John? Or to preach the gospel, like Paul?

---

1. Aune, *Prophecy in Early Christianity*, 338

Conclusion

Prophecy as Preaching Christ

We have argued that the whole of 1 Corinthians 14 is a comprehensive contrast between the gifts of tongues and prophecy, in which tongues is produced without the active engagement of the speaker's mind ("For if I pray in a tongue . . . my mind is unfruitful," 1 Cor 14:14), but prophecy involves and requires the active engagement of the speaker's mind (1 Cor 14:19). So prophecy is not simply intelligible speech (as all agree), but also *intelligent* speech. The focus of this prophetic speech must be the gospel because only the gospel converts people (1 Cor 14:24–25). In other words, the prophesying Paul is talking about must overlap with what we call "gospel preaching" today.

There is evidence for this much earlier in the epistle. We read that when Paul preaches the gospel to non-Christians, he speaks only of "Jesus Christ and him crucified" (1 Cor 2:2), since Christ is the "the wisdom of God" (1:24). On the other hand, when he speaks to Christians ("among the mature" 2:6), he says that speaks "a secret and hidden wisdom of God" (2:7). Since he has already identified the wisdom of God with Christ, Paul must mean that his message to Christians is as Christ-centered as his message to non–Christians; and the fact that this is a wisdom "which God decreed before the ages for our glory" (2:7) is clearly a reference to the gospel mystery.

Paul then describes his ministry as expressing the *Spirit-revealed message of Christ in Spirit-taught words to spiritual people* (2:10, 13). Given the historic synonymy between Spirit-enabled speech and prophecy, by emphasizing the involvement of the Spirit at every stage of its production, Paul must want us to understand that he is referring to *prophecy*, and that he is describing his own prophetic practice. Thus, Gillespie argues that prophecy is the "unlabeled subject matter" of 1 Corinthians 2:6–16 (*FT*, 65).

Upbuilding, Exhortation, and Consolation.

Paul tells us that "the one who prophesies speaks to people for their upbuilding and encouragement and consolation" (1 Cor 14:3). Many commentators consider that this verse describes the effects of prophecy but tells us nothing beyond that about what prophecy actually is. However, these are three common effects of all gospel word ministry and are picked up in many texts describing Paul's word ministry: for example, we read that Paul and Barnabas went about "strengthening the souls of the disciples [*upbuilding*], encouraging them to continue in the faith [*exhortation*], and saying that through many tribulations we must enter the kingdom of God [*consolation*]" (Acts 14:22). When we see the prophets Paul and Barnabas typically engaged in an activity so closely matching the characteristics of prophecy described in 1 Corinthians 14:3, we must suspect that what they are doing constitutes their *typical prophesying*.

We are given a further description of this kind of prophetic ministry in Acts 15, where we read that Judas and Silas were able to encourage and strengthen the church *because they were prophets* (Acts 15:32). In other words, their encouraging constituted their prophesying. We know much about the content of their prophesying, since we are told that Judas and Silas used "many words" (Acts 15:32) to communicate the "same things" (Acts 15:27) as the apostolic letter from the Council of Jerusalem, including, presumably, its basis in Amos 9:11–12 (Acts 15:16–18). These prophets clearly explained doctrine and expounded Scripture, and this activity constituted their prophesying. As Hill says, "As pastoral preachers the New Testament prophets teach and give instruction on what the Christian way requires of individual believers and of the community"[2]

Below we summarize our findings by noting, on the one hand, the constants in prophetic speech throughout Scripture and, on the other hand, how prophecy seems to undergo a transformation in the New Testament.

Some Constants of Prophetic Speech

In the course of our study, we have seen a number of constants in prophetic speech in both Testaments:

1. Prophecy is people speaking with God's authority, or rather, God speaking through people, to communicate his will; prophecy involves speaking the word of God.

2. Scripture was written by means of a special gift of prophecy. All Scripture may therefore be called prophecy, and all who wrote it may be described as prophets.

3. All prophecy is clearly Spirit-inspired speech, but we contend further that all Spirit-inspired (or Spirit-enabled) speech is prophecy. We have seen evidence for this in the fact that prophesying is the verbal

---

2. Hill, "Christian Prophets as Teachers or Instructors in the Church", in Panagopoulos, *Prophetic Vocation*, 116–17

evidence of Spirit-filling (1 Sam 10:6; Num 11:25; Acts 2:17, 19:6; 1 Cor 2:7–13, 12:3, 14:1). This suggests that any verbal evidence of Spirit-filling may be described as prophesying.

4. Two of the main purposes of prophecy are to deliver God's covenant to his people and to recall God's people to that covenant.

5. In both Testaments, to claim to be speaking from God whilst speaking from one's own heart, mind, or imagination is a wicked and grievous sin (Ezek 13:1–3 cf. Matt 7:21–23).

6. Old Testament prophets operated under a prophetic call, following a divine encounter, including visions of "the word of the Lord" (that is, the Lord). The New Testament apostles likewise had a divine encounter during which they received a prophetic calling (e.g. Matt 28:19–20; Gal 1:15–16) to preach the gospel, "the word of the Lord."

7. In both Testaments, although always originating in the Spirit of God, prophecy *normally* involves the actively engaged mind (and heart and soul) of the prophet; but *on occasion* it miraculously bypasses the conscious thought processes of the prophet.

The Transformations of Prophecy

Although some aspects of Old Testament prophecy continue into the New, this is not the whole story. Times of revolution invariably entail a corresponding lexical revolution: consider the impact of the technological revolution of recent years on words such as "mouse," "boot," "surf," etc. Likewise, the birth of the church brought with it a corresponding revolution in vocabulary: new words were needed ("Christian"), and old words gained new, technical meanings (such as the Greek words for "gospel," "apostle," "church").[3] We suggest that the language and nature of prophecy does not escape the revolution instigated by Jesus and undergoes a major transformation under the new covenant.

1. The Messiah whom the prophets predicted by the Spirit, Christians today proclaim by the same Spirit (1 Pet 1:11–12). Messianic prediction is superseded by messianic proclamation.

---

3. It would be linguistic Luddism to insist that the word "mouse" must only ever be used to refer to a rodent; but it is no less Luddite to insist that Paul's theological discourse in Romans, for example, is not prophetic simply because it does not cohere to the familiar styles of the Old Testament literary prophets. Words move on.

2. Nevertheless, prediction persists in the New Testament in the form of the proclamation of the gospel message of salvation and judgment.

3. Under the old covenant, the Holy Spirit fell on and spoke through only a few, whereas under the new covenant, all Christians, as those indwelt by the Spirit, are able to speak in the power of the same Spirit (Acts 2:17).

4. The role of the apostles subsumes and surpasses that of the Old Testament prophets: the apostles are *super*-prophets. Old Testament prophets could only point to a king whom the apostles knew intimately, and to a kingdom the apostles inhabited. As the supreme interpreters of the words and works of Christ, the apostles are "greater" than the prophets (Matt 11:9–11), and their message is far more glorious; however, they are reticent to describe themselves as prophets (as were Moses and Jesus before them) because although the term is an *accurate* description of their role, it is not an *adequate* one.

5. The Great Commission (Matt 28:18–20) is the prophetic calling of all Christians to build the church.

6. Speech that is empowered by the Spirit (1 Cor 2:4) is associated with the message of the cross of Christ (1 Cor 1:17, 18, 24) and the glorification of Christ (John 16:14). All Christian speech that faithfully glorifies Christ and proclaims his word is thus Spirit-enabled (1 Cor 12:3), and it is this speech that Paul seeks to encourage in 1 Corinthians 14.

7. Under the ministry of the apostles, the Spirit-led communication of the Spirit-revealed mystery of Christ becomes the dominant congregational manifestation of the prophetic gift (1 Cor 2:13; Acts 15:27).

8. As the canon is delivered, New Testament prophecy transforms from the gift through which Scripture is given into the gift through which Scripture is explained and applied to life. Prophecy both interprets Scripture and interprets events, people and cultures in the light of Scripture. As God's word is preached today it continues to exercise its prophetic power and accomplishes its divine purposes (Isa 55:11). Prophecy both originates in revelation and effects it.

9. New Testament prophecy also effects *paraklēsis* (exhortation, encouragement) (1 Cor 14:3). Luke translates "Barnabas" ("Son of prophecy" in Hebrew) as "Son of encouragement" in Greek (Acts 4:36), which

suggests that, at least for Luke, *paraklēsis* and prophecy are virtually synonymous. Prophets are repeatedly described as bringing *paraklēsis* (Acts 4:36, 11:23, 15:32), and *paraklēsis* is always tightly associated both with the work of the Holy Spirit (John 14:26) and with the exegesis of Scripture (Acts 13:15ff., 15:32; Rom 15:4; Heb 13:22). *Paraklēsis* involves exhortation to live in the light of God's promised eschatological realities, and all such speech constitutes prophecy.

In summary, we argue that, although some aspects of Old Testament prophecy continue into the New, beginning with Peter's speech at Pentecost, a glorious new form of prophesying appears—gospel word ministry. We could say that this is simply a continuation of Old Testament prophecy but is a butterfly really a continuation of a caterpillar? It might be more accurate to say that in the New Testament prophecy undergoes a substantial transformation or metamorphosis.

Beyond Explaining Doctrine

We have strongly emphasized the doctrinal content of prophesying. However, to characterize all Paul's writing as "explaining doctrine" would be radically to underestimate the scope of his word ministry. A quick glance at 2 Corinthians, for example, shows us how much broader Paul's word ministry is than simply teaching doctrinal propositions; that letter is an expression of his love and parental concern for the welfare of his flock: he shares his heart, and recounts his experiences as a servant of Christ, exhorting the Corinthians to imitate his life. At the end of the epistle, Paul says that what he has written has been "all for your upbuilding, beloved" (2 Cor 12:19). So the entire preceding letter has had upbuilding as its goal (a key effect of prophecy in 1 Corinthians 14:3).

In other words, Paul speaks as one formed and shaped into the likeness of Christ to form and shape others into the same likeness. Prophetic speech cannot be reduced to explaining doctrine, although it certainly includes it: it is, in Thiselton's phrase, "preaching, pastorally contextualized" (*FEC*, 1140). More than that, it is the verbal output of a life-on-life disciple-making ministry: it is sacrificial, upbuilding love expressing itself in speech.

Word and Spirit

How can we begin, however remotely, to follow Paul's example in ministering to others?

As we approach Scripture humbly and seek to interpret it, *it interprets us*: through Scripture, God the Holy Spirit addresses us. We may be challenged by what we read, perhaps rebuked, or shown some aspect of God's character and be moved to worship him; or we may come across a passage that sheds light on some issue we are facing. In short, we get God's perspective on our life, his wisdom for our lives. The Spirit also works in us to respond to what we read, and so, day by day, we are changed to become more like Christ (2 Cor 3:18).

As we seek to help other Christians around us—perhaps those new to the faith—we pray for them, asking God to show us how we might help them grow. Having been formed by Scripture ourselves, we are enabled to play a role in forming others into the likeness of Christ too. Thus, the Spirit uses his sword, the word of God (Eph 6:17), to change both us and those around us. This seems to me to be the heart of the prophetic act.

This collaboration of God's word and Spirit is vital. Without a racket in his hand even Roger Federer would be terrible at tennis; it is his skill *with the racket* that makes him so formidable. Likewise, it is Scripture that makes the man of God "complete, equipped for every good work" (2 Tim 3:17). To attempt to speak on behalf of God *without Scripture* would be as foolish as trying to play tennis without a racket. Scripture is prophecy and prophecy (almost always) involves Scripture, appropriately expressed and applied.

Miraculous Prophesying?

Should we expect miraculous prophesying today, however rarely? The predictions of Agabus in Acts 11 and 21 (concerning a famine and the persecution of Paul) are often cited as examples of the kind of fallible impression that might be expected in prophecy today. However, we contend that

- these predictions are without error;
- they are miraculous perceptions of particular occurrences of End Time events (persecution and famine) promised by Jesus which were given not in order that suffering might be avoided, but in order to

Conclusion

support Christians through it (much as an airline pilot might warn his passengers of turbulence ahead).

So these predictions are remarkable events and do not serve as a very good model for the reporting of random, fallible impressions and pictures today. Nevertheless, since God is as powerful and gracious as ever, he does certainly, on occasion, give miraculous warnings or encouragements today (as in the example of Spurgeon described in Appendix II below). Miracles can and do happen, and so, on occasion, does miraculous prophesying. But we should not let the miraculous, or the requirement for spontaneity, limit and define what qualifies as prophetic speech.

In Scripture, God has provided us with a six-lane highway and a map for our journey. The overwhelming bulk of prophetic traffic will follow this map down this highway. Occasionally, and remarkably, God may choose to take us another way; that is to say, God routinely communicates through Scripture, but he does not limit himself always and entirely to communicating only through Scripture. However, if we do find ourselves driving down a dirt track, it may well also indicate a navigational error!

Today, for example, in a prayer meeting, a Christian may sense a sudden urge to pray for a particular situation or a person. She may have no idea if the Spirit is really leading, or if she has just had a random thought. When she reports this sense to others, how then should she introduce it? Given the uncertain origin, she should be careful not to seek to inject extra divine authority by declaring outright, "The Holy Spirit is saying . . ." or "The Lord is saying . . ." (I would be wary of saying even, "I sense the Spirit is saying . . .") She could simply say, "Can we pray for x?" Why say more than that? Jesus might say, "Anything beyond this comes from the evil one" (Matt 5:37, NIV). We should always remember that, in the Old Testament, claiming that the Lord had spoken when he had not was a crime punishable by death (Deut 18:20).

Is it likely that Corinthian congregational prophecy included reports of impressions such as these? Is this what Paul was seeking to encourage? Because such reports do not fulfill the requirements of intelligent, gospel-centered speech laid out in 1 Corinthians 14, I do not think that this is what Paul has primarily in mind.

A Definition of Prophecy

From 1 Corinthians 2:10, 13 we suggest that New Testament prophecy is

> *the Spirit-revealed wisdom of God in Christ*
> *imparted in Spirit-taught words to people of the Spirit*

A longer-form definition might be as follows:

> Pauline congregational prophecy is speaking on behalf of God, under the enabling of the Holy Spirit, to conform people into the likeness Christ. From an encounter with God in the study of Scripture and in prayer, the New Testament prophet gains insight into God's purposes in Christ for individuals, churches, and cultures, which he/she discloses, building faith, exhorting to right living, consoling during suffering, and reminding of God's promises of salvation and judgment. Although prophecy is principally discourse addressed to the church, it also proclaims Christ to an unbelieving world.

Should We Use the Term "Prophecy" Today, and if so, How?

If Paul talks of all Spirit-inspired speech as prophesying, so, one could argue, should we; and if Paul fights to reclaim the language of prophecy from an abuse of the term by others (in his case, the Corinthians), so also should we. The best way to counter the many erroneous conceptions of prophecy today must be by laboring to re-tether it to Scripture and the message of Christ. With this in mind, it would seem acceptable to describe a sermon today as "prophetic" as a way of declaring that one considers it to be Spirit-enabled. Likewise, any speech from a fellow Christian could be described as "prophetic" simply as a way of indicating that God has spoken through it. It would also be legitimate to describe someone as a "prophet" as a way of indicating that he/she has a special gift of interpreting people or cultures in the light of Scripture—always remembering that *we are all prophets now*.

On the other hand, one could argue, since the terminology of prophecy is so open to misunderstanding, and the consequences of these misunderstandings can be so serious, there is an equally strong case for avoiding use of the term altogether. After all, "if a brother is grieved by what you eat, you are not walking in love" (Rom 14:15). If the use of a word (and that is really all that is at issue here) causes offense to some, perhaps it should be abandoned.

My own view is that it is certainly legitimate to use the term today but only if one is very careful to avoid offense by clearly explaining what one means by it.

Appendix I

The Interpretation of Tongues

> The one who prophesies is greater than the one who speaks in tongues, unless someone interprets, so that the church may be built up. (1 Cor 14:5)

ALTHOUGH PAUL CONTRASTS TONGUES and prophecy in 1 Corinthians 14, commentators sometimes make the point that *interpreted* tongues appear to be functionally equivalent to prophecy. For that reason, it is appropriate to make a few remarks on the interpretation of tongues as part of this study of prophecy.

Thiselton argues that Paul always encourages and expects people *to interpret their own tongues*, as in 1 Corinthians 14:13 ("Therefore, one who speaks in a tongue should pray that he may interpret"). Thiselton maintains that the unwarranted insertion of "*someone*" in many translations of 1 Corinthians 14:5 ("unless someone interprets") is "disastrously misleading"[1] since the text says only, "unless *he* interprets." Thus, "*The Greek does not mention any agent other than the one who speaks in tongues, who remains the subject of the verb.*"[2]

The word "someone" is inserted by ESV, NIV, et al., but NASB and NKJV are more faithful to the text:

---

1. *FEC* 1098.
2. *FEC* 1098.

Appendix I

greater is one who prophesies than one who speaks in tongues, *unless he interprets,* so that the church may receive edifying. (1 Cor 14:5 NASB)

for he who prophesies is greater than he who speaks with tongues, *unless indeed he interprets*, that the church may receive edification. (1 Cor 14:5 NKJV)

This text is straightforward enough. However, 1 Corinthians 14:27–28 is a much trickier passage:

> If any speak in a tongue, let there be only two or at most three, and each in turn, and let someone interpret. But if there is no one to interpret, let each of them keep silent in church and speak to himself and to God. (1 Cor 14:27–28)

The Greek is, *"Eite glossē tis lalei, kata duo ē to pleiston treis, kai ana meros, kai heis diermēneutō· ean de mē ē hermeneutēs sigatō en ekklesia, heautō de laleitō kai tō theō.*

Fee says, "here and in 12:10 and 28–30 it is assumed that the interpretation will be given to someone else."[3] But is it really "assumed" that the interpreter is not the tongues speaker? The text says literally, "but if not an interpreter" which could just as easily mean "but if *he* is not an interpreter" as "but if *there* is not an interpreter."

A further issue with the NIV and ESV translations of 1 Corinthians 14:27–28 is that neither does justice to the conditional statement that opens the text: "If anyone speaks in a tongue . . ." Where is the main clause following this conditional clause? Both translations simply insert verbs where none exists:

> let there be two or at most three (ESV)
>
> two—or at the most three—should speak (NIV)

But this is entirely unnecessary: the main clause becomes quite clear as soon as one reads the word "*kai*" ("and" or "also") as "*also,*" a possibility both translations ignore. The structure of the sentence becomes:

> "If anyone speaks in a tongue . . . let one also interpret"

So we can now propose a translation that captures the possible variant readings:

3. Fee, *First Epistle to the Corinthians*, 692. Although the *heis* in this case could refer to one of the two or three tongues-speakers.

The Interpretation of Tongues

"If anyone speaks in a tongue (two or at most three at a time, and in turn) let one ["someone" or "him"] also interpret; but if [he is or there is] not an interpreter, let him keep silent."

It is becoming increasingly likely that the same person is being referred to in both clauses: "If anyone speaks in a tongue . . . *one should also interpret.*"

"One"

On the word *heis* ("one" in "one should interpret"), it is certainly tempting to read this numerically, because of its proximity to *duo* (two) and *treis* (three). But it may not be intended that way. Thiselton says,

> both *BDF* and *BAGD*, together with H. D. Betz in *EDNT*, firmly agree that the numeral *heis* . . . passes regularly "from the force of a numeral . . . to that of *tis* (indefinite article) . . . parallelled in English ['one speaks . . . '] . . . The numeral may serve to denote "*someone . . . exactly the same thing as the indef.* Art. . . . someone, . . . Mk. 10:17 . . . Lk. 24:18."[4]

Thiselton quotes Betz, "In koine Greek the use of *heis* is extended so that it increasingly takes the place, e.g., of the indefinite pronoun *tis*."[5]

It may also be significant that *heis* can also be used *emphatically*—"one and the same"[6] (see, for example, 1 Cor 12:11: "all these are empowered by one and the same Spirit")—and this could be decisive here: "If anyone speaks in a tongue . . . let *one and the same person* also interpret."

Articulation rather than Interpretation

On *diermeneuō* ("interpret") Thiselton says,

> We have argued consistently that all (or at least virtually all) the relevant passages in 12:1–14:26 which use *diermeneuō* or *hermeneuō* (especially 14:6 [*sic*: intends 14:5?] and 14:13) are more likely to refer to the persons who speak in tongues as themselves articulating what had otherwise been inexpressible in everyday speech.[7]

---

4. *FEC*, 1137–38.
5. Betz, in *EDNT*, 1:399, in *FEC*, 1138.
6. *AG*, 230.
7. *FEC*, 1137.

Appendix I

Thiselton argues that the word *diermeneuō* refers to *explaining an experience beyond words*. He cites an example of the word from Josephus which talks of the impossibility of *putting into words* the wonders of Herod's palace. In another example, Philo describes the role of Aaron as *putting into words* what Moses wanted to say. In both cases, the words "translate" would make no sense, and "interpret" misses the point. Thiselton reports that three-quarters of the uses of *diermeneuō* in Philo refer to the articulation of thoughts or feelings in intelligible speech,[8] and argues that in Paul the contrast is between precognitive experience and linguistic articulation.

Our translation of 14:27–28 now becomes,

> "If anyone speaks in a tongue (two or at most three at a time, and in turn), one [one and the same person] should also put it into intelligible words; but if he can't put it into words, let him keep quiet."

This seems very reasonable: tongues speech is given by "my spirit" (1 Cor 14:14), which means, according to Thiselton, "my innermost spiritual being,"[9] albeit that part of me that is under the control of the Holy Spirit. Who better to articulate what originates from *my* spirit than *me*? For, "who knows a person's thoughts except the spirit of that person, which is in him" (1 Cor 2:11)?

Paul has already made it clear that he expects the person who speaks in tongues to pray for the ability to interpret his own tongues (14:13). If he had wanted to allow third-party interpretation in 14:27, surely he would have been more explicit.

Finally, third-party interpretation raises a huge question which Paul fails to address, namely, how can members of the congregation, charged to be as wise as serpents and as innocent as doves, know with confidence that what the interpreter is saying relates *in any way* to what the tongue speaker has said? How can the accuracy of the interpretation be tested?

No: it makes far more sense to assume that Paul is referring to people interpreting *their own* tongues.

1 Corinthians 12:10

> to another various kinds of tongues, to another the interpretation of tongues (1 Cor 12:10).

8. *FEC*, 1099.
9. *FEC*, 1110.

The Interpretation of Tongues

This text is often quoted by those who argue that the gift of tongues and the gift of interpretation can reside in different people.[10]

The response must be that it would have been unduly pedantic of Paul to say, "some have the gift of tongues, *of which some* also have the gift of interpreting tongues." By the same token, he "should" have said, "to some the working of miracles, *of which some* will have gifts of healing" (12:9–10). In this text, Paul is simply saying that gifts are variously distributed; he is not discussing what different gifts a single individual might have, or how the gifts relate to each other.

---

10. E.g, by Fee, *First Epistle to the Corinthians*, 598–99.

Appendix II

The Danger of Narrow Appeals to History

IT IS CLEARLY IMPORTANT to explore how prophecy has been understood in church history. However, it can be tempting to appeal to history simply to support a particular viewpoint. Thus, Grudem gives a number of examples in support of his view (Grudem, *GP*, 347–359), while MacArthur gives a set of examples that all support a contrary view (MacArthur, 251–261). However, since neither author considers historical examples that run contrary to his own position, neither can be said to be studying history properly.

The danger is highlighted by the fact that both Grudem and MacArthur quote Charles Spurgeon in support of their positions. Thus, Grudem quotes Spurgeon: "*God sometimes guides his servants to say what they themselves would never have thought of uttering*" (Grudem, *GP*, 356).

On one occasion while Spurgeon was preaching, he felt led to point to a man in the crowd and say, "There is a man sitting there who is a shoemaker; he keeps his shop open on Sundays, it was open last Sunday morning, he took ninepence, and there was fourpence profit out of it; his soul is sold to Satan for fourpence!" (ibid., 357).

This insight apparently turned out to be correct and had a powerful effect on the man to whom it was addressed. Spurgeon continues, "*I could tell as many as a dozen similar cases in which I pointed to someone in the hall without having the slightest knowledge of the person, or any idea that what I said was right, except that I believe that I was moved by the Spirit to say it.*" (ibid.)

Appendix II

Grudem quotes these remarkable stories to support his own position that miraculous prophecies still happen today.

On the other hand, MacArthur records a quotation from Spurgeon in support of his own very different view:

> Take care never to impute the vain imaginings of your fancy to him [the Holy Spirit]. I have seen the Spirit of God shamefully dishonored by persons—I hope they were insane—who say that they have had this and that revealed to them. There has not for some years passed over my head a single week in which I have not been pestered by the revelations of hypocrites or maniacs. Semi–lunatics are very fond of coming to me with messages from the Lord to me, and it may spare them some trouble if I tell them once for all that I will have none of their stupid messages . . . Never dream that events are revealed to you by heaven, or you may come to be like those idiots who dare impute their blatant follies to the Holy Ghost . . . *Whatever is to be revealed by the Spirit to any of us is in the word of God already*—he adds nothing to the Bible, and never will. (MacArthur, 130–1, italics mine).

He also quotes Spurgeon as saying, "apostles . . . were needed temporarily . . . Prophets, too, were in the early church" (ibid., 259).

What are we to make of these apparently contradictory comments by Spurgeon? Perhaps he changed his opinion over time. Or perhaps, although he occasionally did give Spirit-enabled insights, he was reluctant to identify them as prophecy. Whatever the case, the key point must be that, without a more thorough understanding of Spurgeon, it would be dangerous to be dogmatic about his position on prophecy. The theological position of historical figures is not always unequivocal, fixed over time, and easily represented by one or two quotations; a more thorough knowledge of the historical figure in question would be needed for an accurate perspective on their views.

It is right to appeal to church history; but we must be careful that we do not simply cherry-pick texts that support the points we wish to make. We need to be just as careful when we do history as when we do theology.

Bibliography

Aune, David E. *Prophecy in Early Christianity and the Ancient Mediterranean World.* Grand Rapids: Eerdmans, 1991.
Bennett, Dennis, and Rita Bennett. *The Holy Spirit and You.* Alachua, FL: Logos, 1971.
Bertin, Jonathan. "A Syntactical and Exegetical Analysis of Key Passages in Their Own Terms Concerning the Continuity of Prophets Today, Heb 2:1–4, Eph 2:20 & 1 Cor 14, with a Biblical Theological Integration." MA diss., Oak Hill College, 2017.
Bock, Darrell L. *Acts.* Grand Rapids: Baker Academic, 2007.
Boring, M. E. *The Continuing Voice of Jesus: Christian Prophecy and the Gospel Tradition.* Louisville: Westminster John Knox, 1991.
———. *Sayings of the Risen Jesus.* Cambridge: Cambridge University Press, 1982.
Bratcher, Dennis. "The Prophetic 'Call' Narrative: Commissioning into Service." http://www.crivoice.org/prophetcall.html.
Calvin, John. *Commentary on the Epistles of Paul the Apostle to the Corinthians.* Translated by J. Pringle. Edinburgh: The Calvin Translation Society, 1848.
Carson, D. A. *Exegetical Fallacies.* Grand Rapids: Baker Academic, 1996.
———. "Getting Excited about Melchizedek (TGC 2011)." Filmed April 14, 2011. Video, 1:01:52. https://www.youtube.com/watch?v=RY-qfjGaBpg.
———. *Showing the Spirit.* Grand Rapids: Baker, 1987.
Conzelmann, Hans. *1 Corinthians: A Commentary on the First Epistle to the Corinthians.* Minneapolis: Augsberg Fortress, 1975.
Cothenet, Édouard. "Les prophètes chrétiens comme exégètes charismatiques de l'écriture." In *Prophetic Vocation in the New Testament and Today,* edited by J. Panagopoulos, 77–107. Leiden: E. J. Brill, 1977.
Cranfield, C. E. B. *Romans: A Shorter Commentary.* Edinburgh: T. & T. Clark, 1985.
Dunn, James, D. G. *The Christ and the Spirit, vol. 2: Pneumatology.* Edinburgh: T. & T. Clark, 1998.
Eichholz, Georg. *Was heißt charismatische Gemeinde? 1. Korinter 12.* (Theologische Existenz Heute, 77) Munich: Kaiser, 1960.
Ellis, E. Earle. *Prophecy & Hermeneutic in Early Christianity.* Eugene, OR: Wipf & Stock, 1978.
Fascher, Erich. *Prophētēs: Eine Sprach–und Religions-geschichtliche Untersuchen.* Giessen, Germany: Töpelmann, 1927.
Fee, Gordon D. *The First Epistle to the Corinthians.* Grand Rapids: Eerdmans, 1987.
Forbes, Christopher. *Prophecy and Inspired Speech in Early Christianity and its Hellenistic Environment.* Tübingen: J. C. B. Mohr, 1995.

Gaffin, Richard B., Jr. *Perspectives on Pentecost*. Phillipsburg, NJ: Presbyterian and Reformed, 1979.
Garland, David E. *1 Corinthians*. Grand Rapids: Baker Academic, 2003.
Gentry, Kenneth L. *The Charismatic Gift of Prophecy: A Reformed Response to Wayne Grudem*. Eugene, OR: Wipf & Stock, 2000.
Gillespie, Thomas W. *The First Theologians*. Grand Rapids: Eerdmans, 1994.
Grudem, Wayne. *1 Peter*. Nottingham, UK: IVP, 1988.
———. *The Gift of Prophecy in 1 Corinthians*. Eugene: Wipf & Stock, 1999.
Grudem, Wayne A., ed. *Are Miraculous Gifts for Today?: Four Views* Grand Rapids: Zondervan, 1996.
Hays, J. Daniel, *The Message of the Prophets: A Survey of the Prophetic and Apocalyptic Books of the Old Testament*. Grand Rapids: Zondervan, 2010.
Heiser, Michael S. *The Unseen Realm*. Bellingham, WA: Lexham, 2015.
Hill, David. *New Testament Prophecy*. London: Marshall, Morgan & Scott, 1979.
Hoehner, Harold. *Ephesians: An Exegetical Commentary*. Grand Rapids: Baker Academic, 2002.
Hooker, M. D. "Hard Sayings: 1 Cor 3:2." *Theology* 69 (1966) 19–22.
Käsemann, Ernst. *Commentary on Romans*. Grand Rapids: Eerdmans, 1994.
———. *Exegetische Versuche und Besinnungen*: Erster Und Zweiter Band. Göttingen: Vandenhoeck & Ruprecht, 1964.
———. *New Testament Questions for Today*. London: SCM, 2012.
Keller, Timothy, J. *Center Church*. Grand Rapids: Zondervan, 2012.
———. *Preaching*. London: Hodder & Stoughton, 2015.
Kensky, Meira. *Trying Man, Trying God: The Divine Courtroom in Early Jewish and Christian Literature*. Tübingen: J. C. B. Mohr, 2010.
Knowles, Robert, *Relating Faith*, Paternoster, Milton Keynes, 2014.
MacArthur, John. *Strange Fire*. Nashville: Thomas Nelson, 2013.
Malherbe, A. J. "'Pastoral Care' in the Thessalonian Church." *New Testament Studies* 36 (1990) 375–91.
Marshall, I. Howard. *Acts*. Leicester, UK: IVP, 1980.
Marshall, I. Howard, and Philip H. Towner. *A Critical and Exegetical Commentary on The Pastoral Epistles*. London: T. & T. Clark, 2004.
Moltmann, Jürgen. *The Trinity and the Kingdom: The Doctrine of God*. Minneapolis: Fortress, 1993.
Motyer, Alec B. "Prophecy." In *NBD*, 1037–46.
Mounce, R. H. "Preaching." In *NBD*, 1023–24.
Müller, Ulrich B. *Prophetie und Predigt im Neuen Testament*. Studien zum Neuen Testament 10. Gütersloh: Gütersloher Verlagshaus Mohn, 1975.
Myers, J. M., and Edwin D. Freed. "Is Paul also among the Prophets?" *Interpretation* 20.1 (1966) 40–53.
O'Brien, Peter T. *The Letter to the Ephesians*. Grand Rapids: Eerdmans, 1999.
Packer, J. I. "Inspiration." In *NBD*, 564–66.
Panagopoulos, J., ed. *Prophetic Vocation in the New Testament and Today*. Leiden: E. J. Brill, 1977.
Peterson, David G. *The Acts of the Apostles*. Grand Rapids: Eerdmans, 2009.
Reiling, Jannes. "Prophecy, the Spirit and the Church." In *Prophetic Vocation in the New Testament and Today*, edited by J. Panagopoulos, 58–76. Leiden: E. J. Brill, 1977.

Bibliography

Robertson, A., and A. Plummer. *A Critical and Exegetical Commentary on the First Epistles of St Paul to the Corinthians*. Edinburgh: T. & T. Clark, 1911.

Robertson, A. T. *A Grammar of the Greek New Testament in the Light of Historical Research*. New York: Hodder & Stoughton, 1934.

Robinson, D. W. B. "Charismata Versus Pneumatika: Paul's Method of Discussion." *The Reformed Theological Journal* 31 (1972) 49–55.

Ruthven, Jon Mark. *On the Cessation of the Charismata: The Protestant Polemic on Post-biblical Miracles*. Tulsa, OK: Word & Spirit, 2011.

Ryle, Gilbert. *The Concept of Mind*. London: Penguin, 2000.

Sandnes, Karl Olav. *Paul—One of the Prophets?* Tübingen: J. C. B. Mohr, 1991.

Schütz, John Howard. *Paul and the Anatomy of Apostolic Authority*. Louisville: Westminster John Knox, 2007.

Schreiner, Thomas. "Why I am a Cessationist." https://www.thegospelcoalition.org/article/why-i-am-a-cessationist/.

Silva, Moisés. *New International Dictionary of New Testament Theology and Exegesis*. Grand Rapids: Zondervan, 2014.

Stählin, Gustav. "*paramutheomai*." In *TDNT*, 5:814–23.

Storms, C. Samuel. "A Third Wave Response." In *Are Miraculous Gifts for Today?: Four Views*, edited by Wayne A. Grudem, 318–26. Grand Rapids: Zondervan, 1996.

Stronstad, Roger. *The Prophethood of All Believers: A Study in Luke's Charismatic Theology*. Cleveland: CPT, 2010.

Thiessen, Gerd. *Psychological Aspects of Pauline Theology*. Minneapolis: Fortress, 1987.

Thiselton, Anthony C. *The Holy Spirit*. London: SPCK, 2013.

Turner, Max. *The Holy Spirit and Spiritual Gifts*. Peabody, MA: Hendrickson, 1996.

Vielhauer, Philipp. *Oikodome: Das Bild vom Bau in der christichen Literatur vom Neuen Testament bis Clemens Alexandrinus*. Karlsruhe-Durlach, 1939.

Wallace, Daniel B. *Greek Grammar Beyond the Basics*. Grand Rapids: Zondervan, 1997.

Watson, David. *Discipleship*. London: Hodder & Stoughton, 1981.

www.ingramcontent.com/pod-product-compliance
Lightning Source LLC
Chambersburg PA
CBHW070251230426
43664CB00014B/2494